Lecture Notes in Economics and Mathematical Systems

438

Springer
Berlin
Heidelberg
New York
Barcelona
Budapest
Hong Kong
London
Milan
Paris
Santa Clara
Singapore
Tokyo

Antonio Villar

General Equilibrium
with Increasing Returns

 Springer

Author

Prof. Dr. Antonio Villar
University of Alicante
Department of Economics
03071 Alicante, Spain
e-mail: villar@merlin.fae.ua.es

339.5
V7lg

Library of Congress Cataloging-in-Publication Data

Villar, Antonio, 1954-
   General equilibrium with increasing returns / Antonio Villar.
      p.   cm. -- (Lecture notes in economics and mathematical
   systems ; 438)
   Includes bibliographical references.
   ISBN 3-540-61152-5 (alk. paper)
   1. Economies of scale--Mathematical models. 2. Equilibrium
   (Economics)--Mathematical models.   I. Title. II. Series.
   HD69.S5V545 1996
   339.5--dc20
                                                       96-16807
                                                       CIP

ISBN 3-540-61152-5 Springer-Verlag Berlin Heidelberg New York

© Springer-Verlag Berlin Heidelberg 1996
Printed in Germany

The use of general descriptive names, registered names, trademarks, etc. in this
publication does not imply, even in the absence of a specific statement, that such
names are exempt from the relevant protective laws and regulations and therefore
free for general use.

Typesetting: Camera ready by author
SPIN: 10516265   42/3142-543210 - Printed on acid-free paper

Preface

This is a book on general equilibrium in which firms are allowed to exhibit increasing returns to scale (more precisely, in which the convexity of production sets is not assumed). As such, it provides a full fledged general equilibrium model and analyzes the chief questions concerning existence and optimality.

Increasing returns is a topic which many economists find it to be simultaneously very *important*, very *difficult* and very *discouraging*. It is very important because it refers to a well established technological phenomenon which is essentially incompatible with the functioning of competitive markets. It is very difficult because the standard concepts and tools for the analysis fail (in particular, the supply mappings are not well defined). It is very discouraging because the available models do not seem to solve the basic questions: *Normative* models where nonconvex firms follow marginal pricing do not achieve efficient outcomes, and *positive* models cannot incorporate monopolistic competition as a way of defining the behavior of those firms with increasing returns to scale.

I would like to think that this monograph will contribute to show that "the increasing returns question" is neither too difficult nor too discouraging. Concerning the difficulty, it will be shown that the analysis can be carried out with essentially the same tools as those applicable to the standard competitive model. As for the relevance of the results available, let me point out the following.

1.- There are abstract existence results for general equilibrium models with increasing returns, under very weak assumptions. These results, however, have not yet provided definite advances on the main positive problem associated with increasing returns: the modelling of imperfectly competitive markets.

2.- The results concerning efficiency are partly negative. The extension of the second welfare theorem to economies with non-convex production sets points out that marginal pricing is a necessary condition for optimality. Yet, a number of robust examples show that marginal pricing equilibria are not generally Pareto optimal, may even be unable to satisfy production efficiency, and can be dominated by other equilibria.

The good side of these negative results is that there is a sound understanding of the difficulties involved in the allocation of resources through a market mechanism with nonconvex technologies. This knowledge provides clues which are precise enought to allow for positive results in more specific models.

Aims and Scope

This book offers a formal and systematic *exposition* of some of the main results on the existence and optimality of equilibria in economies where production sets are not assumed to be convex. There is an explicit attempt and making of it a suitable reference both for *graduate students*, and *researchers* with liking for general equilibrium (not necessarily specialists in mathematical economics).

With this twofold purpose in mind, the work has been written according to three key principles:

(i) The first one is to provide a **unified approach** to the problems involved. For that we construct a basic model which is rich enough to encompass the different models appearing throughout, and derive all the results as corollaries of a reduced number of general theorems.

(ii) The second one, is to carry out the analysis maintaining a relatively **low mathematical complexity**. Thus, when the estimated cost of generality exceeds the benefit of simplicity, we shall state and prove the theorems under assumptions which need not be the most general ones.

(iii) The third one refers to the search for a highly **self-contained exposition**. In particular, detailed proofs of the chief results and explanations of the main concepts are provided.

Since there are clear trade-offs between these principles, let us be precise on the chosen level of formal complexity: everyone familiar with the standard general equilibrium model (or endowed with an equivalent mathematical background), should not have any problem in going through this one. In particular, let us point out that all the action occurs in the $\mathbb{R}^l$ world.

The book may well be considered as a graduate textbook in general equilibrium. It contains all the basic elements for that (i.e., consumers and producers theory, equilibrium existence theorems, analysis of the efficiency of equilibrium allocations).

There is no "Mathematical Appendix" here. K. Border's (1985) book, *Fixed Point Theory with Applications to Economics and Game Theory*, is well suited for the mathematics which might be required. We shall refer to this book for those formal concepts and results which are supposed to be known.

Outline of Contents

The work is organized in ten chapters, which are gathered into three parts. Let us summarize here the contents of what follows.

(i) The first part, contains the basic model. Chapters 1, 2 and 3 present the fundamentals of a general equilibrium model: commodities and prices (chapter 1), consumers (chapter 2) and firms (chapter 3). All this is rather standard. Chapter 4 analyzes the existence of general equilibrium in a model where firms' behaviour is defined in terms of abstract pricing rules.

(ii) Part II is normative. It is devoted to the analysis of marginal pricing (a pricing rule satisfying the necessary conditions for optimality), and the efficiency of the associated equilibrium allocations. Chapters 5 and 6 deal with *marginal pricing* and *two-part tariffs*, respectively. Chapter 7 refers to the efficiency problem. It is shown there that every efficient allocation can be decentralized as a marginal pricing equilibrium, but also that marginal pricing equilibria are not generally Pareto optimal.

(iii) Part III is positive. It analyzes the family of *loss-free pricing rules* (those in which the equilibrium of firms involves non-negative profits), focusing on two main categories: profit maximization, both constrained and unconstrained, and average cost pricing (chapters 8 and 9). Chapter 10 presents a positive model where the equilibrium is defined, according to the classical tradition, by the equalization of firms' profitability.

The specific models presented in parts II and III illustrate the flexibility of the pricing rule approach for the analysis of general equilibrium, and add some flesh to the abstract framework of part I.

In order to facilitate the reading, assumptions, theorems, propositions, lemmata, corollaries and remarks are numbered consecutively within each chapter, preceeded by the chapter number (e.g., proposition 5.3 corresponds to the third proposition in the fifth chapter). The reader will find at the end of the book a short summary of the notation and definitions used along the text, as well as an analytical index of the assumptions and results. That is intended to serve as a quick reference for the reading and the location of the main concepts.

What's new?

The book contains some original research and a novel presentation fo some of the topics involved. Let me refer to these aspects now.

Chapter 4 presents a general equilibrium model and an abstract existence result which do not require the assumption of continuous wealth funcitons (the continuity of these mappings is only assumed on the set of production equilibria). This allows to treat the cases of marginal pricing, two-part tariffs and loss-free pricing as particular cases of this model, and derive the corresponding existence results as corollaries of a single theorem.

Chapter 5 includes a self-contained discussion of Clarke normal cones, and derives the main properties of the marginal pricing rule in a relatively simple way.

Chapter 6 exploits the generality of the existence result in chapter 4, and presents a model with two-part tariffs which extends that in Brown, Heller & Starr (1992).

Chapter 8 provides a common treatment to the models by Scarf (1986) and Dehez & Drèze (1988a, b), as particular instances of *constrained profit maximization.*

Finally, chapter 10 is brand new. It contains a model in which firms are created by consumers who seek for the maximum profitability of their investment. Thus in equilibrium all firms are equally profitable. Interestingly enough, this is an equilibrium concept with competitive features which does not depend on the convexity assumption.

Acknowledgments

I would like to thank those comments and remarks made to different parts of this work by Subir Chattopadhyay, Ana Guerrero, Thorsten Hens, Martine Quinzii, Walter Trockel and Rajiv Vohra. I am most grateful to Ana B. Ania, Carlos Alós and Carmen Herrero who read the whole manuscript and made very useful suggestions. Needless to say that all remaining errors are my own, and that I will be pleased in receiving comments, suggestions or criticisms.

Thaks are due to Vera Emmen and Mercedes Mateo, who helped me with the editing.

Financial support from the Dirección General de Investigación Científica y Técnica, under project PB92-0342 is gratefully acknowledged.

A Personal Remark

I first conceived the possibility of writing a monograph on general equilibrium with increasing returns during my visit to Stanford University (the academic year of 1992-93). That was mostly due to the influence of the works of J.M. Bonnisseau, B. Cornet, E.

Dierker, A. Mas-Colell and R. Vohra, after a workshop on this topic, held in Alicante [a first contribution on this appeared in Villar (1992, ch.4)]. Stanford provided a stimulating environment and the opportunity of writing a first manuscript.

The publication of Martine Quinzii's (1992) book, *Increasing Returns and Efficiency*, killed the project: Martine's book is an excellent work, carefully written and cleverly articulated. Most of the things covered by my old notes were already there, but much better told.

In spite of that, my interest on the topic has continued ever since. In 1994-95 I had to teach a course in general equilibrium with nonconvex technologies, for the students of the Q.E.D. program[1]. That forced me to write extensive notes on this issue, now with a very specific orientation: to serve as a course-book. After polishing and reshaping all the material previously accumulated, I came up with a nice bunch of written pages. As William Thomson put it once, I had reached the stage at which "life becomes miserable", that is, I started to seriously considering the possibility of making a book out of these notes. The final excuse was that now the appoach seemed to be different from (and complementary to) Martine's monograph. Be as it may, here we go.

A. Villar
Alicante, February 1996.

---

[1]The Quantitative Economics Doctorate, a doctoral program jointly developed by the Universities of Alicante, Bielefeld, Copenhaguen, Lisbon and Vienna.

CONTENTS

Part I

THE BASIC MODEL

Most economies organize their economic activity through the functioning of markets. Myriads of individual economic agents take decisions according to their private interests, whose interaction results in an allocation of resources. The production and exchange of commodities is at the centre of the picture: consumers demand commodities and supply labour services, firms produce commodities according to the technological knowledge, and commodities flow across agents by means of an exchange process which is realized through markets and prices.

General equilibrium models try to capture the logics of this complex net of interactions viewing the economic system as a whole, that is, taking into account all the simultaneous interdependencies established among economic agents (as opposed to partial equilibrium models, which typically concentrate on the analysis of specific markets or decision units). The first concern of general equilibrium theory refers to the analysis of conditions ensuring that all the actions taken independently by economic agents are simultaneously feasible. When all agents are realizing their plans, it is said that an *equilibrium* exists. An equilibrium is thus a situation in which agents do not find beneficial to change their actions. Needless to say that the nature of such an equilibrium depends on the behaviour of economic agents, and that the feasibility of the joint schedule may not correspond to a socially desirable state of affairs.

The analysis of the social desirability of equilibrium outcomes comes next in the agenda of general equilibrium theory. Suppose that the economy is arranged in such a way that all agents are simultaneously realizing their plans. Can the economy do better?. If this were the case, there would be scope for the intervention of some authority (the Government, say), because changing the spontaneous allocation of resources would result in a better state. The key questions are, of course, what "better" means, and whether such an authority will be able to improve the social situation.

There are many ways of ranking the outcomes of an economy, but there is a simple principle which seems difficult to object: no resource allocation can be considered satisfactory if it were possible to improve the situation of all the members of the society. This is the Pareto principle, which is to be understood as a minimal test of economic *efficiency*. Note that there may well be allocations passing this test which can be deemed socially undesirable. To be clear: We are not saying that the Pareto principle ensures good outcomes, what we are saying is that one should be worried about those outcomes which do not pass such a simple test.

The existence and efficiency of equilibrium allocations in market economies are the themes of this book. Different equilibrium models will be analyzed, and their efficiency properties discussed. In order to do so, this part of the book is devoted to the construction of a general equilibrium model in which production sets are not assumed to be convex. All the remaining discussion refers to specific models which are particularizations of this *basic model*.

Chapter 1 introduces the increasing returns question, refers to the pricing rule approach, and specifies the framework (commodities, prices, agents). Chapter 2 is devoted to the modelling of consumers (including the study of consumption sets, preferences, budget constraints and demand mappings). Chapter 3 deals with the technology and the behaviour of firms (thus, production sets, returns to scale and pricing rules are the subject of this chapter). Finally, chapter 4 presents a rather general equilibrium existence theorem, for an economy in which firms' behaviour is modelled in terms of abstract pricing rules.

Chapter 1

INTRODUCTION

1.1 EQUILIBRIUM AND INCREASING RE-TURNS

The standard Arrow-Debreu-McKenzie general equilibrium model of a competitive economy, provides a basic tool for the understanding of the functioning of *competitive markets*. It allows us to give a positive answer to the old question concerning the capability of prices and markets to coordinate economic activity in a decentralized framework. This model shows that, under a set of well specified assumptions, markets are in themselves sufficient institutions for the efficient allocation of resources. This may be called the *Invisible Hand Theorem*, and summarizes the most relevant features of competitive markets: the equilibria constitute a nonempty subset of the set of efficient allocations.

The *existence* of a competitive equilibrium is usually obtained by applying a fixed point argument. The strategy of the proof consists of identifying the set of competitive equilibria with the set of fixed points of a suitable mapping, and making use of Kakutani's fixed point theorem. For this approach to work, one has to be able to ensure that the set of attainable allocations of the economy is nonempty and bounded, and that the excess demand mapping is an upper hemicontinuous correspondence, with nonempty, closed and convex values. The convexity of preferences and of consumption and production sets allows one to obtain an excess demand mapping with such properties, when agents behave as payoff maximizers at given prices.

On the other hand, the *efficiency* of competitive equilibria is derived from two basic features. The first one refers again to the fact that agents behave as payoff maximizers at given prices, so that each agent equates her marginal rates of transformation to the relative prices (and hence, in equilibrium, they become equal for *all agents*). The second one is that *each variable affecting the payoff function of an individual has associated with it a price, and belongs to her choice set* (so that prices turn out to be sufficient information, enabling the exploitation of all benefits derived from production and exchange). The equalization of prices and marginal rates of transformation is a necessary condition for optimality, which under the assumption of convex preferences and choice sets (and complete markets) turns out to be sufficient as well.

Implicit in both results is the hypothesis of well informed decision makers. Thus, price-taking behaviour, perfect information, complete markets and quasi-concave payoff functions defined over convex choice sets are the key elements for the Invisible Hand Theorem to hold. This in turn points out that there are many relevant instances in which this Theorem does not work, either because competitive equilibria do not belong to the set of efficient allocations, or because they simply do not exist (externalities, asymmetric information, oligopolistic competition, etc.). The presence of increasing returns to scale (or more general forms of non-convex technologies) is a case in point.

The convexity of production sets can be derived from the combination of two primitive hypotheses: *Additivity* and *divisibility*. The additivity assumption says that if two production plans are technologically feasible, a new production plan consisting of the sum of these two will also be possible. Divisibility says that if a production plan is feasible, then any production plan consisting of a reduction in the scale of the former will also be feasible (non-increasing returns to scale). When these hypotheses hold, production sets turn out to be convex cones. While the additivity assumption seems hard to reject on economic or engineering grounds[1], the divisibility assumption is much more debatable, both theoretically and empirically. Hence the main sources of nonconvexities in production can be related to a failure in the divisibility assumption, that is, to the presence of *indivisibilities, fixed costs* or *increasing returns to scale* [see Mas-Colell (1987, IV-VI) and Guesnerie (1990, 5.1) for a brief discussion concerning the origin and classes of nonconvexities].

The presence of increasing returns in a market economy leads naturally

---

[1]Even though the theory allows for general convex sets, it is difficult to explain the lack of additivity. In some cases it is attributed to the existence of some limitation of inputs. But this cannot be part of the technological description of the economy, once *all* commodities are taken into account. Furthermore, allowing for some input restrictions in the description of production sets implies that we are admitting the existence of a procedure of allocating such scarce inputs, outside the market mechanism; in this case the first welfare theorem cannot be applied (it would be possible that a different allocation of these scarce inputs would result in a Pareto superior state).

to large scale firms. This involves a substantial change in the nature of market competition: firms with increasing returns to scale may well behave as monopolies, because they are able to affect market prices. Indeed, profit maximizing behaviour at given prices and increasing returns turn out to be incompatible (the supply mapping is not defined for non-zero outputs). This suggests two different (and complementary) lines of analysis. The first one is positive, and refers to the introduction of monopolistic competition in the study of market equilibria. The second one is normative, and focuses on the regulation of monopolies. Partial equilibrium analysis has produced many results in these lines of research.

General equilibrium models face serious difficulties in the presence of non-convex technologies, when there are finitely many firms and non-convexities are not negligible. Such difficulties are both analytical and theoretical and have mainly to do with the fact that the supply correspondence may not be convex-valued or even defined, so that the existence of equilibrium will typically fail. This implies that, if we want to analyze a general equilibrium model allowing for non-convex technologies, *we must permit the firms to follow more general rules of behaviour*, and suitably *re-define the equilibrium notion*. This will, however, imply that the *identification between equilibrium and optimum will no longer hold* (the Invisible Hand Theorem now splits into two halves). Thus the existence of equilibria under nonconvex technologies, and the analysis of their optimality properties become now two very different questions.

1.2 THE PRICING RULE APPROACH

The modern approach to these problems consists of building up a general equilibrium model which constitutes a genuine extension of the standard one. For that, an equilibrium for the economy is understood as a price vector, a list of consumption allocations, and a list of production plans such that: (a) consumers maximize their preferences subject to their budget constraints; (b) each individual firm is in "equilibrium" at those prices and production plans; and (c) the markets for all goods clear. It is the nature of the equilibrium condition (b) which establishes the difference with respect to the Walrasian model. The central question now becomes the following: *How to model consistently the behaviour of non-convex firms*, according to relevant positive and/or normative criteria.

A very general and powerful way of dealing with this question consists of associating the equilibrium of firms with the notion of a *pricing rule*, rather than to that of a supply correspondence. A pricing rule is a mapping from each firm's set of efficient production plans to the price space. The graph of such a mapping describes the prices-production pairs which a firm finds "acceptable" (a pricing rule may be thought of as the inverse mapping of a generalized "supply correspondence"). The advantage of formulating the problem in this way is twofold: (1) The notion of a pricing rule is an abstract construct which permits one to model different types of behaviour, and thus to analyze situations where profit maximization is not applicable. (2) These mappings may be upper hemicontinuous and convex-valued, even when the supply correspondence is not so, making it possible to use a fixed point argument (on the "inverse supply" mapping), in order to get the existence of an equilibrium.

As for the ways of modelling the behaviour of non-convex firms in terms of pricing rules, let us point out that both positive and normative approaches are possible. *Positive models* intend to describe plausible behaviour of firms in the context of unregulated markets, while *normative models* typically associate non-convex firms with public utilities (which may be privately owned but regulated). Models within the first category include constrained profit maximization (i.e., situations where firms maximize profits in the presence of some type of quantity constraint), and average cost (or more generally, mark-up) pricing. Normative models concentrate over two main pricing rules: marginal (cost) pricing, and regulation under break-even constraints (including the case of two-part tariffs, which may satisfy both criteria).

1.3   THE SETTING

Let us now briefly describe the background of the analysis, that is, the specification of those elements defining the basic framework of the modelling: (i) *Commodities and prices*, which are the variables of the problem; and (ii) *The agents*, which are the relevant decision units. The specification of these elements provides the implicit assumptions under which the whole book is constructed.

There is a fixed number ℓ of commodities (where ℓ is a natural number, with $1 \leq \ell < +\infty$). Each commodity is a good or service fully specified in terms of its physical properties and its availability (*when* the good is available, *where* is it available). Consequently, two goods or services which are physically identical, but are available at different dates (or in different locations), will be considered as two different commodities. Observe that $\ell < +\infty$ implies that both the number of dates and the number of locations contemplated in the model are finite.

The quantity of a commodity will be represented by a real number. This amounts to saying that we assume that commodities are perfectly divisible. This is certainly an over-simplification of the real world economies: objects such as computers, refrigerators or lorries are indivisible, so that 0.34 of one of these commodities makes little sense. Yet this is partly an interpretative issue. One may well consider that the commodities are not the goods themselves, but the *services* provided by these goods (i.e., time of computing or refrigeration facilities, or transport capacity measured in Tons per Km.). This way of looking at commodities makes the divisibility assumption more palatable.

Remark 1.1.- Observe that this interpretation implies that we are transforming the indivisibility problem in a problem of non-convexities in production: The firm which produces "computing facilities", say, will hardly have a convex production set.

The above specifications can be summarized by saying that we take $\mathbb{R}^\ell$ (the vector space obtained by replicating ℓ times the real numbers) as the *commodity space.*[2]

Each commodity $h = 1, 2, \ldots, \ell$ will have associated with it a real number p_h representing its price. The number p_h is to be interpreted as the amount to be paid here and today by a good or service, with precise physical characteristics, which will be delivered in a well specified date and location. In principle prices may be positive, zero or negative. Positive prices indicate that the corresponding commodity is "desirable". Zero prices may be interpreted as the definition of "free-goods": nobody is willing to pay a positive amount for the right to enjoy these goods. Finally, negative prices are to be interpreted as the cost of disposing of unwanted commodities (i.e., these are actually "bads", rather than goods). We shall concentrate on the case of non-negative prices (this can be derived in most cases from the "free-disposal" assumption over production sets, to be discussed later on). Thus, a *price system* will be represented by a vector $\mathbf{p} \in \mathbb{R}^\ell_+$.

Observe that $\mathbf{p}$ is a point in $\mathbb{R}^\ell$, which is precisely the commodity space. This introduces an implicit assumption which is essential: there is a price for each commodity. That is, commodities that will be available in future dates (or in different locations) have a well defined price, so that the costs and benefits of those actions concerning production and consumption can

---

[2]Note that taking $\mathbb{R}^\ell$ as the commodity space is a convenient assumption, since it exhibits very good operational properties. In particular, it provides both a vector space structure and a suitable topology (e.g., the scalar product is a well defined and continuous operation).

be properly evaluated. This is usually expressed by saying that *markets are complete.*

Economic agents are the decision units of the model (the "actors" of the story told in the next pages). There will be three types of agents: *Consumers, Firms* and *the Government.* Of these three categories, only the first two will be explicitly modelled, while "the Government" will appear as a Central Agency carrying some regulation policies (such as taxes or pricing schemes), and enforcing the property rights.

Consumers are the agents making consumption plans (i.e., deciding the demand for goods and services and the supply of labour, under the restriction of their available wealth). There will be a given number m of them. The *ith* consumer's choice set will be represented by a subset X_i of $\mathbb{R}^\ell$ (called consumption set), while u_i will denote her way of ranking the available alternatives (called her utility function).

Firms decide about production (and, possibly, about pricing policies), under the restriction of their technological knowledge. There will be a given number n of firms. The *jth* firm's choice set will be represented by a subset Y_j of $\mathbb{R}^\ell$ (called production set), while ϕ_j is meant to describe the way of choosing alternatives (called pricing rule).

It will be assumed that *all agents take their decisions under certainty,* that is, with a perfect knowledge of all variables affecting their opportunity sets and their choice mappings. This, combined with the implicit assumption of complete markets, implies that our setting is essentially static: all relevant information is available when agents take decisions.

In summary, we introduce the following:

Preliminary Axiom.- $\mathbb{R}^\ell$ is the commodity space, and $\mathbf{p} \in \mathbb{R}^\ell_+$ is a price system. There are m consumers and n firms, taking decisions under certainty conditions.

We call *economy* to a specification of the m consumers, the n firms (with their choice sets and choice criteria), and a vector $\omega \in \mathbb{R}^\ell$ which describes the initial resources (to be interpreted as those commodities which are available before production takes place). An economy can thus be described by:

$$E = \{(X_i, \; u_i)_{i=1}^m ; (Y_j, \; \phi_j)_{j=1}^n ; \omega\}$$

The functioning of an economy can be thought of as a process through which the initial endowments are transformed in nature, composition, availability and distribution across agents. The outcome of this process will depend not only upon the specifics of the economy (as described by the elements in E), but also upon the institutional framework (in particular concerning the property rights and the nature of the interactions between economic agents). That is why the outcome of economic activity is usually considered as a *resource allocation* process, and each of the different institutional frameworks (the different ways of organizing economic activity) for the economies under consideration, as a *resource allocation mechanism.*

1.4 FINAL COMMENTS

There is a number of papers which survey the recent literature on general equilibrium with increasing returns. Among them let us mention the following: Mas-Colell (1987) contains a simplified exposition of the problems and lines of research related to equilibrium models with increasing returns. Cornet (1988) provides a short review to general equilibrium with non-convex technologies, following the pricing rule approach; his paper is an Introduction to the special issue of the **Journal of Mathematical Economics** where many of the recent contributions appear. Dehez (1988) and Brown (1991) are much more comprehensive papers, well articulated and informative. Dehez's paper focuses more on interpretative issues, while Brown's work contains a very good systematization of the analytical underpinnings of these models. Guesnerie (1990) and Quinzii (1992) provide illuminating discussions of the normative aspects of the topic. Sharkey (1989) surveys the problem from a game theoretic viewpoint. Villar (1994a) is a summary of the results presented in this monograph.

The exposition of the setting is mostly a brief summary of Chapter 2 of Debreu's *Theory of Value.* The reader is referred to it for additional details.

Chapter 2

CONSUMERS

2.1 CONSUMPTION SETS

A **consumer** is an individual agent (a single household or a family) who takes consumption decisions, that is, decisions referring to the demand for goods and services and the supply of different types of labour. It will be assumed that there is a fixed number m of consumers, indexed by $i = 1, 2, ..., m$.

The choice set for the ith consumer is given by a subset X_i of $\mathbb{R}^\ell$ which describes feasible consumption vectors. By "feasible" it is meant here that they consist of combinations of consumption goods and labour which can be physically (including the individual biological constraints) realized. A **consumption plan** for the ith consumer is thus an ℓ-dimensional vector $\mathbf{x}_i \in X_i$. A consumption plan specifies some amounts of goods and labour which the ith consumer is able to realize. Those goods and services that the consumer demands will be denoted by positive numbers, while her supply of productive factors (different types of labour) will be denoted by negative ones.[1]

The ith consumer's **consumption set** $X_i \subset \mathbb{R}^\ell$, is the set of all feasible consumption plans for the ith consumer. The next figure illustrates a consumption set in $\mathbb{R}^2$, where commodity 1 corresponds to a consumption good (corn) while commodity 2 is a productive factor (labour).

---

[1] One can also take $X_i \subset \mathbb{R}^\ell_+$, by properly specifying the productive factors that might be supplied by the ith consumer [on this see Arrow & Hahn (1971, Chap. 3)].

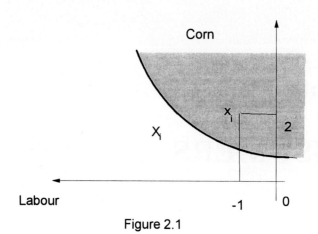

Figure 2.1

Point $\mathbf{x}_i = (-1, 2)$ represents a consumption plan, while the set $X_i \subset \mathbb{R}^2$ gives us the *ith* consumer's consumption set.

Remark 2.1.- Note that consumption sets inform about things such as the maximum number of hours a consumer can supply, the minimum requirements of goods and services a consumer needs in order to survive, and the consumption-labour combinations which are biologically feasible. They thus contain relevant information about the possibilities of the economy.

Concerning consumption sets we shall assume the following:

A.2.1.– For every $i = 1, 2, \ldots, m$, X_i is a nonempty closed and convex subset of $\mathbb{R}^\ell$, bounded from below (that is, there is $\mathbf{c}_i \in \mathbb{R}^\ell$ such that $\mathbf{c}_i \leq \mathbf{x}_i$, $\forall \mathbf{x}_i \in X_i$).

Besides nonemptyness, the first part of this assumption is partly technical (closedness simply says that if $\{\mathbf{x}_i^\nu\}$ is a sequence in X_i converging to a point $\mathbf{x}_i' \in \mathbb{R}^\ell$, then $\mathbf{x}_i' \in X_i$). It also says that if two consumption plans are feasible, so will be any intermediate combination (that is, if $\mathbf{x}_i, \mathbf{x}_i'$ are in X_i, then $[\lambda \mathbf{x}_i + (1 - \lambda)\mathbf{x}_i']$ is also in X_i, for any scalar λ in the closed interval $[0, 1]$). It is also assumed that X_i is bounded from below; this is a natural assumption, since demands are denoted by nonnegative numbers, and the amount of labour a consumer can supply cannot exceed 24 hours a day. Note that if one takes $X_i = \mathbb{R}_+^\ell$ assumption (A.2.1) is automatically satisfied.

The *ith* consumer's economic problem consists of choosing a best consumption plan among those which belong to X_i and are *affordable* (note that this is something else than being physically realizable). Modelling that requires to be precise about the ith consumer's way of ranking alternative consumption plans, and about her (budget) restrictions. This is what is done in the next sections.

2.2 PREFERENCES

In order to model the way in which a consumer ranks different consumption plans we shall assume that there is a binary relation $\succeq_i$ defined over X_i. Let $\mathbf{x}_i, \mathbf{x}'_i$ be points in X_i; then $\mathbf{x}'_i \succeq_i \mathbf{x}_i$ means that $\mathbf{x}'_i$ is *at least as good as* $\mathbf{x}_i$, from the *ith* consumer's viewpoint. We shall refer to $\succeq_i$ as the *ith* consumer's **preference relation**.

Concerning this preference relation we postulate a number of axioms which provide a suitable basis for the modelling of consumers' behaviour. These axioms will be gathered into three different groups. The first group of axioms (completeness and transitivity) refers to order properties; they ensure that the preference relation is a complete preorder. The second group (continuity and convexity) introduces a rich analytical structure. The reader will observe that the first group of axioms is independent of the assumptions on X_i established in (A.2.1), whereas the second one is not. Finally, the third group refers to alternative notions of non-satiation.

2.2.1 Order properties

Let us start by presenting and discussing the first group of axioms:

(COMP).- (COMPLETENESS)
   Let $\mathbf{x}_i, \mathbf{x}'_i \in X_i$, then:

$$[\mathbf{x}_i \succeq_i \mathbf{x}'_i \text{ or } \mathbf{x}'_i \succeq_i \mathbf{x}_i]$$

(TRA).- (TRANSITIVITY)
   Let $\mathbf{x}_i, \mathbf{x}'_i, \mathbf{x}''_i \in X_i$, then:

$$[\mathbf{x}_i \succeq_i \mathbf{x}'_i \ \& \ \mathbf{x}'_i \succeq_i \mathbf{x}''_i] \Longrightarrow \mathbf{x}_i \succeq_i \mathbf{x}''_i$$

Axiom (COMP) discards the presence of alternatives that the *ith* consumer cannot compare. Observe that it implies that $\succeq_i$ is also *reflexive*. The transitivity axiom is to be understood as a property of "consistency in the evaluation". Nevertheless, even under certainty, transitivity can be violated in some cases; the best known examples are those in which the *ith* consumer has imperfect discriminatory power (inaccurate perception), or when the *ith* agent is actually a family and takes decisions by majority voting.

Axioms (COMP) and (TRA) imply that $\succeq_i$ is a *complete preference preorder*. This preorder reflects the *ith* consumer's evaluation of alternative consumption plans. From this preference preorder we can deduce a new binary relation, called **indifference relation** and denoted by $\sim_i$, which is defined as follows: Given $\mathbf{x}_i, \mathbf{x}_i'$ in X_i,

$$\mathbf{x}_i \sim_i \mathbf{x}_i' \Longleftrightarrow [\mathbf{x}_i \succeq_i \mathbf{x}_i' \ \& \ \mathbf{x}_i' \succeq_i \mathbf{x}_i]$$

to be read as $\mathbf{x}_i$ is *indifferent* to $\mathbf{x}_i'$, meaning that both consumption plans are equally satisfactory from the *ith* consumer's point of view.

Remark 2.2.- Note that "being indifferent" and "being non-comparable" are two logically distinct statements. The first one says $\mathbf{x}_i \succeq_i \mathbf{x}_i'$ *and* $\mathbf{x}_i'$ $\succeq_i \mathbf{x}_i$, while the second one asserts that *neither* $\mathbf{x}_i \succeq_i \mathbf{x}_i'$ *nor* $\mathbf{x}_i' \succeq_i \mathbf{x}_i$.

The indifference relation is obviously reflexive, symmetric (i.e., $\mathbf{x}_i \sim_i \mathbf{x}_i'$ implies $\mathbf{x}_i' \sim_i \mathbf{x}_i$), and transitive. It is thus an *equivalence relation* whose classes are called *indifference classes* (or *curves*). Let $\mathbf{x}_i'$ be a point in X_i. Call $I(\mathbf{x}_i')$ the set of points in X_i which are indifferent to $\mathbf{x}_i'$, that is,

$$I(\mathbf{x}_i') = \{\mathbf{x}_i \in X_i \ / \ \mathbf{x}_i \sim_i \mathbf{x}_i'\}$$

Axioms (COMP) and (TRA) over $\succeq_i$ imply that $\sim_i$ is an equivalence relation so that it generates a partition over X_i, that is:

$$I(\mathbf{x}_i') \neq \emptyset \text{ for each } \mathbf{x}_i' \in X_i$$

$$\bigcup_{x_i \in X_i} I(\mathbf{x}_i') = X_i$$

$$I(\mathbf{x}_i') \bigcap I(\mathbf{x}_i'') \neq \emptyset \Longrightarrow I(\mathbf{x}_i') \equiv I(\mathbf{x}_i'')$$

We can define now a third binary relation, called **strict preference** and denoted by $\succ_i$, as follows: for any two consumption plans $\mathbf{x}_i, \mathbf{x}_i' \in X_i$

$$\mathbf{x}_i \succ_i \mathbf{x}_i' \Longleftrightarrow [\mathbf{x}_i \succeq_i \mathbf{x}_i' \ \& \ \mathbf{x}_i' \notin I(\mathbf{x}_i)]$$

The expression $\mathbf{x}_i \succ_i \mathbf{x}'_i$ is to be read as $\mathbf{x}_i$ *is preferred to* $\mathbf{x}'_i$ *by the ith consumer.* Assumptions (COMP) and (TRA) imply that this relation is *irreflexive* ($\mathbf{x}_i$ cannot be preferred to itself) and *asymmetric* (that is, $\mathbf{x}_i \succ_i \mathbf{x}'_i$ implies that $\mathbf{x}'_i$ cannot be preferred to $\mathbf{x}_i$). Therefore, this relation induces a complete and strict ordering over the indifference classes [the elements of the quotient set $(X_i/ \sim_i)$].

Summing up: Assumptions (COMP) and (TRA) over the preference relation $\succeq_i$ enable to partition the consumption set into classes which gather consumption bundles which are indifferent for the *ith* consumer, and are completely ordered by $\succ_i$. The consumer's choice problem thus consists of selecting a consumption bundle which is maximal in the subset of the affordable ones (i.e., a bundle in the "highest" indifference class attainable).

2.2.2 Analytical axioms

In order to formalize these axioms, we shall implicitly assume that (A.2.1) holds. Consider the following definitions, which provide additional qualifications to the preference relation:

Definition 2.1.-
    A preference relation $\succeq_i$ defined over a topological space X_i is **continuous** if, for every $\mathbf{x}_i \in X_i$, the sets:
$$B_i(\mathbf{x}_i) \equiv \{\mathbf{x}'_i \in X_i \ / \ \mathbf{x}'_i \succ_i \mathbf{x}_i\}$$
$$W_i(\mathbf{x}_i) \equiv \{\mathbf{x}'_i \in X_i \ / \ \mathbf{x}_i \succ_i \mathbf{x}'_i \}$$
are open sets in X_i.

Observe that $B_i(\mathbf{x}_i)$ is the set of consumption plans which are *better than* $\mathbf{x}_i$, while $W_i(\mathbf{x}_i)$ is the set of options which are *worse than* $\mathbf{x}_i$. Continuity says that these sets are open. The intuition is clear: Let $\mathbf{x}_i$, $\mathbf{x}'_i$ be points in X_i such that $\mathbf{x}'_i \succ_i \mathbf{x}_i$; then, points which are "close enough" to $\mathbf{x}'_i$ will also be preferred to $\mathbf{x}_i$. More formally, $\succeq_i$ is continuous if for any $\mathbf{x}_i, \mathbf{x}'_i \in X_i$ with $\mathbf{x}'_i \succ_i \mathbf{x}_i$ there are neighbourhoods $\epsilon(\mathbf{x}'_i)$ and $\delta(\mathbf{x}_i)$ such that, for each $\mathbf{z} \in \epsilon(\mathbf{x}'_i)$ we have $\mathbf{z} \succ_i \mathbf{x}_i$, and for each $\mathbf{z} \in \delta(\mathbf{x}_i)$, $\mathbf{x}'_i \succ_i \mathbf{z}$.

We introduce then the following axiom:

(CONT).- (CONTINUITY)
    $\succeq_i$ is continuous.

Consider now the following sets:
$$BE_i(\mathbf{x}_i) \equiv \{\mathbf{x}'_i \in X_i/\mathbf{x}'_i \succeq_i \mathbf{x}_i\}$$
$$WE_i(\mathbf{x}_i) \equiv \{\mathbf{x}'_i \in X_i/\mathbf{x}_i \succeq_i \mathbf{x}'_i\}$$

These are the *better or equal than* and the *worse or equal than* sets. By complementarity, the continuity of $\succeq_i$ can equally be defined by requiring these sets to be closed in X_i. Observe that this implies that *indifference classes are closed*, since we can write: $I(\mathbf{x}_i) \equiv BE_i(\mathbf{x}_i) \cap WE_i(\mathbf{x}_i)$. Furthermore, it is clear by (COMP) that $BE_i(\mathbf{x}_i^\circ) \cup WE_i(\mathbf{x}_i^\circ) = X_i$.

It is interesting to note that the order axioms are not independent from the continuity axiom. In particular:

Proposition 2.1.- [Schmeidler (1971)]
Let $\succeq_i$ be a preference relation defined over a connected[2] subset X_i of a topological space. Suppose that $\succeq_i$ is transitive and continuous in X_i, and that there are elements $\mathbf{x}_i$, $\mathbf{x}_i'$ in X_i such that $\mathbf{x}_i \succ_i \mathbf{x}_i'$. Then, $\succeq_i$ is also complete.

Proof.-
(We drop the subscripts to make notation simpler)
Let us show first that for all $\mathbf{x}, \mathbf{x}' \in X$ such that $\mathbf{x} \succ \mathbf{x}'$ one has

$$T = \{\mathbf{z} \,/\, \mathbf{z} \succ \mathbf{x}'\} \;\bigcup\; \{\mathbf{z} \,/\, \mathbf{x} \succ \mathbf{z}\} = X \qquad [1]$$

By definition, $T \subset T' = \{\mathbf{z} \,/\, \mathbf{z} \succeq \mathbf{x}'\} \bigcup \{\mathbf{z} \,/\, \mathbf{x} \succeq \mathbf{z}\}$. To see that the converse inclusion also holds, let $\mathbf{r} \in \{\mathbf{z} \,/\, \mathbf{z} \succeq \mathbf{x}'\}$, and suppose that $\mathbf{r}$ does not belong to $\{\mathbf{z} \,/\, \mathbf{z} \succ \mathbf{x}'\}$. We can write then $\mathbf{x}' \succeq \mathbf{r}$. Since $\mathbf{x} \succ \mathbf{x}'$, it follows from transitivity that $\mathbf{x} \succ \mathbf{r}$, and hence that $\mathbf{r}$ is a point in $\{\mathbf{z} \,/\, \mathbf{x} \succ \mathbf{z}\}$. The same reasoning applies for the case $\mathbf{x} \succeq \mathbf{r}$.

Therefore, $T = T' \neq \emptyset$ (since $\mathbf{x} \succ \mathbf{x}'$ by assumption). But being X a connected set, T open and T' closed (by continuity), it follows that $T = T' = X$. That proves[3] the equality postulated in [1]. Suppose now that preferences are not complete. Let then $\mathbf{v}, \mathbf{w} \in X$ non-comparable. According to [1], if $\mathbf{x} \succ \mathbf{x}'$,

$$\{\mathbf{z} \,/\, \mathbf{z} \succ \mathbf{x}'\} \;\bigcup\; \{\mathbf{z} \,/\, \mathbf{x} \succ \mathbf{z}\} = X$$

so that, either $\mathbf{v} \succ \mathbf{x}'$, or $\mathbf{x} \succ \mathbf{v}$. Without loss of generality, let $\mathbf{v} \succ \mathbf{x}'$. We would have:

$$\{\mathbf{z} \,/\, \mathbf{z} \succ \mathbf{x}'\} \;\bigcup\; \{\mathbf{z} \,/\, \mathbf{v} \succ \mathbf{z}\} = X$$

Hence, $\mathbf{w} \succ \mathbf{x}'$ or $\mathbf{v} \succ \mathbf{w}$. Being $\mathbf{w}, \mathbf{v}$ non-comparable, it follows that

---

[2]Let X be a subset of a topological space S. X is **connected** if it cannot be expressed as the union of two nonempty and disjoint open subsets of S. Intuitively, X is connected if it is "made of a single piece".

[3]Let us recall here that a nonempty subset T of a connected topological space X can only be open and closed in X if it is precisely X.

$$\mathbf{w} \succ \mathbf{x'} \ \& \ \mathbf{v} \succ \mathbf{x'}$$

Thus, the open sets $\{\mathbf{z} \ / \ \mathbf{v} \succ \mathbf{z}\}, \{\mathbf{z} \ / \ \mathbf{w} \succ \mathbf{z}\}$ have a nonempty and open intersection. Furthermore, $\{\mathbf{z} \ / \ \mathbf{v} \succ \mathbf{z}\} \cap \{\mathbf{z} \ / \ \mathbf{w} \succ \mathbf{z}\}$ is not X (by construction). We can show now the following equality:

$$\{\mathbf{z} \ / \ \mathbf{v} \succ \mathbf{z}\} \cap \{\mathbf{z} \ / \ \mathbf{w} \succ \mathbf{z}\} = \{\mathbf{z} \ / \ \mathbf{v} \succeq \mathbf{z}\} \cap \{\mathbf{z} \ / \ \mathbf{w} \succeq \mathbf{z}\}$$

Let $\mathbf{v} \succeq \mathbf{z}, \mathbf{w} \succeq \mathbf{z}$. The fact that $\mathbf{z} \succeq \mathbf{v}$ and the transitivity of the preference relation imply that $\mathbf{w} \succeq \mathbf{v}$, which goes against the assumption. On the other hand, $\mathbf{z} \succeq \mathbf{w}$ and transitivity would imply $\mathbf{v} \succeq \mathbf{w}$. Thus, the only possibility would be $\mathbf{v} \succ \mathbf{z}$ and $\mathbf{w} \succ \mathbf{z}$, so that the previous inequality holds. But then we have a nonempty and open set in the left hand side, which is equal to a nonempty and closed one in the right hand side. This can only be if both are equal to X, which are not by hypothesis. Then the relation $\succeq$ must be complete. ♠

The case of a preference relation which satisfies (COMP) and (TRA) but it is not continuous is the **lexicographic ordering**. For $X_i = \mathbb{R}^2_+$ this ordering can be defined as follows: given $\mathbf{x} = (x_1, x_2), \mathbf{z} = (z_1, z_2) \in X_i$,

$$\mathbf{z} \succ \mathbf{x} \ \text{if} \ \begin{cases} \text{(i) } z_1 > x_1, \text{ or} \\ \text{(ii) if } z_1 = x_1, \ y \ z_2 > x_2 \end{cases}$$

The next figure shows clearly that the set $B_i(\mathbf{x})$ is neither open nor closed.

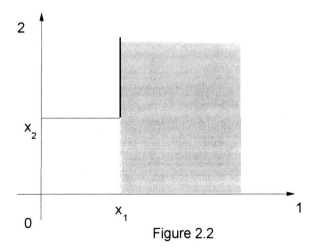

Figure 2.2

Let us consider now a series of alternative axioms on the *convexity of preferences*. They are presented in decreasing order of generality. Convexity is a postulate on the *liking of variety*: intermediate combinations of consumption bundles tend to be more appreciated. The particularities of the different axioms will be clear along the discussion.

(WCONV).- (WEAK CONVEXITY)

Let X_i be convex. For all $\mathbf{x}_i, \mathbf{x}'_i \in X_i$, every scalar $\lambda \in [0,1]$,

$$\mathbf{x}_i \succeq_i \mathbf{x}'_i \Longrightarrow [\lambda \mathbf{x}_i + (1-\lambda)\mathbf{x}'_i] \succeq_i \mathbf{x}'_i$$

In words: a preference relation is convex if any convex combination of two consumption plans is at least as good as the less preferred one. Thus the convexity of preferences pictures a consumer who likes variety: a combination of any two consumption bundles never makes the consumer worse off. When preferences satisfy (COMP), (TRA), (CONT) and (WCONV), then the better than sets $B_i(\mathbf{x}_i)$ are open convex sets (and the better or equal than sets are closed convex sets). These axioms are compatible with the presence of *thick* indifference curves (that is, curves with nonempty interior).

A slightly more demanding axiom is the following:

(CONV).- (CONVEXITY)

Let X_i be convex. For all $\mathbf{x}_i, \mathbf{x}'_i \in X_i$, every scalar $\lambda \in (0,1]$,

$$\mathbf{x}_i \succ_i \mathbf{x}'_i \Longrightarrow [\lambda \mathbf{x}_i + (1-\lambda)\mathbf{x}'_i] \succ_i \mathbf{x}'_i$$

It can be shown [e.g. Debreu (1959, p. 60)] that, under (COMP), (TRA) and (CONT), Convexity implies Weak Convexity. Moreover, it follows from (CONV) that if $\mathbf{x}'_i$ is not a *bliss point* (a maximum of $\succeq_i$ over X_i), then the set $I_i(\mathbf{x}'_i)$ has a nonempty interior.

The next figure shows the class of indifference curves which are compatible with the axioms established so far, in the simplified world of two goods (labour and corn).

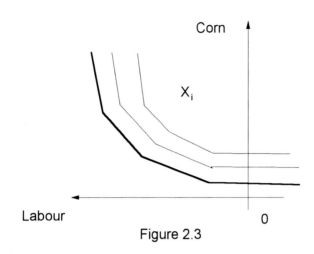

Figure 2.3

It can be seen that (CONV) is still a relatively mild assumption, which permits the presence of *segments* in the indifference curves. A stricter assumption which eliminates this possibility is the following:

(SCONV).- (STRONG CONVEXITY)
   Let X_i be convex. For all $\mathbf{x}_i, \mathbf{x}_i' \in X_i$, any $\lambda \in (0, 1)$,

$$\mathbf{x}_i \succeq_i \mathbf{x}_i' \implies [\lambda \mathbf{x}_i + (1 - \lambda)\mathbf{x}_i'] \succ_i \mathbf{x}_i'$$

This axiom says that if $\mathbf{x}_i$ is better than $\mathbf{x}_i'$, then every intermediate bundle will also be preferred to $\mathbf{x}_i'$. This obviously excludes the possibility of indifference curves with segments.

2.2.3 Axioms of non-satiation

Axioms of non-satiation introduce the idea that, in any relevant economic problem, the available commodities are always *scarce* relative to the needs and desires of consumers. Some will postulate that this is the essence of economic problems. The following axioms, presented in a decreasing level of generality, provide alternative formalizations of this general idea:

(NS) (NON-SATIATION)
For every $\mathbf{x}_i \in X_i$ there exists $\mathbf{x}_i' \in X_i$ such that $\mathbf{x}_i' \succ_i \mathbf{x}_i$.

(LNS) (LOCAL NON-SATIATION)
For every $\mathbf{x}_i \in X_i$, any scalar $\alpha > 0$, there exists $\mathbf{x}_i' \in N_\alpha(\mathbf{x}_i) \cap X_i$ such that $\mathbf{x}_i' \succ_i \mathbf{x}_i$ (where $N_\alpha(\mathbf{x}_i)$ denotes a ball of centre $\mathbf{x}_i$ and radius α).

(SM) (SEMIMONOTONICITY)
For all $\mathbf{x}_i \in X_i$ there exists some j (which might well depend on $\mathbf{x}_i$) such that $\mathbf{x}_i + \lambda \mathbf{e}^j \succ_i \mathbf{x}_i$, for all $\lambda > 0$, where $\mathbf{e}^j \in \mathbb{R}^\ell$ is a vector whose components are all zero except the jth one, which is equal to one.

(NS) simply says that for any given consumption bundle, there always exists some preferred one. Local Non-Satiation is more precise: it says that *arbitrarily close* to any consumption bundle, there always exists a better one. Finally, Semimonotonicity establishes that for any given $\mathbf{x}_i \in X_i$, one can find better alternatives by increasing the amount of some commodity. When this property holds for some commodity j independently of the bundle $\mathbf{x}_i$ under consideration, we say that good j is a **desirable** commodity for the *ith* consumer.

It is immediate to check that (SM) implies (LNS) which in turn implies (NS). It is also easy to see that none of this axioms prevents the possibility that the *ith* consumer gets satiated with respect to some good; what certainly precludes is the possibility of satiation with respect to all commodities simultaneously. Local Non-Satiation directly implies that indifference curves have empty interior, and that the maximal elements cannot be interior points of the choice set. These properties also derive from the combination of (CONV) and (NS). Indeed, it can be shown that, under (COMP), (TRA) and (CONT), Weak Convexity and Local Non-Satiation hold if and only if (CONV) and (NS) hold.

A substantially stronger axiom in this family is the following:

(MON).- (MONOTONICITY)
Let $\mathbf{x}_i, \mathbf{x}_i' \in X_i$ be such that $\mathbf{x}_i >> \mathbf{x}_i'$. Then $\mathbf{x}_i$ is better than $\mathbf{x}_i'$.

This axiom provides an extremely simple specification of the idea of non-satiation. It says "the more, the better".[4] Even though this axioms is useful in facilitating the proofs of some theorems, it is very restrictive. It asks

---

[4]There is a weaker version, known as **weak monotonicity**, which says that $\mathbf{x}_i \geq \mathbf{x}_i'$ implies $\mathbf{x}_i \succeq_i \mathbf{x}_i'$. And there is also a stronger version, called **strong monotonicity**, which says that $\mathbf{x}_i > \mathbf{x}_i'$ implies $\mathbf{x}_i \succ_i \mathbf{x}_i'$.

the consumer to always prefer additional amounts of commodities. It is not difficult to find everyday life examples of goods that some people find desirable whereas some other deeply reject (think of commodities such as fast-food, acid music, or economic theory lectures).

Remark 2.3.- If a preference preorder satisfies (CONT), (CONV) and (NS), then it has closed indifference curves with empty interior, and the better than sets turn out to be convex. This suggests that any point in the boundary of a better than set can be supported by a hyperplane (to be understood as a linear price system).

The following assumption gathers in a single hypothesis the axioms that will be used in order to model the behaviour of consumers:

<u>A.2.2.-</u> For all $i = 1, 2, \ldots, m$, $\succeq_i$ is a complete, transitive, continuous, weakly convex and locally non-satiated preference preordering.

2.3   THE UTILITY FUNCTION

We have seen that, under assumptions (COMP) and (TRA), a preference relation generates a partition over the consumption set, via the indifference relation. The following question arises naturally in this context: Can we associate a real number to each indifference class, so that the order induced by the relation $\succeq_i$ translates into an order over real numbers?. Or, more formally: is there any real-valued function which enables a numerical representation of the preference relation?. If such a mapping exists, the *ith* consumer's choice problem can be formulated as the maximization of a real-valued function (rather than as the search for maximal elements of a binary relation). This formulation is usually easier to handle (and allows us to apply a number of well established mathematical results, when such a function is continuous).

<u>Definition 2.2.-</u>
A real-valued function $u_i : X_i \longrightarrow \mathbb{R}$ **represents** a preference relation $\succeq_i$ over X_i if, for any $\mathbf{x}_i, \mathbf{x}'_i \in X_i : u_i(\mathbf{x}_i) \geq u_i(\mathbf{x}'_i) \Longleftrightarrow \mathbf{x}_i \succeq_i \mathbf{x}'_i$.
Function u_i is called a **utility function.**

Three remarks are in order:
(i) By definition, for any increasing function $f : \mathbb{R} \longrightarrow \mathbb{R}$, we have:

$$f\left[u_i(\mathbf{x}_i)\right] \geq f\left[u_i(\mathbf{x}'_i)\right] \Longleftrightarrow u_i(\mathbf{x}_i) \geq u_i(\mathbf{x}'_i) \Longleftrightarrow \mathbf{x}_i \succeq_i \mathbf{x}'_i$$

so that u_i simply *represents* $\succeq_i$, and its actual values are not relevant magnitudes.

(ii) Note also that for such a representation being a useful tool (in the sense of allowing for the formulation of the consumer's choice problem as a maximization problem), the utility function should be continuous.

(iii) The existence of such a function is not an immediate problem when X_i is not countable, and the preference relation is not trivial (i.e., not all elements in X_i are indifferent).

It turns out that the continuity of the preference relation is the key assumption for the existence of a continuous utility function, when X_i is taken to be a connected subset of $\mathbb{R}^{\ell}$. The next result is a powerful tool in the analysis of consumer choices, and will be presented without proof. A detailed proof of a slightly less general result, which is nevertheless adequate for our purposes, is presented in the Appendix:

Proposition 2.2.- [Debreu (1959, 4.6)]

Let $\mathbf{X}_i$ be a connected subset of $\mathbb{R}^{\ell}$, and $\succeq_i$ a preference relation satisfying assumptions (COMP), (TRA) and (CONT). Then, there exists a continuous function $\mathbf{u}_i{:}\mathbf{X}_i \to \mathbb{R}$ which represents this preference relation.

The following result is obtained:

Theorem 2.1.-

Let $\succeq_i$ be a preference relation defined over a connected subset $\mathbf{X}_i$ of $\mathbb{R}^{\ell}$. Suppose furthermore that there are at least two elements $\mathbf{x}_i, \mathbf{x}_i' \in \mathbf{X}_i$ such that $\mathbf{x}_i \succ_i \mathbf{x}_i'$. Then, $\succeq_i$ can be represented by a continuous utility function if and only if it is transitive and continuous.

Proof.-

($\Longrightarrow$) Follows directly from Propositions 2.1 and 2.2.

($\Longleftarrow$) If $u_i : X_i \to \mathbb{R}$ is continuous over X_i, then it is a single-valued mapping defined for all $\mathbf{x}_i$ (hence $\succeq_i$ is complete); furthermore, since it applies over $\mathbb{R}$ it preserves the natural order of the real numbers (so that $\succeq_i$ is transitive). Finally, continuity implies that the inverse image of open sets are open; in particular, the sets of points $\mathbf{x}_i \in X_i$ such that $u_i(\mathbf{x}_i) > u_i(\mathbf{x}_i')$ [resp. $u_i(\mathbf{x}_i) < u_i(\mathbf{x}_i')$], are open (and hence the better and worse than sets are open, so that $\succeq_i$ is continuous).♠

Therefore, under assumptions (TRA) and (CONT), every nontrivial preference relation defined over a connected subset of $\mathbb{R}^{\ell}$ can *equivalently* be described by a real-valued function. We shall use the utility representation, since it makes easier the exposition. The search for maximal elements will then be formulated as the maximization of a continuous real valued function (let us recall here that Weierstrass theorem ensures that such a maximum will exist over any compact nonempty subset of X_i).

Let us consider now the following definition:

Definition 2.3.- (QUASI-CONCAVITY)
   (i) A function $F : \mathbb{R}^n \to \mathbb{R}$ is **quasi-concave** if, for all $\mathbf{x}, \mathbf{y} \in \mathbb{R}^n$, every $\lambda \in [0, 1]$, we have:

$$F(\mathbf{x}) \geq F(\mathbf{y}) \Longrightarrow F[\lambda \mathbf{x} + (1 - \lambda)\mathbf{y}] \geq F(\mathbf{y})$$

   (ii) Function F is **semi-strictly quasi-concave** if, for all $\mathbf{x}, \mathbf{y} \in \mathbb{R}^n$, every $\lambda \in (0, 1]$, we have:

$$F(\mathbf{x}) > F(\mathbf{y}) \Longrightarrow F[\lambda \mathbf{x} + (1 - \lambda)\mathbf{y}] > F(\mathbf{y})$$

   (iii) Function F is **strictly quasi-concave** if, for all $\mathbf{x}, \mathbf{y} \in \mathbb{R}^n$, every $\lambda \in (0, 1)$, we have:

$$F(\mathbf{x}) \geq F(\mathbf{y}) \Longrightarrow F[\lambda \mathbf{x} + (1 - \lambda)\mathbf{y}] > F(\mathbf{y})$$

These definitions are obviously linked to the alternative notions of convex preferences presented above. In particular, (WCONV) is equivalent to the quasi-concavity of u_i, (CONV) is equivalent to the semi-strict quasi-concavity of u_i, and (SCONV) is equivalent to the strict quasi-concavity of u_i. Observe that when we maximize a semi-strictly quasi-concave function over a convex set, any maximum turns out to be a *global maximum* (by the Local-Global theorem [5]). This is important because usual methods that enable to find extremal points only allow to identify local extrema. It is easy to see that if one maximizes a strictly quasi-concave function over a convex set, then if a solution exists it will be unique.

The following result gives us the additional properties derived from the convexity assumption:

---

[5]The Local-Global theorem can be stated as follows: Let $U : D \to \mathbb{R}$ be a continuous and semi-estrictly quasi-concave function, whenre D is a convex subset of $\mathbb{R}^n$. Then, any maximum of U over D is a global maximum.

Corollary 2.1.-

Let $\succeq_i$ be a nontrivial preference relation, defined over a convex subset $X_i \subset \mathbb{R}^\ell$ that satisfies (TRA), (CONT) and (WCONV). Then, there is a continuous and quasi-concave utility function $u_i : X_i \to \mathbb{R}$ which represents $\succeq_i$.

The following assumption is a rewriting of (A.2.2) in terms of utility functions:

A.2.2'.- For all $i = 1, 2, \ldots, m$, $u_i : X_i \to \mathbb{R}$ is a continuous and quasi-concave utility function satisfying local non-satiation.

2.4   WEALTH RESTRICTIONS

Let $\mathbf{p} \in \mathbb{R}^\ell_+$, be a price vector, and $\mathbf{x}_i \in X_i$, a consumption plan. The ith consumer's **expenditure** is given by the scalar product

$$\mathbf{p}\mathbf{x}_i = \sum_{k=1}^{\ell} p_k x_{ik}$$

Note that, according to the sign convention, $\mathbf{p}\mathbf{x}_i$ actually describes the difference between the cost of goods and services demanded (those commodities with positive entries), and the revenue obtained by selling factors (those commodities with negative ones).

A scalar $r_i \in \mathbb{R}$ will denote the ith consumer's **wealth**, to be understood as an expenditure capacity which is not related to the income obtained from the supply of factors (we can think of r_i as the net worth of the ith consumer's assets). Throughout this chapter r_i will be considered as a given magnitude (even though later on will be treated as a function, depending on market prices and firms' production).

The ith consumer's *wealth constraint*, which determines what is affordable to her, can be expressed as the set of consumption plans $\mathbf{x}_i$ in X_i satisfying: $\mathbf{p}\mathbf{x}_i \leq r_i$. Let us define the ith consumer's **budget correspondence** as a mapping $\gamma_i : \mathbb{R}^\ell_+ \times \mathbb{R} \to X_i$ given by:

$$\gamma_i(\mathbf{p}, r_i) \equiv \{\mathbf{x}_i \in X_i \ / \ \mathbf{p}\mathbf{x}_i \leq r_i\}$$

Two immediate (but relevant) properties of this correspondence are the following:

(i) γ_i is homogeneous of degree zero in $(\mathbf{p}, r_i)$, that is, for every $\lambda > 0$, $\gamma_i(\lambda \mathbf{p}, \lambda r_i) = \gamma_i(\mathbf{p}, r_i)$.

(ii) When X_i is a convex set, $\gamma_i(\mathbf{p}, r_i)$ is convex, for every $(\mathbf{p}, r_i)$ in $\mathbb{R}_+^\ell \times \mathbb{R}$.

Nothing ensures however that $\gamma_i(\mathbf{p}, r_i)$ is nonempty. Hence, at some points of the analysis below, we shall state properties of γ_i in a restricted domain, i.e., for those values in a subset $D_i \subset \mathbb{R}_+^\ell \times \mathbb{R}$, where $\gamma_i(\mathbf{p}, r_i) \neq \emptyset$. The reader should clearly understand both that $\gamma_i(\mathbf{p}, r_i)$ may be empty, and that such a subset D_i can always be found (provided X_i is nonempty).

Remark 2.4.- Most of the results presented below are established under the assumption that X_i is compact. This is to be interpreted as saying that the results hold over any compact subset of X_i. Conditions will eventually be given for this to apply (namely, hypotheses ensuring that the set of attainable consumptions is compact, so that nothing outside this compact set is relevant for the actual functioning of the economy).

For a given $\mathbf{p} \in \mathbb{R}_+^\ell$, let $b_i(\mathbf{p})$ denote the minimum of the scalar product $\mathbf{p}x_i$ over X_i. The number $b_i(\mathbf{p})$ gives us the minimum worth at prices $\mathbf{p}$ of a feasible consumption bundle, for the ith consumer. Observe that this minimum exists, because X_i is closed and bounded from below, and $\mathbf{p}x_i$ is a continuous function.

The main result concerning the budget correspondence is the following:

Proposition 2.3.- [Debreu (1959, 4.8 (1))]

Let $X_i \subset \mathbb{R}^\ell$ be compact and convex, and assume that γ_i is nonempty valued for every $(\mathbf{p}, r_i) \in D_i \subset \mathbb{R}_+^\ell \times \mathbb{R}$. Let $(\mathbf{p}^o, r_i^o)$ be a point in D_i such that $r_i^o > b_i(\mathbf{p}^o)$. Then, γ_i is continuous in $(\mathbf{p}^o, r_i^o)$.

Proof.-

In order to prove that γ_i is continuous in $(\mathbf{p}^o, r_i^o)$ we have to show that it is both upper and lower hemicontinuous at this point.

(i) Let us show first that γ_i is upper hemicontinuous at $(\mathbf{p}^o, r_i^o)$. Let $\{\mathbf{p}^q, r_i^q\}$ be a sequence in D_i converging to $(\mathbf{p}^o, r_i^o)$, and let $\{\mathbf{x}_i^q\}$ be a sequence in X_i converging to $\mathbf{x}_i^o$, such that $\mathbf{x}_i^q \in \gamma_i(\mathbf{p}^q, r_i^q)$ for all q. One has to show that $\mathbf{x}_i^o \in \gamma_i(\mathbf{p}^o, r_i^o)$ (because γ_i is compact valued), that is, $\mathbf{p}^o \mathbf{x}_i^o \leq r_i^o$.

We know by assumption that $\mathbf{p}^q \mathbf{x}_i^q \leq r_i^q$ for all q. Taking limits as $q \to \infty$ (and bearing in mind that the continuity of the scalar product enables to write the limit of the product as the product of the limits), one gets:

$$\lim_{q \to \infty} \mathbf{p}^q \mathbf{x}_i^q = \mathbf{p}^o \mathbf{x}_i^o \qquad \lim_{q \to \infty} r_i^q = r_i^o$$

Suppose, by way of contradiction, that $\mathbf{p}^o \mathbf{x}_i^o > r_i^o$. Then there will exist some q' such that, $\mathbf{p}^q \mathbf{x}_i^q > r_i^q$, for all $q > q'$. But this contradicts the hypothesis that $\mathbf{x}_i^q \in \gamma_i(\mathbf{p}^q, r_i^q)$ for all q. Hence $\mathbf{x}_i^o \in \gamma_i(\mathbf{p}^o, r_i^o)$, that is, γ_i is upper hemicontinuous at this point.

(ii) We shall show now that γ_i is lower hemicontinuous at $(\mathbf{p}^o, r_i^o)$.

Consider a sequence $\{\mathbf{p}^q, r_i^q\}$ in D_i converging to $(\mathbf{p}^o, r_i^o)$, and let $\mathbf{x}_i^o$ be a point in $\gamma_i(\mathbf{p}^o, r_i^o)$ (that is, $\mathbf{x}_i^o \in X_i$ and $\mathbf{p}^o \mathbf{x}_i^o \leq r_i^o$). We have to show that there is a sequence $\{\mathbf{x}_i^q\}$ in X_i such that $\mathbf{x}_i^q \to \mathbf{x}_i^o$ and, for all q, $\mathbf{x}_i^q \in \gamma_i(\mathbf{p}^q, r_i^q)$ (that is, $\mathbf{p}^q \mathbf{x}_i^q \leq r_i^q$).

There are two possible cases:

a) $\mathbf{p}^o \mathbf{x}_i^o < r_i^o$. Then, for all $q > q'$ (where q' is a big enough number), $\mathbf{p}^q \mathbf{x}_i^o < r_i^q$. We can define then the following sequence: For $q \leq q'$, take $\mathbf{x}_i^q$ to be an arbitrary point in $\gamma_i(\mathbf{p}^q, r_i^q)$; for $q > q'$, take the constant sequence $\mathbf{x}_i^q = \mathbf{x}_i^o$. It is immediate to check that this sequence satisfies the lower hemicontinuity conditions.

b) $\mathbf{p}^o \mathbf{x}_i^o = r_i^o$. Choose a point $\mathbf{x}_i' \in X_i$ such that $\mathbf{p}^o \mathbf{x}_i' < r_i^o$ (which exists by assumption). As $(\mathbf{p}^q, r_i^q) \to (\mathbf{p}^o, r_i^o)$, there exists q' big enough so that, for all $q > q'$ one has: $\mathbf{p}^q(\mathbf{x}_i' - \mathbf{x}_i^o) < 0$. The straight line through $(\mathbf{x}_i', \mathbf{x}_i^o)$ has the following equation: $\mathbf{x}_i = \mathbf{x}_i^o + \lambda(\mathbf{x}_i' - \mathbf{x}_i^o)$, with $\lambda \in \mathbb{R}$. The hyperplane $H^q = \{\mathbf{z} \in \mathbb{R}^\ell \ / \ \mathbf{p}^q \mathbf{z} = r_i^q\}$ intersects this line at the point:

$$\mathbf{z}^q = \mathbf{x}_i^o + \frac{r_i^o - \mathbf{p}^q \mathbf{x}_i^o}{\mathbf{p}^q(\mathbf{x}_i' - \mathbf{x}_i^o)}(\mathbf{x}_i' - \mathbf{x}_i^o)$$

which is well defined for all $q > q'$, and satisfies $\mathbf{z}^q \to \mathbf{x}_i^o$ (see the figure). Let us define now a sequence $\{\mathbf{x}_i^q\}$ as follows:

(1) For $q \leq q'$ take $\mathbf{x}_i^q$ as an arbitrary point in $\gamma_i(\mathbf{p}^q, r_i^q)$.

(2) For $q > q'$:

(2.1) $\mathbf{x}_i^q = \mathbf{z}^q$, if $\mathbf{z}^q$ belongs to the segment $[\mathbf{x}_i^o, \mathbf{x}_i']$, which is contained in X_i, a convex set (that is, $\mathbf{x}_i^q = \mathbf{z}^q$ if and only if $0 \leq \frac{r_i^o - \mathbf{p}^q \mathbf{x}_i^o}{\mathbf{p}^q(\mathbf{x}_i' - \mathbf{x}_i^o)} \leq 1$).

(2.2) $\mathbf{x}_i^q = \mathbf{x}_i^o$ otherwise.

It is obvious that $\{\mathbf{x}_i^q\} \subset X_i$ and that $\mathbf{x}_i^q \in \gamma_i(\mathbf{p}^q, r_i^q)$ for all q, with $\{\mathbf{x}_i^q\} \to \mathbf{x}_i^o$ (note that as $q \to \infty$, $H^q \to H^o = \{\mathbf{z} \in \mathbb{R}^\ell / \mathbf{p}^o \mathbf{z} = r_i^o\}$, so that $\mathbf{x}_i^o \in H^o$). Therefore, γ_i is lower hemicontinuous in this case as well.

That completes the proof. ♠

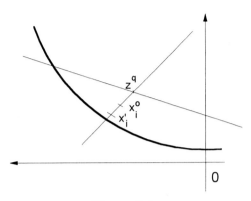

Figure 2.4

Concerning the assumptions of Proposition 2.3, the next figure illustrates the difficulties emerging when $b_i(\mathbf{p}^o) = r_i^o$:

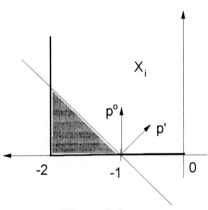

Figure 2.5

Let $(\mathbf{p}, r_i) \to (\mathbf{p}^o, r_i^o) = [(0,1),0]$ in Figure 2.5, so that the wealth hyperplane rotates over the point $\mathbf{x}_i = (-1,0)$. While $\mathbf{p} \neq \mathbf{p}^o$, the budget set $\gamma_i(\mathbf{p}, r_i)$ (the shaded area in the figure) moves approaching the segment $[-1, -2]$. Yet, $\gamma_i(\mathbf{p}^o, r_i^o) = [0, -2]$.

Remark 2.5.- The restriction $r_i > b_i(\mathbf{p})$ is usually called the *cheaper point requirement*, because it asks for the existence of points in X_i which cost less than r_i, at prices $\mathbf{p}$.

2.5   CONSUMER'S BEHAVIOUR

We have already modelled the ith consumer's way of ranking alternatives (consumption bundles), and the restrictions involved in the choice problem. It is now time to model consumers' behaviour. To make things simpler, we shall assume that assumptions (A.2.1) and (A.2.2') hold throughout this section. Under these assumptions, the equilibrium of the *ith* consumer can be expressed as the solution to the following program:

$$Max.\ u_i\left(\mathbf{x}_i\right)$$
$$s.t. \qquad\qquad\qquad\qquad [P]$$
$$\mathbf{x}_i \in \gamma(\mathbf{p},r_i)$$

The basic idea is thus the following: the *ith* consumer's behaviour is characterized by the choice of a best affordable option in X_i (which obviously depends on prices and wealth). The selected options are called the *ith* consumer's demand. More formally, the *ith* consumer's **demand correspondence** is a mapping $\xi_i : \mathbb{R}^\ell_+ \times \mathbb{R} \to X_i$, which associates to each pair $(\mathbf{p},r_i)$ in $\mathbb{R}^\ell_+ \times \mathbb{R}$ the set of solutions to program [P] above. Observe that, since the budget correspondence is homogeneous of degree zero, $\forall \lambda > 0$, $\xi_i(\lambda\mathbf{p}, \lambda r_i) = \xi_i(\mathbf{p}, r_i)$ (i.e., the demand correspondence inherits the zero homogeneity property).

The following theorem tells us the key properties of the demand correspondence, when the consumption set is taken to be compact, and the budget set is nonempty (i.e., when we restrict the domain of γ_i to the set D_i). Part (i) establishes that the demand correspondence is nonempty, compact and convex valued. Part (ii) says that the demand is an upper hemicontinuous correspondence, provided the budget set has a nonempty interior.

The next Lemma, known as the **Maximum Theorem**, will facilitate the proof of the Theorem (and it is a most useful tool for many other purposes):

Lemma 2.1.- [Berge (1963, III.3)]

Let $D \subset \mathbb{R}^k$ and $\mathbf{X} \subset \mathbb{R}^\ell$ **compact. Let** $\gamma : D \rightarrow \mathbf{X}$ **be a continuous correspondence,** $u : \mathbf{X} \rightarrow \mathbb{R}$ **a continuous function, and** $\xi : D \rightarrow \mathbf{X}$ **be given by:** $\xi(\mathbf{d}) = \{\mathbf{x} \in \gamma(\mathbf{d}) \,/\, u(\mathbf{x})$ *is maximum*$\}$**. Then,** ξ **is upper hemicontinuous in** D**. Furthermore, the function** $v(\mathbf{d}) = u(\mathbf{x})$ **for** $\mathbf{x} \in \xi(\mathbf{d})$ **is continuous.**

Proof.-

As X is compact, it suffices to show that for all sequences $\{\mathbf{d}^n\} \subset D$, $\{\mathbf{x}^n\} \subset X$, converging to $\mathbf{d}^\circ, \mathbf{x}^\circ$, respectively, and such that $\mathbf{x}^n \in \xi(\mathbf{d}^n)$ for all n, it follows that $\mathbf{x}^\circ \in \xi(\mathbf{d}^\circ)$.

Hence, let $\{\mathbf{d}^n\} \subset D$ be a sequence converging to $\mathbf{d}^\circ$, and $\{\mathbf{x}^n\} \subset X$ a sequence converging to $\mathbf{x}^\circ$ such that $\mathbf{x}^n \in \xi(\mathbf{d}^n)$ for all n. As $\mathbf{x}^n \in \gamma(\mathbf{d}^n)$ for all n, and γ is upper hemicontinuous, it follows that $\mathbf{x}^\circ \in \gamma(\mathbf{d}^\circ)$. Moreover, as γ is lower hemicontinuous, for any $\mathbf{z} \in \gamma(\mathbf{d}^\circ)$ there exists a sequence $\{\mathbf{z}^n\} \subset X$ converging to $\mathbf{z}$ such that $\mathbf{z}^n \in \gamma(\mathbf{d}^n)$, for all n. Thus, $u(\mathbf{x}^n) \geq u(\mathbf{z}^n)$ for all n [because $\mathbf{x}^n$ maximizes u over $\gamma(\mathbf{d}^n)$], and, in the limit: $u(\mathbf{x}^\circ) \geq u(\mathbf{z})$. As this inequality holds for every $\mathbf{z} \in \gamma(\mathbf{d}^\circ)$, we have shown that $\mathbf{x}^\circ \in \xi(\mathbf{d}^\circ)$.

Let now $\{\mathbf{d}^n\} \rightarrow \mathbf{d}^\circ$, with $\mathbf{x}^n \in \xi(\mathbf{d}^n)$ for all n. As X is compact, we can take $\{\mathbf{x}^n\} \rightarrow \mathbf{x}^\circ \in X$. We have $v(\mathbf{d}^n) = u(\mathbf{x}^n)$. As u is continuous, by applying the former reasoning we conclude: $v(\mathbf{d}^n) = u(\mathbf{x}^n) \rightarrow u(\mathbf{x}^\circ) = v(\mathbf{d}^\circ)$. ♠

Theorem 2.2.-

Under assumptions (A.2.1) and (A.2.2'), let $\mathbf{X}_i$ **be compact, and** $\gamma_i : D_i \rightarrow \mathbf{X}_i$ **nonempty. Then, for all** $(\mathbf{p}, r_i)$ **in** D_i**:**

(i) $\xi_i(\mathbf{p}, r_i)$ **is nonempty, compact and convex.**

(ii) ξ_i **is upper hemicontinuous in** $(\mathbf{p}, r_i)$**, provided** $r_i > b_i(\mathbf{p})$**.**

Proof.-

(i) We know that, under the assumptions of the theorem, program $[P]$ has a solution, since $\gamma_i(\mathbf{p}, r_i)$ is nonempty and compact-valued, and u_i is a continuous function (Weierstrass' Theorem). Now observe that the set $\xi_i(\mathbf{p}, r_i)$ of solutions to $[P]$ can be expressed as the intersection of the two following sets: $\gamma_i(\mathbf{p}, r_i)$ (which is compact and convex, by construction), and

$$\{\mathbf{x}_i \in X_i \,/\, u_i(\mathbf{x}_i) \geq \max u_i(\mathbf{x}_i') \text{ with } \mathbf{x}_i' \in \gamma_i(\mathbf{p}, r_i)\}$$

which is compact (since X_i is compact, and u_i is continuous), and convex (since u_i is quasi-concave).

(ii) Proposition 2.3 ensures that γ_i is continuous in this case. Lemma 2.1 gives us the desired result. ♠

Remark 2.6.- Note that when X_i is not compact, the nonemptyness of $\gamma_i(\mathbf{p}, r_i)$ does not ensure that program [P] has a solution.

The next figure illustrates the equilibrium of an individual consumer.

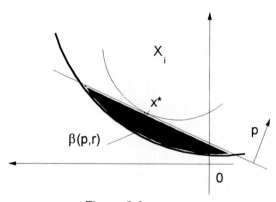

Figure 2.6

The next results tell us about the relationships between expenditure minimization and utility maximization. Proposition 2.4 establishes that the consumer expends all her wealth, and that those consumption plans which are preferred to her demand are more expensive. Proposition 2.5 in turn gives us sufficient conditions for expenditure minimization to imply utility maximization.

Proposition 2.4.-
    Under assumptions (A.2.1) and (A.2.2'), let $\mathbf{x}_i^* \in \xi_i(\mathbf{p}, r_i)$. Then:
    (a) $\mathbf{p}\mathbf{x}_i^* = r_i$
    (b) $u_i(\mathbf{x}_i') \geq u_i(\mathbf{x}_i^*)$ implies $\mathbf{p}\mathbf{x}_i' \geq \mathbf{p}\mathbf{x}_i^*$ (with $\mathbf{p}\mathbf{x}_i' > \mathbf{p}\mathbf{x}_i^*$ if the inequality is strict).
    Proof.-
    (a) Suppose $\mathbf{p}\mathbf{x}_i^* < r_i$. Then $\mathbf{x}_i^*$ is an interior point of $\gamma_i(\mathbf{p}, r_i)$, and we can find a ball $N_\delta(\mathbf{x}_i^*)$ which is contained in $\gamma_i(\mathbf{p}, r_i)$. By (CONV) and (NS) there will exist $\mathbf{x}_i \in N_\delta(\mathbf{x}_i^*)$ which is better than $\mathbf{x}_i^*$, against the assumption.
    (b) Suppose now that $u_i(\mathbf{x}_i') \geq u_i(\mathbf{x}_i')$ with $\mathbf{p}\mathbf{x}_i' < \mathbf{p}\mathbf{x}_i^* = r_i$. Then $\mathbf{x}_i' \in int\gamma_i(\mathbf{p}, r_i)$, so that cannot be at least as good as a maximizer $\mathbf{x}_i^* \in \xi_i(\mathbf{p}, r_i)$. In particular, if we assume that $u_i(\mathbf{x}_i') > u_i(\mathbf{x}_i^*)$ and $\mathbf{p}\mathbf{x}_i' \leq \mathbf{p}\mathbf{x}_i^*$, then $\mathbf{x}_i' \in$

$\gamma_i(\mathbf{p}, r_i)$ and $\mathbf{x}_i^*$ would not be a maximizer of the preference relation over $\gamma_i(\mathbf{p}, r_i)$. ♠

Proposition 2.5.-
    Under assumptions **(A.2.1), (A.2.2')**, let $\mathbf{p}^* \in \mathbb{R}_+^\ell$, $\mathbf{x}_i^* \in X_i$ **be such that $\mathbf{x}_i^*$ minimizes $\mathbf{p}^*\mathbf{x}_i$ over $BE(\mathbf{x}_i^*)$, with $\mathbf{p}^*\mathbf{x}_i^* > b_i(\mathbf{p}*)$. Then, $\mathbf{x}_i^*$ is a maximizer of u_i over the set** $A_i(\mathbf{p}*, \mathbf{x}_i^*) = \{ \mathbf{x}_i \in X_i \;/\; \mathbf{p}^*\mathbf{x}_i \le \mathbf{p}^*\mathbf{x}_i^* \}$.
    Proof.-
    Let $\mathbf{x}_i' \in A_i(\mathbf{p}^*, \mathbf{x}_i^*)$. If $\mathbf{p}^*\mathbf{x}_i' < \mathbf{p}*\mathbf{x}_i^*$, then $\mathbf{x}_i' \notin BE(\mathbf{x}_i^*)$. Suppose then that $\mathbf{p}^*\mathbf{x}_i' = \mathbf{p}^*\mathbf{x}_i^*$. By assumption, there is some $\mathbf{z} \in X_i$ such that $\mathbf{p}^*\mathbf{z} < \mathbf{p}^*\mathbf{x}_i^*$. Define then $\mathbf{x}_i(\alpha) = \alpha\mathbf{x}_i' + (1 - \alpha)\mathbf{z}$, for α in $[0, 1]$. For every $\alpha < 1$ one has $\mathbf{p}^*\mathbf{x}_i(\alpha) < \mathbf{p}^*\mathbf{x}_i' = \mathbf{p}^*\mathbf{x}_i^*$, with $u_i(\mathbf{x}_i^*) > u_i[\mathbf{x}_i(\alpha)]$ [that is, $\mathbf{x}_i(\alpha)$ is not in $BE(\mathbf{x}_i^*)$]. As α goes to 1, $\mathbf{x}_i(\alpha)$ tends to $\mathbf{x}_i'$, and $u_i(\mathbf{x}_i^*) \ge u_i[\mathbf{x}_i(\alpha)]$, for all α in $[0, 1)$. The continuity of the utility function implies that, in the limit, $u_i(\mathbf{x}_i^*) \ge u_i[\mathbf{x}_i(1)] = u_i(\mathbf{x}_i')$.♠
    It is worth understanding what happens if $\mathbf{x}_i^*$ minimizes $\mathbf{p}^*\mathbf{x}_i$ over $BE_i(\mathbf{x}_i^*)$. The following figure illustrates this case.

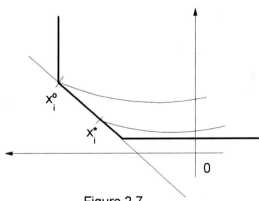

Figure 2.7

    Given a consumption set $X_i \subset \mathbb{R}^\ell$ for each consumer $i = 1, 2, \ldots, m$, the **aggregate consumption set** X, is given by:

$$X \equiv \sum_{i=1}^{m} X_i$$

Under assumption (A.2.1), X is a nonempty and convex set, bounded from below. It can also be shown that it is closed[6]. For our purposes it suffices to note that if every X_i is compact, then X is also compact.

The **aggregate demand correspondence** can be defined as a mapping ξ from $\mathbb{R}^\ell \times \mathbb{R}^m$ into X, such that, for every $(\mathbf{p}, \mathbf{r}) \in \mathbb{R}^\ell \times \mathbb{R}^m$ (where $\mathbf{r}$ is the vector representing the *wealth distribution*), it gives us:

$$\xi(\mathbf{p}, \mathbf{r}) \equiv \sum_{i=1}^{m} \xi_i(\mathbf{p}, r_i)$$

This is again a zero homogeneous mapping. That means that only relative prices actually matter for consumers' decisions. Moreover, non-satiation implies that demand mappings are not defined for $\mathbf{p} = \mathbf{0}$. This allows one to restrict the price space to the price simplex $\mathbb{P} \subset \mathbb{R}^\ell_+$, given by:

$$\mathbb{P} = \{\mathbf{p} \in \mathbb{R}^\ell_+ \ / \ \sum_{h=1}^{\ell} p_h = 1\}$$

This derives from the homogeneity property, because for any $\mathbf{p} \in \mathbb{R}^\ell_+$ for which $\xi_i(\mathbf{p}, r_i) \neq \emptyset$ for all i, one has $\sum_{h=1}^{\ell} p_h > 0$, so that multiplying by $\lambda = 1 / \sum_{h=1}^{\ell} p_h$ makes of $\lambda \mathbf{p}$ a point in the simplex.

Call now D to that subset of $\mathbb{P} \times \mathbb{R}^m$ where $\gamma_i(\mathbf{p}, r_i) \neq \emptyset$ for all i simultaneously. The following properties follow immediately from the above results:

Corollary 2.2.-
    Under assumptions (A.2.1) and (A.2.2'), let X_i be compact for every i, and $D \subset \mathbb{P} \times \mathbb{R}^m$ such that $\gamma_i : D_i \to X_i$ is nonempty for all i. Then, for all $(\mathbf{p}, \mathbf{r})$ in D:
    (i) $\emptyset \neq \xi(\mathbf{p}, \mathbf{r})$, compact and convex.
    (ii) ξ is upper hemicontinuous in $(\mathbf{p}, \mathbf{r})$, whenever $r_i > b_i(\mathbf{p})$ for all i.

---

[6]This is a difficult result having to do with the properties of asymptotic cones [see Debreu 4.3(1), Herrero (1982)].

2.6 FINAL COMMENTS

This chapter is a summary of the standard consumer theory, as in Debreu (1959), or Arrow & Hahn (1971). Alternative sources abound, and we shall simply refer to the works of Deaton & Muellbauer (1980) and Barten & Böhm (1982) for additional developments and references.

Let us conclude by commenting on some specifics of the way of modelling consumer behaviour:

(i) An alternative way of modelling the consumer's choice problem consists of using *choice functions* rather than preference relations. Yet, if one imposes minimal consistency properties, both approaches essentially coincide. See Suzumura (1983, ch. 2) for a discussion.

(ii) The transitivity and completeness of the preference relation can be dispensed with in order to ensure the existence of maximal elements, when one introduces the convexity and continuity assumptions. On this see Shafer (1974), Mas-Colell (1974), Shafer & Sonnenschein (1975), Walker (1977), Llinares (1995), and the discussion in Florenzano (1981) and Border (1985, Ch. 7).

(iii) Concerning the modelling of consumer behaviour as an optimization problem, let us refer to Takayama (1985,ch.I) for a detailed discussion [see Bazaraa & Shetty (1979) for a guide on convexity and optimization]. The classic works of Kuhn and Tucker (1951), Arrow, Hurwicz and Uzawa (1961), and specially Arrow and Enthoven (1961) are still worth reading.

2.7 APPENDIX

The Existence of a Continuous Utility Function

The next result is a particular case of proposition 2.2. Yet, it is general enough for our purposes, and has a rather intuitive proof (that will be developed in detail).

Proposition 2.6.-
Let $X_i \subset \mathbb{R}^\ell$ be a convex set, and let $\succeq_i$ be a binary relation on X_i which satisfies (COMP), (TRA), (CONT) and (LNS). Then, $\succeq_i$ can be represented by a continuous utility function, $u : X_i \to \mathbb{R}$.

Proof.-

The proof will be divided into three parts, to make things easier. An explicit utility function will be proposed first. Then, we shall see that this function actually represents the preference relation. Finally, we shall show that this is a continuous function. Subscripts will be omitted in order to simplify notation.

(i) Let $\mathbf{x}^0$ be an arbitrary point in X (that will be taken as a reference point), and let $d : X \to \mathbb{R}$ be a function given by $d(\mathbf{x}) = \|\mathbf{x} - \mathbf{x}^0\|$ (that is, for each $\mathbf{x} \in X$ it gives us the euclidean distance between $\mathbf{x}$ and $\mathbf{x}^0$). For any subset $T \subset X$, the expression $d(T)$ denotes the distance between $\mathbf{x}^0$ and T (that is, $d(T) = \min d(\mathbf{x})$ with $\mathbf{x} \in T$). Define now $u : X \to \mathbb{R}$ as follows:

(a) $u(\mathbf{x}^0) = 0$.

(b) For $\mathbf{x} \in X$ such that $\mathbf{x} \succeq \mathbf{x}^0$, $u(\mathbf{x}) = d[BE(\mathbf{x})]$, that is, $u(\mathbf{x}) = \min d(\mathbf{x}')$, with $\mathbf{x}' \in BE(\mathbf{x})$.

(c) For $\mathbf{x} \in X$ such that $\mathbf{x}^0 \succeq \mathbf{x}$, $u(\mathbf{x}) = -d[WE(\mathbf{x})]$, that is, $u(\mathbf{x}) = -\min d(\mathbf{x}')$, with $\mathbf{x}' \in WE(\mathbf{x})$.

The utility of a consumption bundle $\mathbf{x} \in X$ is thus defined as the distance between the reference point $\mathbf{x}^0$ and the set of alternatives which are better or equal than $\mathbf{x}$ (resp. worse or equal than $\mathbf{x}$, depending upon the ranking of $\mathbf{x}$ versus $\mathbf{x}^0$). The continuity of the preference relation and the distance function ensure that u is well defined for all $\mathbf{x} \in X$.

(ii) To show that this function u actually *represents* the preference relation $\succeq$, it suffices to show that the following relations hold:

$$\mathbf{x} \sim \mathbf{x}' \implies u(\mathbf{x}) = u(\mathbf{x}') \qquad [1]$$
$$\mathbf{x} \succ \mathbf{x}' \implies u(\mathbf{x}) > u(\mathbf{x}') \qquad [2]$$

This is so because $[u(\mathbf{x}) > u(\mathbf{x}') \ \& \ \mathbf{x} \sim \mathbf{x}']$ is not compatible with [1], whereas $[u(\mathbf{x}) = u(\mathbf{x}') \ \& \ \mathbf{x} \succ \mathbf{x}']$ is not compatible with [2].

Implication [1] follows trivially from the definition of u, because (COMP) and (TRA) imply that $BE(\mathbf{x}) = BE(\mathbf{x}')$, whenever $\mathbf{x} \sim \mathbf{x}'$.

Let us check that [2] also holds. To see this let us assume that $\mathbf{x} \succ \mathbf{x}'$, and consider the following cases:

a) $\mathbf{x} \succ \mathbf{x}' \succeq \mathbf{x}^o$. Transitivity implies that $BE(\mathbf{x}) \subset BE(\mathbf{x}')$, so that $u(\mathbf{x}) \geq u(\mathbf{x}')$.

b) $\mathbf{x}^o \succeq \mathbf{x} \succ \mathbf{x}'$. By (TRA) $WE(\mathbf{x}') \subset WE(\mathbf{x})$, hence $d[WE(\mathbf{x})] \leq d[WE(\mathbf{x}')]$, that is, $u(\mathbf{x}) \geq u(\mathbf{x}')$.

c) $\mathbf{x} \succ \mathbf{x}^o \succeq \mathbf{x}'$ (or $\mathbf{x} \succeq \mathbf{x}^o \succ \mathbf{x}'$). In this case we have: $u(\mathbf{x}) \geq 0$ and $u(\mathbf{x}') \leq 0$.

Therefore, $\mathbf{x} \succ \mathbf{x}'$ implies $u(\mathbf{x}) \geq u(\mathbf{x}')$. It remains to show that these numbers are different. Looking for a contradiction, let us suppose that $u(\mathbf{x}) = u(\mathbf{x}')$ with $\mathbf{x} \succ \mathbf{x}'$.

Observe first that $u(\mathbf{x}) = 0$ implies $\mathbf{x} \sim \mathbf{x}^o$. To see this notice that (COMP) ensures that $\mathbf{x} \succeq \mathbf{x}^o$ or $\mathbf{x}^o \succeq \mathbf{x}$. Suppose $\mathbf{x} \succeq \mathbf{x}^o$ and $u(\mathbf{x}) = 0$. It follows that $d[BE(\mathbf{x})] = 0$, so there exists $\mathbf{x}'' \in BE(\mathbf{x})$ such that $d(\mathbf{x}'') = 0$. But this is possible only if $\mathbf{x}^o \in BE(\mathbf{x})$, and we would have $\mathbf{x}^o \succeq \mathbf{x}$ (hence: $\mathbf{x} \sim \mathbf{x}^o$). The same reasoning applies to the case $\mathbf{x}^o \succeq \mathbf{x}$. This proves that $\mathbf{x} \succ \mathbf{x}'$ implies $u(\mathbf{x}) \neq 0$ (otherwise the transitivity of the indifference relation would imply $\mathbf{x} \sim \mathbf{x}'$). Therefore, $\mathbf{x} \succ \mathbf{x}'$ and $u(\mathbf{x}) = u(\mathbf{x}') = 0$ cannot hold together.

Consider now the case $u(\mathbf{x}) = u(\mathbf{x}') > 0$, and let $\tilde{\mathbf{x}} \in X$ be a point such that $d(\tilde{\mathbf{x}}) = u(\mathbf{x})$. As $\tilde{\mathbf{x}} \in BE(\mathbf{x})$, we know that $\tilde{\mathbf{x}} \succeq \mathbf{x} \succ \mathbf{x}'$. The continuity of preferences ensures that we can find a scalar $\alpha \in (0,1)$ small enough so that $[(1-\alpha)\tilde{\mathbf{x}} + \alpha \mathbf{x}^o] \succeq \mathbf{x}'$, that is $[(1-\alpha)\tilde{\mathbf{x}} + \alpha \mathbf{x}^o] \in BE(\mathbf{x}')$. We can write then:

$$u(\mathbf{x}') \leq d[(1-\alpha)\tilde{\mathbf{x}} + \alpha \mathbf{x}^o] = \|(1-\alpha)\tilde{\mathbf{x}} + \alpha \mathbf{x}^o - \mathbf{x}^o\|$$

$$= (1-\alpha)\|\tilde{\mathbf{x}} - \mathbf{x}^o\| = (1-\alpha)d(\tilde{\mathbf{x}}) = (1-\alpha)u(\mathbf{x})$$

That is, $u(\mathbf{x}') = u(\mathbf{x}) \leq (1-\alpha)u(\mathbf{x})$, which can only occur if $u(\mathbf{x}) = 0$. But we had already discarded this possibility, hence $\mathbf{x} \succ \mathbf{x}'$ implies $u(\mathbf{x}) > u(\mathbf{x}')$.

The case $u(\mathbf{x}) = u(\mathbf{x}') < 0$ can be analyzed along the same lines, by taking $\tilde{\mathbf{x}} \in WE(\mathbf{x}')$ such that $-d(\mathbf{x}') = u(\mathbf{x}')$.

Therefore, function u represents $\succeq$.

(iii) To prove that u is a continuous function we have to show that, for any scalar $a \in \mathbb{R}$, the sets $U(a^+) = \{\mathbf{x} \in X \ / \ u(\mathbf{x}) \geq a\}$, $U(a^-) = \{\mathbf{x} \in X \ / \ u(\mathbf{x}) \leq a\}$ are closed.

Let us show firs that $U(a^+)$ is a closed set. Let $\{\mathbf{x}^n\} \to \mathbf{x}$ be a sequence in X such that $u(\mathbf{x}^n) \geq a$ for all n, and let $\mathbf{x}'$ be such that $d(\mathbf{x}') = u(\mathbf{x}) > 0$ (that is, we assume $\mathbf{x} \succ \mathbf{x}^o$). By (LNS) there exists $\mathbf{z} \in X$, arbitrarily close to $\mathbf{x}'$ such that $\mathbf{z} \succ \mathbf{x}'$. By (TRA) $\mathbf{z} \succ \mathbf{x}$. Now (CONT) implies that for a big enough n onwards, $\mathbf{z} \succeq \mathbf{x}^n$. Hence, $u(\mathbf{z}) \geq u(\mathbf{x}^n) \geq a$. But $\mathbf{z}$ can be chosen as close to $\mathbf{x}'$ as we wish. As $\mathbf{z} \succ \mathbf{x}^o$, $d(\mathbf{z}) \geq u(\mathbf{z}) \geq a$, and $d(.)$ is continuous, it follows that $d(\mathbf{x}') \geq a$. Thus, $u(\mathbf{x}) = u(\mathbf{x}') = d(\mathbf{x}') \geq a$, because $\mathbf{x}' \sim \mathbf{x} \succ \mathbf{x}^o$.

Let now $\{\mathbf{x}^n\} \to \mathbf{x}$ be a sequence in X such that $u(\mathbf{x}^n) \geq a$ for all n, with $\mathbf{x}^o \succeq \mathbf{x}$. By (TRA) $\mathbf{x}^o \succeq \mathbf{x}^n$, for all n. By definition, $u(\mathbf{x}^n) = -\min\{d(\mathbf{z}) \ / \ \mathbf{z} \in WE(\mathbf{x}^n)\} = -d(\hat{\mathbf{x}}^n)$, con $\mathbf{x}^n \sim \hat{\mathbf{x}}^n$ for all n. As $u(\mathbf{x}^n) = -d(\hat{\mathbf{x}}^n) \geq a$, we can write: $d(\hat{\mathbf{x}}^n) \leq -a$ for all n, so that the sequence $\{\hat{\mathbf{x}}^n\}$ is bounded from above. Let $\{\hat{\mathbf{x}}^{n_k}\}_k$ be a subsequence converging to $\hat{\mathbf{x}}$. The continuity of the distance function implies that $u(\hat{\mathbf{x}}) = -\min\{d(\mathbf{z}) \ / \ \mathbf{z} \in WE(\hat{\mathbf{x}})\} \geq -d(\hat{\mathbf{x}}) \geq a$. By (CONT) $\mathbf{x} \sim \hat{\mathbf{x}}$ and hence $u(\mathbf{x}) = u(\hat{\mathbf{x}}) \geq a$, according to part (ii) above.

This proves that $U(a^+)$ is a closed set.

Let us show now that the set $U(a^-)$ is also closed. Let $\{\mathbf{x}^n\} \to \mathbf{x}$ be a sequence such that $u(\mathbf{x}^n) \leq a$, and $\mathbf{x} \succeq \mathbf{x}^o$. Let $\mathbf{x}'^n$ be such that $d(\mathbf{x}'^n) = u(\mathbf{x}^n)$ for each n. By construction $u(\mathbf{x}'^n) \leq a$. The sequence $\{\mathbf{x}'^n\}$ is bounded so it converges to a point $\mathbf{x}'$ such that $u(\mathbf{x}') \leq a$. According to part (ii), $\mathbf{x}'^n$ is indifferent to $\mathbf{x}^n$ for all n, and $\mathbf{x}^n \to \mathbf{x}$. Consider now the sequence $\{\mathbf{x}'^n\} \to \mathbf{x}'$; by (CONT) we conclude that $\mathbf{x}'$ is indifferent to $\mathbf{x}$, so that $u(\mathbf{x}') = u(\mathbf{x}) \leq a$.

Take now $\{\mathbf{x}^n\} \to \mathbf{x}$, with $u(\mathbf{x}^n) \leq a$, and $\mathbf{x}^o \succ \mathbf{x}$. If $\mathbf{z} \succeq \mathbf{x}$ for all $\mathbf{z} \in X$, then we would have $\mathbf{x}^n \succeq \mathbf{x}$ and, by (ii), $a \geq u(\mathbf{x}^n) \geq u(\mathbf{x})$ (what proves the result). Suppose then that these is some $\mathbf{z}$ in X such that $\mathbf{x} \succ \mathbf{z}$. If there is some n for which $\mathbf{x}^n \succeq \mathbf{x}$ we would have again that $u(\mathbf{x}) \leq a$. Consider the last possible alternative: $\mathbf{x} \succ \mathbf{x}^n$ for all n. From some n onwards we shall have $\mathbf{x}^o \succ \mathbf{x} \succ \mathbf{x}^n \succ \mathbf{z}$, by (CONT). Let $\{\tilde{\mathbf{x}}^n\}$ be a sequence such that $\tilde{\mathbf{x}}^n \sim \mathbf{x}^n$, with $u(\mathbf{x}^n) = -d(\tilde{\mathbf{x}}^n)$. By (ii) we know that $u(\mathbf{z}) < u(\mathbf{x}^n) = -d(\tilde{\mathbf{x}}^n)$, so that $d(\tilde{\mathbf{x}}^n) < -u(\mathbf{z})$ for all n. Thus $\{\tilde{\mathbf{x}}^n\}$ is bounded and we can find a subsequence $\{\tilde{\mathbf{x}}^{n_k}\}_k$ converging to some $\tilde{\mathbf{z}}$. By (CONT) $\tilde{\mathbf{z}} \sim \mathbf{x}$, so: $u(\mathbf{x}) = u(\tilde{\mathbf{z}}) = -d(\tilde{\mathbf{z}}) \leq a$, because $d(.)$ is continuous, $\{\tilde{\mathbf{x}}^{n_k}\}_k \to \tilde{\mathbf{z}}$, and $-d(\tilde{\mathbf{x}}^n) = u(\mathbf{x}^n) \leq a$ for all n. That is, $u(\mathbf{x}) \leq a$.

This proves that $U(a^-)$ is a closed set.

The proof is in this way completed.♠

Chapter 3

FIRMS

3.1 PRODUCTION SETS

Production refers to a technological process which *transforms* certain commodities (inputs) into different ones (outputs). "Transformation" here has to be interpreted following the notion of commodities adopted in chapter 1 (thus, transporting a commodity to a different place, or keeping it until the next period constitute transformations). In the context of a market economy, these transformation processes are carried out within *firms*, which are therefore the decision units concerning production. A firm is actually a rather complex entity which typically involves collective decisions, information and incentive problems, etc. Here it will simply be identified with a set of technological possibilities and a criterion of choice. It will be assumed throughout that there is a given number n of firms, indexed by $j = 1, 2, \ldots, n$.

A **production plan** for the jth firm, denoted by $\mathbf{y}_j \in \mathbb{R}^\ell$, specifies the amounts of (net) inputs which are required in order to obtain some well specified amounts of (net) outputs. Outputs will be represented by positive numbers, while inputs by negative ones. A simple illustration of this way of describing production, for $\ell = 2$, is the following: Suppose that we can produce 300 Tons of corn using 50 Tons of corn and 1,000 hours of labour time. The corresponding production plan will be given by $\mathbf{y} = (-1,000,\ 250)$, meaning that we obtain 250 net Tons of corn (that is, 300 Tons of gross output minus 50 Tons used as input) using 1,000 hours of labour.

A **production set** for the jth firm, denoted by $Y_j \subset \mathbb{R}^\ell$, is a set made of all production plans which are possible for the jth firm, according to the technological knowledge available.

Consider the following assumptions concerning these production sets:

<u>A.3.1.-</u> (i) $Y_j \subset \mathbb{R}^\ell$ is closed.

　　　　(ii) $Y_j - \mathbb{R}^\ell_+ \subset Y_j$.

<u>A.3.2.-</u> $\mathbf{0} \in Y_j$.

Part (i) of assumption (A.3.1), referred to as "continuity", is a technical requirement. Formally it amounts to saying that any production plan which can be approximated by a sequence of elements $\{\mathbf{y}^\nu_j\} \subset Y_j$ will also be in Y_j. Part (ii) says that Y_j is a **comprehensive** set, that is: if $\mathbf{y}_j \in Y_j$ and $\mathbf{y}'_j$ is a vector in $\mathbb{R}^\ell$ satisfying $\mathbf{y}'_j \leq \mathbf{y}_j$, then $\mathbf{y}'_j$ will also be in Y_j. In words: If a production plan is possible, it will also be any production plan which uses more inputs or obtains less outputs.

Assumption (A.3.2) establishes that producing nothing (meaning obtaining no outputs and using up no inputs) is always an alternative available for the jth firm (i.e., $\mathbf{0}$ belongs to Y_j). This trivially implies that Y_j is nonempty (and also that we may be calling firm to a rather bodiless entity).

Part (ii) of assumption (A.3.1) and assumption (A.3.2) imply that $-\mathbb{R}^\ell_+ \subset Y_j$, so that the jth firm can freely dispose of any amounts of commodities. That is why these hypotheses are sometimes called "Free-disposal".

The following figure illustrates a production set satisfying assumptions (A.3.1) and (A.3.2). We may think that it corresponds to a firm producing corn (as a net output) and using labour (as a net input).

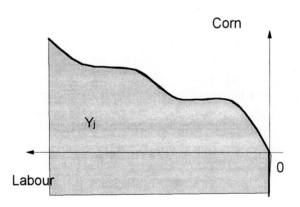

Figure 3.1

Let us introduce a key concept in the theory of production: the notion of production efficiency[1]:

<u>Definition 3.1.-</u>
A production plan $y_j^o \in Y_j$ is **efficient** (resp. **weakly efficient**), if there is no $y_j' \in Y_j$ such that $y_j' > y_j^o$ (resp. $y_j' >> y_j^o$).

In words: An efficient production plan is an input-output combination such that it is not possible to increase any output without decreasing some other, or increasing some inputs. By definition, if y_j is an efficient production plan, then it must be in ∂Y_j (the boundary of the jth firm's production set).

Efficient production plans satisfy a very general and interesting property which can be formalized as follows:

Proposition 3.1.-
Let $Y_j \subset \mathbb{R}^\ell$ be a production set, and let q be a vector in $\mathbb{R}^\ell$ such that $q >> 0$ (resp. $q > 0$). Suppose that, for some $y_j^o \in Y_j$, we have: $qy_j^o \geq qy_j$, $\forall\ y_j \in Y_j$. Then y_j^o is an efficient (resp. weakly efficient) production plan.
(The proof is left as an exercise)

Remark 3.1.- Notice that if we interpret q as a price vector, then this property can be read as follows: Profit maximization at given prices implies selecting efficient production plans. It is worth pointing out that none of the hypotheses in (A.3.1) or (A.3.2) is required for this result.

The next result serves to illustrate a key implication of assumption (A.3.1):

Proposition 3.2.-
Under assumption (A.3.1), a production plan y_j in Y_j is weakly efficient if and only if $y_j \in \partial Y_j$.
(The proof is left as an exercise)

Let y_j be a production plan for the jth firm, $j = 1, 2, \ldots, n$. We call **aggregate production** to the vector

$$y = \sum_{j=1}^{n} y_j$$

Note that when we add up all firms' production plans, all trading among firms cancels out.

---

[1] Let us recall here that notation for vector comparisons is: $\geq, >, >>$.

Similarly, we call **aggregate production set** to the set:

$$Y = \sum_{j=1}^{n} Y_j$$

3.2   RETURNS TO SCALE

A key technological aspect in the modelling of firms refers to the nature of the *returns to scale*. When a firm produces a single output, we say that it exhibits increasing (resp. decreasing) returns to scale when, for every given production plan, multiplying the amounts of inputs by a scalar $t > 1$ implies that the output appears multiplied by a scalar $t' > t$ (resp. $t' < t$); and we talk about constant returns to scale when $t' = t$, for every $t > 0$. When there are several inputs and outputs involved, however, this simple notion cannot be applied. In order to deal with the general case, let us consider the following definitions:

Definition 3.2.-
    Let $\mathbf{y}_j \in Y_j$ be given. **To change the scale of operations** consists of multiplying $\mathbf{y}_j$ by a scalar $\lambda > 0$. When $\lambda > 1$ (resp. $\lambda < 1$) we shall talk about **increasing** (resp. **decreasing**) the scale.

Definition 3.3.-
    Y_j exhibits **non-decreasing returns to scale** when, for each $\mathbf{y}_j \in Y_j$ we can increase arbitrarily the scale of operations (i.e., $[\mathbf{y}_j \in Y_j$ & $\lambda \geq 1] \Longrightarrow \lambda\mathbf{y}_j \in Y_j$). Y_j exhibits **non-increasing returns to scale** when, for each $\mathbf{y}_j \in Y_j$ we can decrease arbitrarily the scale of operations (i.e., if $[\mathbf{y}_j \in Y_j$ and $0 < \lambda \leq 1]$ then $\lambda\mathbf{y}_j \in Y_j$). And Y_j exhibits **constant returns to scale** when, for each $\mathbf{y}_j \in Y_j$ we can change arbitrarily the scale of operations (i.e., $[\mathbf{y}_j \in Y_j$ & $\lambda > 0] \Longrightarrow \lambda\mathbf{y}_j \in Y_j$).

The next figure shows three production sets in $\mathbb{R}^2$, satisfying assumptions (A.3.1) and (A.3.2). Case (a) corresponds to constant returns to scale (in this case the production set is a convex cone with vertex zero). Case (b) illustrates a production set with decreasing returns to scale (note that in this case we also have a convex set). Case (c) depicts a firm with increasing returns to scale; observe that in this case the production set is not convex anymore (that is why it is customary to refer to increasing returns as to the presence of non-convexities in production).

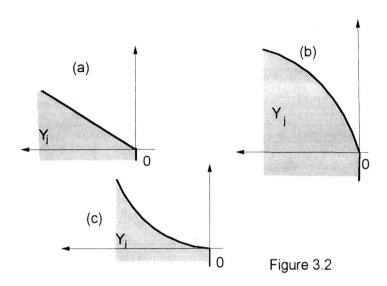

Figure 3.2

Remark 3.2.- Observe that: (i) Production sets may not satisfy any of the above definitions of returns to scale (as in Figure 3.1); in particular, a non-convex production set need not exhibit increasing returns to scale. (ii) Under assumptions (A.3.1) and (A.3.2), a production set is convex if and only if it exhibits non-increasing returns to scale.

The convexity of production sets can be derived from the combination of two primitive hypotheses: *Additivity* and *divisibility*. The additivity assumption says that if two production plans are technologically feasible, a new production plan consisting of the sum of these two will also be possible (that is, $\mathbf{y}'_j, \mathbf{y}''_j \in Y_j \Rightarrow (\mathbf{y}'_j + \mathbf{y}''_j) \in Y_j$). Divisibility says that if a production plan is feasible, then any production plan consisting of a reduction in its scale of operation will also be feasible (non-increasing returns to scale). When these hypotheses hold, production sets turn out to be convex cones. Formally:

Proposition 3.3.-

Under assumptions (A.3.1) and (A.3.2), a production set Y_j satisfies additivity and divisibility if and only if it is a convex cone with vertex 0.

(The proof is left as an exercise)

3.3   ATTAINABLE PRODUCTION PLANS

Let $\omega \in \mathbb{R}^\ell$ denote the vector of **initial endowments** (those amounts of commodities which constitute the aggregate initial holdings of the economy). Let $(\mathbf{x}_i)$ denote a point in $\mathbb{R}^{\ell m}$ describing a consumption plan for every consumer $i = 1, 2, \ldots, m$, and let $(\mathbf{y}_j) \in \mathbb{R}^{\ell n}$ stand for a vector specifying a production plan for each of the n firms.

Consider the following definition:

Definition 3.4.-

The set of **attainable allocations** is given by:

$$A(\omega) \equiv \{[(\mathbf{x}_i), (\mathbf{y}_j)] \in \prod_{i=1}^{m} X_i \times \prod_{j=1}^{n} Y_j \ / \ \sum_{i=1}^{m} \mathbf{x}_i - \omega \leq \sum_{j=1}^{n} \mathbf{y}_j\}$$

That is, the set of attainable allocations for an economy is given by those consumption and production plans which are simultaneously feasible, given the initial endowments. Observe that a positive component in vector $\mathbf{z} = \sum_{i=1}^{m} \mathbf{x}_i - \omega - \sum_{j=1}^{n} \mathbf{y}_j$ (the kth one, say), means that the sum of the aggregate production and the aggregate initial endowment of the kth commodity is insufficient to cover its demand.

The projections of $A(\omega)$ on the spaces containing X_i, Y_j give us the ith **consumer's set of attainable consumptions**, and the jth **firm's set of attainable production plans**, respectively.

Concerning this set we shall assume:

A.3.3.- For each $j = 1, 2, \ldots, n$, any $\omega \in \mathbb{R}^\ell$, the jth firm's set of attainable production plans is compact.

Assumption (A.3.3) introduces an element of realism in the model: It is not possible to obtain unlimited amounts of outputs, when resources are limited.

A related requirement is that in which one postulates that:

$$Y_j \bigcap \mathbb{R}_+^\ell = \{\mathbf{0}\}$$

This may be thought of as involving two different messages. The first one corresponds to (A.3.2): Inaction is a feasible alternative. The second one says that "There is no such a thing as a Free Lunch", that is, any production plan involving strictly positive outputs has to use up some inputs (i.e., it has to contain strictly negative numbers as well). Hence, the only possible common point (if any) between Y_j and $\mathbb{R}_+^\ell$ would be $\{\mathbf{0}\}$ (the origin of the $\mathbb{R}^\ell$ space).

This property, however, does not translate to the aggregate production set Y. Indeed, even if $Y_j \cap \mathbb{R}_+^\ell = \{\mathbf{0}\}$ for all j, we still could have $\sum_{j=1}^{n} Y_j \cap \mathbb{R}_+^\ell \neq \{\mathbf{0}\}$. To see this, suppose that the economy consists of two firms with constant returns to scale, both of which satisfy assumptions (A.3.1) and (A.3.2). Let $\mathbf{y}_1 = (-3,\ 3)$, $\mathbf{y}_2 = (4,\ -2)$ be two efficient production plans for firms 1 and 2, respectively. The aggregate production turns out to be: $\mathbf{y} = \mathbf{y}_1 + \mathbf{y}_2 = (1,\ 1)$, which belongs to the interior of $\mathbb{R}_+^2$, and hence tells us that this economy is actually able to produce without using up inputs.

It is easy to check that, if we assume that $Y \cap (-Y) \subset \{\mathbf{0}\}$ (a property known as irreversibility), then assumptions (A.3.1) and (A.3.2) imply that $Y \cap \mathbb{R}_+^\ell \subset \{\mathbf{0}\}$. From that it follows that, when production sets are convex, the set of attainable production plans is bounded [see Debreu (1959, Ch.5), Herrero (1982)].

When production sets are not convex, however, no simple restriction on individual and/or aggregate production sets yield the boundedness of attainable production plans.

3.4   THE BEHAVIOUR OF FIRMS

Let $\mathbb{F}_j$ denote the jth firm's set of weakly efficient production plans, that is,

$$\mathbb{F}_j \equiv \{\mathbf{y}_j \in Y_j \mid \mathbf{y}_j' >> \mathbf{y}_j \Rightarrow \mathbf{y}_j' \notin Y_j\}$$

$\mathbb{F}$ will stand for the Cartesian product of the n sets of weakly efficient production plans, that is, $\mathbb{F} \equiv \prod_{j=1}^{n} \mathbb{F}_j$. Observe that, under assumption (A.3.1), $\mathbb{F}_j$ corresponds precisely to the boundary of Y_j (see Proposition 3.2). Thus we shall use $\mathbb{F}_j$ and ∂Y_j equivalently.

Denote by $\mathbb{P} \subset \mathbb{R}_+^\ell$ the price simplex, that is,

$$\mathbb{P} = \{\mathbf{p} \in \mathbb{R}_+^\ell \ / \ \sum_{t=1}^{\ell} p_t = 1\}$$

For a point $\mathbf{y}_j \in \mathbb{F}_j$ and a price vector $\mathbf{p} \in \mathbb{P}$, $\mathbf{p}\mathbf{y}_j$ gives us the associated profits [note that since outputs are represented by positive numbers and inputs by negative ones, the scalar product $\mathbf{p}\mathbf{y}_j = \sum_{h=1}^{\ell} p_h y_{jh}$ gives us the profit associated with the pair $(\mathbf{p}, \mathbf{y}_j)$].

Firms' behaviour will now be defined in terms of a *pricing rule*. A pricing rule for the jth firm is usually defined as a mapping Φ_j applying the set of efficient production plans $\mathbb{F}_j$ into $\mathbb{P}$. For a point $\mathbf{y}_j$ in $\mathbb{F}_j$, $\Phi_j(\mathbf{y}_j)$ has to be interpreted as the set of price vectors found "acceptable" by the *jth* firm when producing $\mathbf{y}_j$. In other words, the *jth* firm is in equilibrium at the pair $(\mathbf{p}, \mathbf{y}_j)$, if $\mathbf{p} \in \Phi_j(\mathbf{y}_j)$. Even though in most of the cases the *jth* firm's pricing rule only depends on $\mathbf{y}_j$, we shall adopt here (and in the next chapter) a more general notion of firms' behaviour, by allowing each firm's pricing rule to depend on other firms' actions and "market prices". To do this, let $\tilde{\mathbf{y}} = (\mathbf{y}_1, \mathbf{y}_2, \dots, \mathbf{y}_n)$ denote a point in $\mathbb{F}$. Then,

Definition 3.5.-
  A **Pricing Rule** for the *jth* firm is a correspondence,

$$\phi_j : \mathbb{P} \times \mathbb{F} \to \mathbb{P}$$

A pricing rule is thus a mapping which describes the *jth* firm's set of admissible prices, as a function of "market conditions". That is, $\mathbf{y}_j$ is an equilibrium production plan for the *jth* firm at prices $\mathbf{p}$, if and only if, $\mathbf{p} \in \phi_j(\mathbf{p}, \tilde{\mathbf{y}})$ (where $\mathbf{y}_j$ is precisely the *jth* firm's production plan in $\tilde{\mathbf{y}}$). As for interpretative purposes, we may think of a market mechanism in which there is an auctioneer who calls both a price vector (to be seen as proposed market prices), and a vector of efficient production plans. Then, the *jth* firm checks whether the pair $(\mathbf{p}, \mathbf{y}_j)$ agrees with its objectives (formally, $[(\mathbf{p}, \tilde{\mathbf{y}}), \mathbf{p}]$ belongs to the graph of ϕ_j).
  A situation in which all firms find acceptable the proposed combination between prices and production plans is called a *production equilibrium*. Formally:

Definition 3.6.-
  A pair $(\mathbf{p}, \tilde{\mathbf{y}}) \in \mathbb{P} \times \mathbb{F}$ is a **Production Equilibrium**, relative to the pricing rules $\phi = (\phi_1, \phi_2, \dots, \phi_n)$, if:

$$\mathbf{p} \in \bigcap_{j=1}^{n} \phi_j(\mathbf{p}, \tilde{\mathbf{y}}).$$

We shall denote by **PE** the set of production equilibria.
  Observe that different firms may follow different pricing rules. Furthermore, the pricing rule "may be either endogenous or exogenous to the model, and that it allows both price-taking and price-setting behaviors" [Cf. Cornet (1988, p. 106)].

  Consider now the following definition:

Definition 3.7.-

$\phi_j : \mathbb{P} \times \mathbb{F} \to \mathbb{P}$ is a **Regular Pricing Rule**, if ϕ_j is an upper hemicontinuous correspondence, with nonempty, closed and convex values.

A pricing rule is called *regular* when it satisfies some convenient analytical properties: it is always non-empty valued for any efficient production plan, it has compact and convex images, and its graph is closed.

Remark 3.3.- A correspondence $\Gamma : D \subset \mathbb{R}^\ell \to \mathbb{R}^\ell$ is closed when its graph is closed [that is, if for any sequences $\{\mathbf{z}^\nu\} \subset D, \{\mathbf{f}^\nu\} \subset \mathbb{R}^\ell$, such that $\mathbf{f}^\nu \in \Gamma(\mathbf{z}^\nu)$ for all ν, and $\{\mathbf{z}^\nu\} \to \mathbf{z}, \{\mathbf{f}^\nu\} \to \mathbf{f}$, we have: $\mathbf{f} \in \Gamma(\mathbf{z})$]. A correspondence is closed-valued, when $\Gamma(\mathbf{z})$ is closed, for each $\mathbf{z} \in D$. If Γ is closed and $\Gamma(\mathbf{z})$ is compact, for each $\mathbf{z} \in D$, then Γ is upper hemicontinuous.

Pricing rules may refer to both normative and positive models. Normative models are intended to formalize regulation policies for non-convex firms, mostly in terms of pricing policies which satisfy some desirable properties (they typically aim at first or second best efficiency). Positive models try to describe plausible scenarios of market economies where firms may exhibit increasing returns to scale, and profit maximization at given prices is not applicable. It was already mentioned that different firms may follow different patterns of behaviour, so that models which combine the positive and normative approaches are also possible.

A family of pricing rules which is common in the literature is that in which the losses that firms find acceptable are bounded. This sensible assumption plays a relevant role in the existence of equilibrium, and imposes some structure on production sets for particular pricing rules. Let us present here the definition of these pricing rules (even though we shall use a different assumption in order to prove the chief existence result in chapter 4)

Definition 3.8.-

$\phi_j : \mathbb{P} \times \mathbb{F} \to \mathbb{P}$ is a **Pricing Rule with Bounded Losses**, if there is a scalar $\alpha_j \leq 0$ such that, for each $(\mathbf{p}, \tilde{\mathbf{y}})$ in $\mathbb{P} \times \mathbb{F}$,

$$\mathbf{q}\mathbf{y}_j \geq \alpha_j, \forall\ \mathbf{q} \in \phi_j(\mathbf{p}, \tilde{\mathbf{y}})$$

A pricing rule for the *jth* firm satisfies the *bounded losses* condition if there exists a limit to the losses this firm is ready to admit, for any production plan. A particular case of bounded losses is that in which firms' admissible profits are always nonnegative (known as *loss-free pricing rules*).

Observe that the combination of the notions of bounded-losses and regularity implies a non-trivial structure on the pricing rule. In particular, it prevents a firm from setting:

$$\phi_j(\mathbf{p}, \tilde{\mathbf{y}}) \equiv \{\mathbf{q}^o\}$$

(constant) for all $(\mathbf{p}, \tilde{\mathbf{y}})$ in $\mathbb{P} \times \mathbb{F}$ (which would easily destroy any possibility of equilibria). The reader is encouraged to think about the nature of this implication [Bonnisseau & Cornet (1988a, Remark 2.6) will help].

3.5 FINAL COMMENTS

Let us conclude this chapter by giving a few examples of regular pricing rules that will be analyzed in parts II and III:

(1) Profit maximization at given prices (when production sets are assumed to be convex, or nonconvexities are due to external economies).

(2) Average cost pricing (i.e., firms choose prices so that they just break-even).

(3) Marginal pricing (firms are instructed to sell their outputs at prices which satisfy the necessary conditions for optimality).

(4) Two-Part Marginal pricing (a non-linear price structure which combines marginal and average cost pricing).

(5) Constrained Profit Maximization (a situation in which firms maximize profits at given prices, subject to quantity constraints).

The reader is referred to the classical works of Koopmans (1957), Debreu (1959) and Arrow & Hahn (1971), and the survey by Nadiri (1982), for a more detailed study of production theory. The discussion on the modelling of firms in terms of pricing rules is carried out in next chapters.

Chapter 4

EQUILIBRIUM

4.1 INTRODUCTION

This chapter analyzes the existence of equilibrium in an economy made of those consumers and firms modelled in chapters 2 and 3. The existence result presented refers to an economy in which firms' behaviour is described in terms of *abstract* pricing rules.

The abstract pricing rule approach has to cope with a number of problems when we come to analyze the existence of equilibrium. These problems, which are ones of technique and of substance, do not exist in the standard competitive world, and turn out to be interdependent and to appear simultaneously. Let us briefly comment on them, in order to clarify the nature of the assumptions that we shall meet later on:

1) In the absence of convexity, the set of attainable allocations may not be bounded (see section 3.3). This implies that some hypothesis on the compactness of this set must be introduced, if we want to be able to apply a standard fixpoint argument.

2) When firms do not behave as profit maximizers at given prices, they may suffer losses in equilibrium. This is the case of marginal pricing, which yields negative profits under increasing returns to scale. Hence some restriction on the distribution of wealth must be imposed in order to avoid difficulties for the survival of consumers (and the upper hemicontinuity of the demand mapping). Indeed the survival assumption turns out to be a key element in the shaping of most models with increasing returns.

3) Pricing rules cannot be totally arbitrary. In particular, each firm's pricing rule must exhibit some sensitivity with respect to changes in production, since an equilibrium price vector must belong to the intersection of all firms' pricing rules (think of the case of two firms, each of which only accepts

a single price vector for any possible production plan, and in which the two price vectors differ).

It is worth stressing that the existence result presented here allows for discontinuous wealth functions (continuity is only assumed on the set of production equilibria). This is important because it allows us to deal with income schedules which are relevant but usually difficult to handle in a general equilibrium framework (e.g., two-part tariffs, salaries which include productivity bonuses, etc.).

4.2   THE MODEL

Let us briefly summarize the main features of the economy described in chapters 2 and 3. We consider a market economy with ℓ perfectly divisible commodities, m consumers and n firms. A point $\omega \in \mathbb{R}^\ell$ denotes the vector of initial endowments. For $j = 1, 2, \ldots, n, Y_j \subset \mathbb{R}^\ell$ denotes the jth firm's production set, while $\mathbb{F}_j$ stands for the jth firm's set of weakly efficient production plans, and $\mathbb{F}$ for the Cartesian product of the n sets of weakly efficient production plans, that is $\mathbb{F} \equiv \Pi_{j=1}^n \mathbb{F}_j$. We denote by $\mathbb{P} \subset \mathbb{R}_+^\ell$ the standard price simplex, that is, $\mathbb{P} = \{\mathbf{p} \in \mathbb{R}_+^\ell \; / \; \sum_{t=1}^\ell p_t = 1\}$.

The jth firm's behaviour is described by a pricing rule correspondence $\phi_j : \mathbb{P} \times \mathbb{F} \rightarrow \mathbb{P}$, which establishes the jth firm set of admissible prices, as a function of "market conditions". A production equilibrium is a situation in which all firms find acceptable the proposed combination between market prices and production plans. The set of production equilibria is denoted by **PE**.

The ith consumer is characterized by a triple, $[X_i, u_i, r_i]$, where X_i, u_i stand for the ith consumer's consumption set and utility function, respectively. The term r_i denotes the ith consumer's wealth. Along this chapter, r_i is taken to be a mapping from $\mathbb{P} \times \mathbb{R}^{\ell n}$ into $\mathbb{R}$ so that, for each pair $(\mathbf{p}, \tilde{\mathbf{y}})$, $r_i(\mathbf{p}, \tilde{\mathbf{y}})$ gives us the ith consumer's wealth. Particularizations of this mapping (less general but more informative) will appear later on.

Let $(\mathbf{p}, \tilde{\mathbf{y}}) \in \mathbb{P} \times \mathbb{F}$ be given. Then, consumers' behaviour can be summarized by an aggregate net demand correspondence, that can be written as $\xi(\mathbf{p}, \tilde{\mathbf{y}}) - \{\omega\}$, where $\xi(\mathbf{p}, \tilde{\mathbf{y}}) \equiv \sum_{i=1}^m \xi_i(\mathbf{p}, \tilde{\mathbf{y}})$, and ξ_i stands for the ith consumer's demand correspondence [i.e., $\xi_i(\mathbf{p}, \tilde{\mathbf{y}})$ is the set of solutions to the program: *Max.* $u_i(.)$ subject to $\mathbf{x}_i \in X_i$ and $\mathbf{p}\mathbf{x}_i \leq r_i(\mathbf{p}, \tilde{\mathbf{y}})$].

Remark 4.1.- Observe that since consumers' choices depend on market prices and firms' production, we may think of each ϕ_j as also being dependent on consumers' decisions, that is, $\phi_j(\mathbf{p}, \tilde{\mathbf{y}}) = \Theta_j[\mathbf{p}, \tilde{\mathbf{y}}, \xi(\mathbf{p}, \tilde{\mathbf{y}})]$. This provides enough flexibility to deal with market situations in which firms' target payoffs may depend on demand conditions (as it is the case for Boiteaux-Ramsey prices).

The set of attainable allocations is given by:

$$A(\omega) \equiv \{[(\mathbf{x}_i), (\mathbf{y}_j)] \in \prod_{i=1}^{m} X_i \times \prod_{j=1}^{n} Y_j \ / \ \sum_{i=1}^{m} \mathbf{x}_i - \omega \le \sum_{j=1}^{n} \mathbf{y}_j\}$$

The projection of $A(\omega)$ on the spaces containing X_i, Y_j gives us the *ith* consumer's set of attainable consumptions and *jth* firm's set of attainable production plans, respectively.

For a given $\mathbf{p} \in \mathbb{P}$, $b_i(\mathbf{p})$ denotes the minimum of $\mathbf{p}\mathbf{x}_i$ over X_i. This is clearly a continuous function, by virtue of the Maximum Theorem.

Consider now the following assumptions:

A.4.1.- For each $i = 1, 2, \dots, m$:
    (i) X_i is a nonempty, closed and convex subset of $\mathbb{R}^\ell$, bounded from below.
    (ii) $u_i : X_i \to \mathbb{R}$ is a continuous and quasi-concave function, which satisfies local non-satiation.

A.4.2.- For each firm $j = 1, 2, \dots, n$:
    (i) Y_j is a closed subset of $\mathbb{R}^\ell$.
    (ii) $Y_j - \mathbb{R}_+^\ell \subset Y_j$.
    (iii) For every $\omega' \ge \omega$, the set $A(\omega')$ is bounded.

A.4.3.- For each $j = 1, 2, \dots, n$, ϕ_j is a regular pricing rule.

A.4.4.- Let **PE** stand for the set of production equilibria. Then, the restriction of r_i over **PE** is continuous, with $r_i(\mathbf{p}, \tilde{\mathbf{y}}) > b_i(\mathbf{p})$, and $\sum_{i=1}^{m} r_i(\mathbf{p}, \tilde{\mathbf{y}}) = \mathbf{p}(\omega + \sum_{j=1}^{n} \mathbf{y}_j)$.

Assumption (A.4.1) is standard. It assumes that consumers have complete, continuous and convex preferences, locally non-satiated, which are defined over convex choice sets bounded form below.

Assumption (A.4.2) refers to production sets. Besides closedness, it assumes that Y_j is comprehensive. It also says that it is not possible (either for the *jth* firm or for the economy as a whole) to obtain unlimited amounts of production out of a finite amount of endowments. Observe that under (A.4.2) the set of weakly efficient production plans $\mathbb{F}_j$, consists exactly of those points in the boundary of Y_j (Proposition 3.2). Note that we have not assumed here that $\mathbf{0} \in Y_j$.

Assumption (A.4.3) establishes that each firm's pricing rule is an upper hemicontinuous correspondence with nonempty, compact and convex values.

Assumption (A.4.4) refers to production equilibria. First it assumes the continuity of wealth functions, when restricted to the set of production equilibria (a much weaker requirement than assuming that r_i is continuous over $\mathbb{P} \times \mathbb{F}$). Then, it introduces the "cheaper point" requirement: in a production equilibrium the ith consumer's demand does not minimize $\mathbf{p}\mathbf{x}_i$ over X_i. This implies of course a survival condition (every consumer will survive in equilibrium). Finally, it simply says that total wealth equals the value of the aggregate initial endowments plus total profits.

Notice that assumptions (A.4.1) and (A.4.2) ensure that $A(\omega)$ is compact, but not that it is nonempty (that will follow from the existence theorem).

It was pointed out in the Introduction that the existence of equilibrium cannot be ensured unless pricing rules exhibit some sensitivity to changes in production plans. The next assumption introduces such a requirement by asking every firm to change the price of some commodity, when production plans belong to the boundary of a well defined compact set (which contains in its relative interior the set of all feasible production plans).[1]

In order to formulate this assumption, let us introduce the following notation: For a scalar $k > 0$ let K denote the cube with edge $2k$, that is,

$$K = \{\mathbf{z} \in \mathbb{R}^\ell \ / \ |z_h| \le k, \ for \ all \ h = 1, 2, ..., \ell\}$$

Under assumptions (A.4.1) and (A.4.2) every attainable production and consumption set is compact, so that there exists $k > 0$ such that K contains in its interior all these sets. Call $K_+ = K + \mathbb{R}^\ell_+$, and $\mathbb{F}^*_j = \mathbb{F}_j \cap K_+$ (that is, $\mathbb{F}^*_j$ is a subset $\mathbb{F}_j$ which contains in its relative interior all attainable production plans). Our hypothesis (A.4.5) concerns production plans in $\mathbb{F}^*_j$. This is clearly a *compact set*.[2]

---

[1]This assumption is inspired in Vohra (1988 a), and plays the role of the "bounded losses assumption" in other models.

[2]It is closed because it is the intersection of two closed sets. Suppose that it is not bounded; then there must be some unbounded sequence in $\mathbb{F}_j$ for which some component goes to $+\infty$, contradicting the boundedness of $A(\omega)$.

<u>A.4.5.-</u> Let $(\mathbf{p}, \tilde{\mathbf{y}})$ be given. Suppose that $\mathbf{y}_j \in \mathbb{F}_j^*$ and $\mathbf{p} \notin \phi_j(\mathbf{p}, \tilde{\mathbf{y}})$. Then, for all $\mathbf{q}_j \in \phi_j(\mathbf{p}, \tilde{\mathbf{y}})$ at least one of the following alternatives occurs:

(a) There is a commodity c for which $y_{jc} > -k$ and $p_c \leq q_{jc}$.

(b) There exists a commodity c for which $y_{jc} = -k$ and $p_c - q_{jc} > p_h - q_{jh}$ for all $h \neq c$.

The intuitive explanation of this requirement is the following. Suppose that the jth firm faces a price vector which is not acceptable for a production plan which is not too far from the attainable production set. Assumption (A.4.5) establishes that if the firm were asked to propose a new price vector in these circumstances, then:

(a) It will never propose to reduce the prices of all outputs[3]. Or:

(b) It will propose to reduce *most* the price of one of the inputs being used at the highest possible level.

Assumption (A.4.5) conveys the idea that we exclude profit minimization as a plausible behaviour (so note the connection with the idea of bounded losses). Observe that if $\mathbf{y}_j$ is such that $y_{jc} > -k$ for all c, then (a) is automatically satisfied. Therefore this mild assumption only applies to those production plans which hit the boundary of $\mathbb{F}_j^*$.

Remark 4.2.- It is worth stressing that assumption (A.4.5) will automatically be satisfied by all particular pricing rules considered in later chapters.

The next definition makes it precise the equilibrium notion:

<u>Definition 4.1.-</u>

We shall say that a price vector $\mathbf{p}^* \in \mathbb{P}$, and an allocation $[(\mathbf{x}_i^*), \tilde{\mathbf{y}}^*]$, yield an **Equilibrium** if the following conditions are satisfied:

(α) For each $i = 1, 2, \ldots, m$, $\mathbf{x}_i^*$ maximizes u_i over the set of points $\mathbf{x}_i$ in X_i such that, $\mathbf{p}^* \mathbf{x}_i \leq r_i(\mathbf{p}^*, \tilde{\mathbf{y}}^*)$.

(β) $(\mathbf{p}^*, \tilde{\mathbf{y}}^*)$ is a production equilibrium, that is, $\mathbf{p}^* \in \bigcap_{j=1}^{n} \phi_j(\mathbf{p}^*, \tilde{\mathbf{y}}^*)$.

(γ) $\sum_{i=1}^{m} \mathbf{x}_i^* - \sum_{j=1}^{n} \mathbf{y}_j^* \leq w$, and $\sum_{i=1}^{m} \mathbf{x}_{it}^* - \sum_{j=1}^{n} \mathbf{y}_{jt}^* < w_t \Rightarrow p_t^* = 0$

That is, an Equilibrium is a situation in which: (a) Consumers maximize their preferences subject to their budget constraints; (b) Every firm is in equilibrium; and (c) All markets clear (meaning that net production is greater

---

[3]More precisely: the desired price of some commodity, which does not correspond to an input used at the highest possible level, will not be smaller than its market price.

or equal than net demand on all markets, and that only free goods can be produced in excess).

The main result of this chapter goes as follows:

Theorem 4.1.-
   Let E stand for an economy satisfying assumptions (A.4.1) to (A.4.5). Then an equilibrium exists.

(The proof of this theorem is given in the next section)

The structure of the model (and the proof of the existence theorem) allows us to interpret the functioning of this economy as follows: (a) There is an auctioneer who calls both a price vector (to be seen as proposed market prices), and a vector of efficient production plans. (b) Given these prices and production plans, the ith consumer chooses that consumption bundle which maximizes her utility subject to her wealth constraint. (c) Firms check whether the proposed prices-production pair agrees with their objectives. When this is so, the price vector is a candidate for a market equilibrium. (d) When not all firms agree on the proposed prices-production combination, or markets do not clear, the auctioneer tries a new proposal. For that, she chooses those prices and production plans such that, they maximize the value of the "excess demand" and minimize the distance between each pricing rule and the proposed prices.

Remark 4.3.- Even though in this abstract framework the existence result allows for pricing rules which may depend on $\mathbb{P} \times \mathbb{F}$, in the case of particular pricing rules we shall restrict their domain to the smallest possible one (in particular, pricing rules will appear in most cases as mappings from $\mathbb{F}_j$ into $\mathbb{P}$). It should be clear that this is a particular case of the general setting presented in this chapter.

4.3   THE EXISTENCE OF EQUILIBRIUM

The strategy of the proof of theorem 4.1 goes along the lines of the standard one for convex economies. Namely we shall apply a fixpoint argument over an artificial economy (which satisfies all the required properties for that), and show that this actually corresponds to an equilibrium in the original one.

The reader should notice three different complications that we have to consider in order to apply this scheme. Two of these complications refer to assumption (A.4.4), which establishes conditions on the set of production equilibria only. In particular: Assumption (A.4.4) ensures neither the continuity of wealth functions on $\mathbb{P} \times \mathbb{F}$, nor the minimum wealth requirement for budget sets to be continuous mappings. As for the third complication, let us recall that even though we are describing the behaviour of firms in terms of upper hemicontinuous and convex-valued correspondences (the regular pricing rules), they are defined over nonconvex sets (so that we are not able to directly apply Kakutani's Fixpoint Theorem). These three problems will be "remedied" in the way of constructing the artificial economy where we shall show an equilibrium to exist.

The following preliminary result, which is a variant of the classical Gale-Nikaido-Debreu Lemma, embodies the fixpoint argument required for the proof of the theorem:

Lemma 4.1.-

Let D be a compact and convex subset of $\mathbb{R}^\ell$, and $\Gamma : D \to \mathbb{R}^\ell$ an upper hemicontinuous correspondence, with nonempty, compact and convex values. Then points $\mathbf{x}^* \in D$, $\mathbf{y}^* \in \Gamma(\mathbf{x}^*)$ exist such that $(\mathbf{x} - \mathbf{x}^*)\mathbf{y}^* \leq 0$, for all $\mathbf{x} \in D$.

Proof.-

Let $T = \Gamma(D)$. Since D is compact, T will be a compact set [see for instance Border (1985,11.16)]. Let $Co(T)$ denote the convex hull of T. By construction $Co(T)$ is a compact and convex set. Now define a correspondence $\rho{:}Co(T) \to D$ as follows:

$$\rho(\mathbf{y}) = \{\mathbf{x} \in D \ / \ \mathbf{xy} \geq \mathbf{zy}, \ \forall \, \mathbf{z} \in D\}$$

Clearly ρ is a nonempty, convex-valued correspondence. Furthermore, ρ is upper hemicontinuous in view of the Maximum Theorem (we are maximizing a continuous function over a fixed set, which can trivially be regarded as a continuous correspondence). Define now a new correspondence, ϕ from $D \times Co(T)$ into itself as follows:

$$\phi(\mathbf{x}, \mathbf{y}) = \rho(\mathbf{y}) \times \Gamma(\mathbf{x})$$

By construction, ϕ is an upper hemicontinuous correspondence with nonempty, compact and convex values, mapping a compact and convex set into itself. Thus, Kakutani's fixed point theorem applies and there exists $(\mathbf{x}^*, \mathbf{y}^*) \in \phi(\mathbf{x}^*, \mathbf{y}^*)$, that is,

$$\mathbf{x}^* \in \rho(\mathbf{y}^*), \quad \mathbf{y}^* \in \Gamma(\mathbf{x}^*)$$

By definition of ρ we have:

$$\mathbf{x}^*\mathbf{y}^* = \max \ \mathbf{zy}^*, \ \mathbf{z} \in D$$

and hence the result follows.♠

Under the assumptions of the model, there exists $k > 0$ such that
$$K = \{\mathbf{z} \in \mathbb{R}^\ell \; / \; |z_h| \le k, \; for \; all \; h = 1, 2, ..., \ell\}$$
contains in its interior all production and consumption sets. By letting $K_+ = K + \mathbb{R}_+^\ell$, $K_+^n = (K + \mathbb{R}_+^\ell)^n$ (that is, the n-fold replica of K_+), we define $\mathbb{F}_j^* = \mathbb{F}_j \cap K_+$ and $\mathbb{F}^* \equiv \mathbb{F} \cap K_+^n$. By construction, $\mathbb{F}^*$ is a compact set.

The next Lemma is directed towards the first complication mentioned above:

Lemma 4.2.-

Under assumptions (A.4.1), (A.4.2) and (A.4.4), for every $i = 1, 2, ..., m$, there exists a continuous function $R_i : \mathbb{P} \times \mathbb{F}^* \to \mathbb{R}$ such that $R_i(\mathbf{p}, \tilde{\mathbf{y}}) > b_i(\mathbf{p})$ for all $(\mathbf{p}, \tilde{\mathbf{y}})$ with $R_i(\mathbf{p}, \tilde{\mathbf{y}}) = r_i(\mathbf{p}, \tilde{\mathbf{y}})$ whenever $(\mathbf{p}, \tilde{\mathbf{y}})$ is a production equilibrium.

Proof.-

Under assumptions (A.4.1) and (A.4.2), the set of production equilibria restricted to $\mathbb{F}^*$ is a compact (possibly empty) set. Assumption (A.4.4) ensures that r_i is continuous over the set of production equilibria. Hence the Tietze-Urysohn extension theorem (see the Appendix) ensures the existence of a continuous function $R_i : \mathbb{P} \times \mathbb{F}^* \to \mathbb{R}$ such that $R_i(\mathbf{p}, \tilde{\mathbf{y}})$ coincides with $r_i(\mathbf{p}, \tilde{\mathbf{y}})$ over the set of production equilibria, and $R_i(\mathbf{p}, \tilde{\mathbf{y}}) > b_i(\mathbf{p})$ for all $(\mathbf{p}, \tilde{\mathbf{y}}) \in \mathbb{P} \times \mathbb{F}^*$ (because $b_i(\mathbf{p}) < r_i(\mathbf{p}, \tilde{\mathbf{y}})$ over the set of production equilibria, by assumption, and b_i is continuous and bounded from below).♠

In order to deal with the second type of complication, define a mapping $g : \mathbb{P} \times \mathbb{F}^* \to \mathbb{R}^\ell$, such that it associates with every $(\mathbf{p}, \tilde{\mathbf{y}})$ in the compact set $\mathbb{P} \times \mathbb{F}^*$ the set of points $\mathbf{t}$ which solve the following program:

$$Min. \; dist. \left[\mathbf{t}, \sum_{j=1}^{n} \mathbf{y}_j\right]$$
$$s.t. :$$
$$\mathbf{p}\left(\omega + \mathbf{t}\right) = \sum_{i=1}^{m} R_i\left(\mathbf{p}, \tilde{\mathbf{y}}\right)$$

Observe that the feasible set is convex and the objective function is strictly convex. Therefore, for each $(\mathbf{p}, \tilde{\mathbf{y}})$ in $\mathbb{P} \times \mathbb{F}^*$, there is a unique solution to this program, which varies continuously with $(\mathbf{p}, \tilde{\mathbf{y}})$ (by virtue of the maximum theorem).

Call $\mathbb{F}_j'$ the jth firm's set of **attainable and weakly efficient** production plans, $j = 1, 2, ..., n$. The next lemma deals with the third type of complication mentioned above:

Lemma 4.3.-

Under assumption (A.4.2), $\mathbb{F}_j^*$ can be made homeomorphic to a simplex $S_j = \{ s_j \in \mathbb{R}_+^\ell \ / \ \sum_{i=1}^\ell s_{ij} = 1 \}$, so that the points in $\mathbb{F}_j'$ are mapped into the interior of S_j .

Proof.-

Under assumption (A.4.2), $\mathbb{F}_j'$ is a compact set; furthermore, the way of constructing $\mathbb{F}_j^*$ implies that the set $\mathbb{F}_j^* + \{ke\}$ will be in $\mathbb{R}_+^\ell$, and the set $\mathbb{F}_j'$ $+\{ke\}$ will be in the interior of $\mathbb{R}_+^\ell$ (where e stands for the unit vector in $\mathbb{R}_+^\ell$). Define now a mapping $H_j : S_j \to \mathbb{R}_+^\ell$ as follows (see Figure 4.1):

$$H_j(s_j) = \{\lambda s_j, \lambda \geq 0\} \cap \{\mathbb{F}_j^* + \{ke\}\}$$

Assumption (A.4.2) implies that this mapping is well defined, continuous, onto and that for each $s_j \in S_j$ there exists a unique point $y_j \in \mathbb{F}_j^*$ such that $y_j + ke = H_j(s_j)$ (if there were two one would be strictly smaller than the other, contradicting the fact that both are points in $\mathbb{F}_j^*$).

Consider now the mapping $h_j : S_j \to \mathbb{F}_j^*$ given by:

$$h_j(s_j) = H_j(s_j) - ke$$

This is an onto, continuous function which maps $\mathbb{F}_j'$ into the interior of S_j and gives us the postulated homeomorphism between S_j and $\mathbb{F}_j^*$.♠

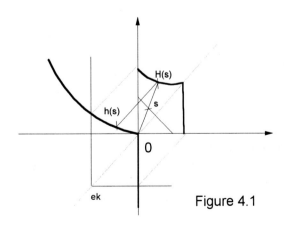

Figure 4.1

For each $j = 1, 2, \ldots, n$, let $\mathbf{h}_j$ denote the continuous mapping which associates to every $\mathbf{s}_j$ in S_j a unique $\mathbf{y}_j$ in $\mathbb{F}_j^*$. Let $\mathbb{S} \equiv \prod_{j=1}^{n} S_j$, and define $\Delta \equiv \mathbb{P} \times \mathbb{S}$; $\mathbf{s} = (\mathbf{s}_1, \ldots, \mathbf{s}_n)$ will denote a point in $\mathbb{S}$. We shall write:

$$\mathbf{h}(\mathbf{s}) \equiv [\mathbf{h}_1(\mathbf{s}_1), \mathbf{h}_2(\mathbf{s}_2), \ldots, \mathbf{h}_n(\mathbf{s}_n)]$$

$$\hat{g}(\mathbf{p}, \mathbf{s}) \equiv g[\mathbf{p}, \mathbf{h}(\mathbf{s})]$$

$$\hat{R}_i(\mathbf{p}, \mathbf{s}) \equiv R_i[\mathbf{p}, \mathbf{h}(\mathbf{s})]$$

which are obviously continuous functions on $\mathbb{S}$ and Δ.

Define a new demand correspondence $\hat{\xi}$, where $\hat{\xi}(\mathbf{p}, \mathbf{s}) \equiv \sum_{i=1}^{m} \hat{\xi}_i(\mathbf{p}, \mathbf{s})$, and $\hat{\xi}_i(\mathbf{p}, \mathbf{s})$ stands for the set of solutions to the program:

$$Max \ u_i(\mathbf{x}_i)$$
$$s.t. \quad : \quad \mathbf{x}_i \in X_i^*$$
$$\mathbf{p} \, \mathbf{x}_i \ \leq \ \hat{R}_i(\mathbf{p}, \mathbf{s})$$

where $X_i^* \equiv X_i \cap K$.

Call $\hat{E}$ the economy constructed in that way, and let $\hat{\zeta}$ be the corresponding excess demand mapping, that is,

$$\hat{\zeta}(\mathbf{p}, \mathbf{s}) \equiv \hat{\xi}(\mathbf{p}, \mathbf{s}) - \{\omega\} - \hat{g}(\mathbf{p}, \mathbf{s})$$

Define now a mapping $\Gamma : \Delta \to \mathbb{R}^{\ell(1+n)}$ as follows:

$$\Gamma(\mathbf{p}, \mathbf{s}) \equiv \begin{bmatrix} \hat{\zeta}(\mathbf{p}, \mathbf{s}) \\ \mathbf{p} - \phi_1[\mathbf{p}, \mathbf{h}(\mathbf{s})] \\ \mathbf{p} - \phi_2[\mathbf{p}, \mathbf{h}(\mathbf{s})] \\ \cdots\cdots\cdots\cdots \\ \cdots\cdots\cdots\cdots \\ \mathbf{p} - \phi_n[\mathbf{p}, \mathbf{h}(\mathbf{s})] \end{bmatrix}$$

Notice that Γ is a correspondence consisting of $(1+n)$ ℓ-vector mappings. The first one corresponds to the excess demand mapping of $\hat{E}$, whilst any of the remaining n can be interpreted as the difference between the price vector proposed by the auctioneer and those prices which are acceptable for each firm.

We are ready now to present our main result:

Theorem 4.1.-

Let E stand for an economy satisfying assumptions (A.4.1) to (A.4.5). Then an equilibrium exists.

Proof.-

Let $\widehat{E}$ stand for the economy defined above. Under the assumptions of the theorem, for every $i = 1, 2, \ldots, m$, the mapping $\gamma_i : \Delta \rightarrow X_i^*$ given by:

$$\gamma_i(\mathbf{p}, \mathbf{s}) = \{ \mathbf{x}_i \in X_i^* \ / \ \mathbf{p} \, \mathbf{x}_i \leq \widehat{R}_i(\mathbf{p}, \mathbf{s}) \}$$

is continuous in $(\mathbf{p}, \mathbf{s})$ (see proposition 2.3), with nonempty, compact and convex values. Therefore, since preferences are assumed to be continuous and convex, for each pair $(\mathbf{p}, \mathbf{s}) \in \Delta$, every $\widehat{\xi}_i$ will be an upper-hemicontinuous correspondence, with nonempty, compact and convex values (theorem 2.2). The way of constructing the $\widehat{g}$ mapping implies that $\widehat{\zeta}$ inherits these properties. Since we have assumed that pricing rules are regular, this also applies to Γ.

Thus, Γ is an upper-hemicontinuous correspondence, with nonempty, compact and convex values, applying a compact and convex set, $\Delta \subset \mathbb{R}_+^{\ell(1+n)}$ into $\mathbb{R}^{\ell(1+n)}$. Then, Lemma 4.1 ensures the existence of points $(\mathbf{p}^*, \mathbf{s}^*)$ in $\Delta, (\mathbf{z}^*, \mathbf{v}^*)$ in $\Gamma(\mathbf{p}^*, \mathbf{s}^*)$ such that,

$$(\mathbf{p}^*, \mathbf{s}^*)(\mathbf{z}^*, \mathbf{v}^*) \geq (\mathbf{p}, \mathbf{s})(\mathbf{z}^*, \mathbf{v}^*)$$

for every pair $(\mathbf{p}, \mathbf{s})$ in Δ. In particular,

$$(\mathbf{p}^*, \mathbf{s}^*)(\mathbf{z}^*, \mathbf{v}^*) \geq (\mathbf{p}, \mathbf{s}^*)(\mathbf{z}^*, \mathbf{v}^*), \forall \mathbf{p} \in \mathbb{P} \qquad [1]$$

$$(\mathbf{p}^*, \mathbf{s}^*)(\mathbf{z}^*, \mathbf{v}^*) \geq (\mathbf{p}^*, \mathbf{s})(\mathbf{z}^*, \mathbf{v}^*), \forall \mathbf{s} \in \mathbb{S} \qquad [2]$$

From [1] it follows that $\mathbf{p}^* \mathbf{z}^* \geq \mathbf{p} \mathbf{z}^*$, for all $\mathbf{p} \in \mathbb{P}$, which implies:

$$\mathbf{p}^* \mathbf{z}^* = \max_j \mathbf{z}_j^*$$

By construction $\mathbf{p}^* \mathbf{z}^* = 0$, so that $\max_j z_j^* = 0$, and hence, $\mathbf{z}^* \leq \mathbf{0}$, with $p_k^* = 0$ whenever $z_k^* < 0$.

Similarly, from [2] it follows that $\mathbf{s}^* \mathbf{v}^* \geq \mathbf{s} \mathbf{v}^*$, for all $\mathbf{s}$ in $\mathbb{S}$, and hence for each $j = 1, 2, \ldots, n$ we have: $\mathbf{s}_j^* \mathbf{v}_j^* = \max_i v_{ij}^*$. This implies that either $v_{kj}^* = \{\max_i v_{ij}^*\}$, or else $s_{kj}^* = 0$, for each k.

We have now the following possibilities:

(a) $\mathbf{s}_j^* \in intS_j, \forall j$. In this case, since $\mathbf{v}_j^* \equiv \mathbf{p}^* - \mathbf{q}_j^*$ consists of the difference between two points in $\mathbb{P}$ (for some $\mathbf{q}_j^* \in \phi_j[\mathbf{p}_j^*, \mathbf{h}(\mathbf{s}^*)]$), it must be the case that $\mathbf{v}_j^* = \mathbf{0}$.

(b) $\mathbf{v}_j^* \neq \mathbf{0}$ for some j, and consequently $\mathbf{s}_j^* \in \partial S_j$. From assumption (A.4.5) it follows that there exists some commodity c for which one of the following relations holds: $(b, 1)$ $s_{jc}^* > 0$ and $p_c^* \leq q_{jc}^*$; or $(b, 2)$ $s_{jc}^* = 0$ and $p_c^* - q_{jc}^* > p_h^* - q_{jh}^*, \forall h \neq c$. The first alternative means that $\max\limits_{i} v_{jk}^* = v_{jc}^* = p_c^* - q_{jc}^* \leq 0$, so that $\mathbf{p}^* - \mathbf{q}_j^* \leq \mathbf{0}$ and consequently $\mathbf{v}_j^* = 0$ (that is, $\mathbf{p}^* \in \phi_j[\mathbf{p}^*, \mathbf{h}(\mathbf{s}^*)]$). The second is incompatible with [2], because it requires $s_{jc}^* > 0$.

Since only (a) or $(b, 1)$ can occur, we know that $\mathbf{v}_j^* = 0$ for all j. Therefore one finds that $\mathbf{p}^* \in \bigcap\limits_{j=1}^{n} \phi_j[\mathbf{p}^*, \mathbf{h}(\mathbf{s}^*)]$, that is, $[\mathbf{p}^*, \mathbf{h}(\mathbf{s}^*)]$ is a production equilibrium of the original economy.

Assumption (A.4.4) ensures in these circumstances that, $\hat{R}_i(\mathbf{p}^*, \mathbf{s}^*) = r_i[\mathbf{p}^*, \mathbf{h}(\mathbf{s}^*)] > b_i(\mathbf{p}^*)$, for all i. Hence $\hat{g}(\mathbf{p}^*, \mathbf{s}^*) = \sum\limits_{j=1}^{n} \mathbf{h}_j(\mathbf{s}_j^*)$, and consequently

$$0 \geq \mathbf{z}^* \in \hat{\xi}(\mathbf{p}^*, \mathbf{s}^*) - \{\omega\} - \sum_{j=1}^{n} \mathbf{y}_j^*$$

Finally, it remains to show that, for all i, $\mathbf{x}_i^*$ maximizes u_i on the set

$$\beta_i(\mathbf{p}^*, \tilde{\mathbf{y}}^*) \equiv \{\mathbf{x}_i \in X_i \ / \ \mathbf{p}^*\mathbf{x}_i \leq r_i(\mathbf{p}^*, \tilde{\mathbf{y}}^*)\}$$

(i.e., that the restriction of consumption plans to X_i^* is actually irrelevant). We know that $\mathbf{x}_i^*$ maximizes u_i on the set of points $\mathbf{x}_i \in X_i^*$ such that $\mathbf{p}^*\mathbf{x}_i \leq r_i(\mathbf{p}^*, \tilde{\mathbf{y}}^*)$. Suppose that there exists some $\mathbf{x}_i'$ in $\beta_i(\mathbf{p}^*, \tilde{\mathbf{y}}^*)$ with $u_i(\mathbf{x}_i') > u_i(\mathbf{x}_i^*)$. Because $\mathbf{x}_i^*$ is feasible, it must be a point in the interior of K. Hence, there will be some $\mathbf{x}_i''$ in the segment $[\mathbf{x}_i^*, \mathbf{x}_i']$, different from $\mathbf{x}_i^*$ but close enough to be in K. Such a point will be in X_i (a convex set). The convexity and non-satiability of preferences imply that $u_i(\mathbf{x}_i'') > u_i(\mathbf{x}_i^*)$, whereas $\mathbf{p}^*\mathbf{x}_i'' \leq r_i(\mathbf{p}^*, \tilde{\mathbf{y}}^*)$, by construction. But this contradicts the fact that $\mathbf{x}_i^*$ maximizes u_i in X_i^*.

The proof is in this way completed.♠

4.4 FINAL COMMENTS

There is a number of existence results which refer to abstract pricing rules, results that can then be particularized so as to encompass most of the pricing rules to be considered in next chapters.

The papers by MacKinnon (1979) and Dierker, Guesnerie & Neuefeind (1985) are pioneering contribution in this area. Bonnisseau & Cornet (1988a) provide an extremely general existence result, for the case in which firms' losses are bounded (this paper may be thought of as a benchmark in the literature on the existence of equilibria with non-convex technologies). Vohra (1988a) presents an alternative existence result, using slightly different assumptions and an easier proof. A degree theoretic existence result can be found in Kamiya (1988) (where the question of uniqueness is also analyzed). Simplified versions of Bonnisseau & Cornet's model appear in Villar (1991),(1994b) where relatively easy existence proofs are provided. See also Bonnisseau (1988), (1991) for a discussion of some interconnections. All these models, however, assume the continuity of wealth functions on the entire domain.

The reader is encouraged to go through Brown's (1991) survey and Bonnisseau & Cornet's (1988a) paper in order to get a deeper review of the existence results.

4.5 APPENDIX

The Tietze-Urysohn Extension Theorem

Proposition 4.1.-
Let **E** be a metric space, **A** a closed subset of **E**, f a continuous bounded mapping of **A** into $\mathbb{R}$. Then there exists a continuous mapping g of **E** into $\mathbb{R}$ which coincides with F in **A** and is such that

$$\sup_{x \in E} g\ (\ \mathbf{x}\ ) = \sup_{y \in A} f(\mathbf{y})\ , \qquad \inf_{x \in E} g\ (\ \mathbf{x}\ ) = \inf_{y \in A} f(\mathbf{y})$$

Proof.- [4]

Without loss of generality, suppose that $\inf_{y \in A} f(y) = 1$, $\sup_{y \in A} f(\mathbf{y}) = 2$
(in case f is constant the result is trivial). Call now $\mathbf{h}(x)$ to the following
mapping: $\mathbf{h}(x) = \inf_{y \in A} [f(y) \cdot d(x,y)]$ (where d stands for distance). Define
$g(x)$ as equal to $f(x)$ for $x \in A$, and equal to $\mathbf{h}(x)/d(x,A)$ for $x \in E - A$.
It follows that $1 \le g(x) \le 2$ for $x \in E - A$. We need to prove that g is
continuous on E. If $x \in A$, g is continuous by assumption. Thus we simply
have to prove that $\mathbf{h}$ is continuous in the open set $E - A$ (because $d(x,A)$ is
continuous and different from zero).

Let $R = d(x,A)$; for $d(x,x') \le \varepsilon < R$, we have $d(x,y) \le d(x',y) + \varepsilon$, hence
$(x) \le (x') + 2\varepsilon$ (since $f(y) \le 2$), and similarly $\mathbf{h}(x') \le \mathbf{h}(x) + 2\varepsilon$, which proves
the continuity of $\mathbf{h}$ in this case.

Suppose now that $x \in \partial A$. Given $\varepsilon > 0$, let $R > 0$ be such that for
$y \in A \cap B(x;R)$ (a ball of centre x and radius R), $| f(y) - f(x) | \le \varepsilon$. Let
$C = A \cap B(x;R), D = A - C$; if $x' \in E - A$ and $d(x,x') \le R/4$, we have, for
each y in $D, d(x',y) \ge d(x,y) - d(x,x') \ge 3R/4$, hence

$$\inf_{y \in A} [f(y) \cdot d(x',y)] \ge 3R/4$$

on the other hand, $f(x)d(x',x) \le 2d(x',x) \le R/2$, and therefore

$$\inf_{y \in A} [f(y) \cdot d(x',y)] = \inf_{y \in C} [f(y) \cdot d(x',y)] =$$

But, as $f(x) - \varepsilon \le f(y) \le f(x) + \varepsilon$ for $y \in C$, and $\inf_{y \in C} d(x',y) = d(x',A)$, we
have

$$[f(x') - \varepsilon]d(x',A) \le \inf_{y \in A}[f(y) \cdot d(x',y)] \le [f(x') + \varepsilon]d(x',A)$$

which proves that $| g(x') - \mathbf{F}(x) | \le \varepsilon$ for $x' \in E - A$ and $d(x,x') \le R/4$. On
the other hand, if $x' \in A$ and $d(x,x') \le R/4$, we have

$$| g(x') - f(x) | = | f(x') - f(x) | \le \varepsilon$$

The proof is in this way completed.♠

---

[4]Borrowed from Dieudonné (1969), pp.89-90.

Part II

MARGINAL PRICING AND THE EFFICIENCY PROBLEM

Marginal pricing may be seen as an abstract principle which derives from the necessary conditions for optimality: if prices do not coincide with marginal rates of transformation, improvements are possible. When production sets are convex, this pricing rule corresponds to profit maximization at given prices, so that it can be identified with competitive behaviour. When production sets are not convex, it can be understood as a regulation policy aiming at Pareto efficiency.

Concerning the welfare properties of marginal pricing, let us advance that, under very general assumptions, any Pareto optimal allocation can be decentralized as a marginal pricing Equilibrium. This amounts to saying that marginal pricing is a necessary condition in order to achieve efficiency through a price mechanism. Yet marginal pricing is far from being sufficient, as will be illustrated by a number of examples. Hence we are facing almost an impossibility result: Under general conditions, there is no way of allocating efficiently the resources through a price mechanism, in the presence of increasing returns to scale (unless we can freely arrange the income distribution).

A more general question arises then: the analysis of the nonemptyness of the core in an economy with increasing returns. It is well known that the core of a standard convex competitive economy is nonempty (indeed, every competitive equilibrium is in the core). One might think that the presence of increasing returns may facilitate the nonemptyness of the core: bigger coalitions are more likely to be more productive organizing the economic activity. This intuition, however, is rather inaccurate: Scarf (1986) shows that if all commodities can be consumed, the core of an economy may be empty unless the aggregate production set is a convex cone

These negative aspects can be summarized in the following *warning*: When production sets are not convex, the necessary conditions for optimality (which lead to marginal pricing) are not sufficient. Furthermore, when there are increasing returns to scale, marginal pricing implies losses, so that it requires the simultaneous design of a system of taxes and transfers, in order to cover the resulting losses. All this points out that marginal pricing is a regulation policy which requires lots of information and control, and may well not achieve its goal.

In spite of these limits in the scope, the models presented in this part are of interest both on their own, and as platforms to build up more specific models with better properties.

Chapter 5 offers a detailed discussion of the Clarke cones (the generalization of the "rates of transformation"), from which marginal pricing derives, and analyzes the existence of equilibrium when firms behave according to this pricing rule. In view of the existence result in chapter 4, the key questions refer to the *regularity* of marginal pricing and the conditions ensuring that assumption (A.4.5) is satisfied. Chapter 6 analyses the existence of Two-Part marginal pricing Equilibrium (a nonlinear pricing principle which combines the necessary conditions for optimality with the absence of losses).

Chapter 7 presents a general version of the Second Welfare Theorem (compatible with the presence of nonconvex production sets), and a number of examples which illustrate the failure of the First Welfare Theorem. It also includes a (rather negative) reference to the nonemptyness of the core of an economy with increasing returns.

Chapter 5

MARGINAL PRICING

5.1 INTRODUCTION

We shall consider here the pricing rule from which most of the existence results on general equilibrium in nonconvex environments originated: the marginal pricing rule[1].

Consider the case in which resources are to be allocated through a price mechanism, and suppose that production sets are assumed to be closed and satisfy free-disposal (that is, $Y_j - \mathbb{R}_+^\ell \subset Y_j$). Then, irrespective of the convexity assumption, a general principle for achieving Pareto optimality is that prices must equal the marginal rates of transformation (both for consumers and firms). If this were not so, it would be possible to reallocate commodities so that someone would be better off.

When production sets have a smooth (i.e. differentiable) boundary, marginal rates of transformation are well defined, and marginal prices coincide with the vector of partial derivatives at every efficient production plan. When production sets are convex but do not have a smooth boundary, one has to take a generalized view of what marginal rates of transformation are. In particular, marginal prices can be associated with the cone of normals which is defined as follows: Let A be a closed and convex subset of $\mathbb{R}^\ell$, and $\mathbf{s} \in A$; the *Normal Cone* of A at $\mathbf{s}$, $\mathbb{N}_A(\mathbf{s})$, is given by:

$$\mathbb{N}_A(\mathbf{s}) \equiv \{\mathbf{p} \in \mathbb{R}^\ell \mid \mathbf{p}(\mathbf{y} - \mathbf{s}) \leq 0, \forall \mathbf{y} \in A\}$$

---

[1]The expression "marginal pricing", instead of the usual "marginal cost pricing" is used in order to remind that in the absence of convexity (more precisely, in the absence of convexity of the iso-outputs sets), this pricing rule may not imply cost minimization. See the discussion in Guesnerie (1990, Section 5.2).

Thus when production sets are convex, marginal pricing implies profit maximization at given prices.

When production sets are neither convex nor smooth, we need a way of extending still further the notion of "marginal rates of transformation". There are several alternatives for that [see Kahn & Vohra (1987, Section 2), Cornet (1990, Appendix) for a discussion], but nowadays the standard definition is based on *Clarke normal cones*. In order to properly define marginal prices in this general context, we shall present first the auxiliary notions of *limsup of a correspondence*, and the *cone of perpendicular vectors*. After that, the concept and main properties of Clarke cones will be analyzed [these are mostly a rephrasing of those in Clarke (1983, Ch.2) and Cornet (1990, Lemma 4)]. Then, we shall be ready to define the notion of marginal pricing, and analyze the most useful properties of this pricing rule.

As for the connection between marginal pricing and profit maximization, let us advance the following: if, for some $\mathbf{p} \in \mathbb{P}$, some $\mathbf{y}'_j$ in Y_j, we have: $\mathbf{p}\mathbf{y}'_j \geq \mathbf{p}\mathbf{y}_j \ \forall \mathbf{y}_j \in Y_j$ (where Y_j is a closed subset of $\mathbb{R}^\ell$), then $\mathbf{p}$ is a marginal price system relative to Y_j at $\mathbf{y}'_j$. In case Y_j is convex, then the converse is also true.

5.2 PRELIMINARIES

This is a purely mathematical section, which is nevertheless quite instructive. It refers to the notions of limsup of a correspondence, and the Clarke cone. The chief properties of marginal pricing rely on the analysis presented here[2].

Definition 5.1.-
  Let $Y \subset \mathbb{R}^\ell$, $\Gamma : Y \to \mathbb{R}^\ell$ a set valued mapping, and $\mathbf{y}^*$ a point in Y. The **limsup** of Γ at y^* is given by:

$$\mathop{Lim\,sup}_{y \to y^*} \Gamma(y) \ \equiv \ \{\mathbf{p} = \lim \mathbf{p}^\nu \ / \ \exists\{\mathbf{y}^\nu\} \subset Y, \{\mathbf{y}^\nu\} \to \mathbf{y}^* \text{ and}$$

$$\mathbf{p}^\nu \ \in \ \Gamma(\mathbf{y}^\nu) \ \forall\nu\}$$

In words: By Limsup of Γ at $\mathbf{y}^*$ we denote the set of all points which are limits of sequences of points $\mathbf{p}^\nu \in \Gamma(\mathbf{y}^\nu)$, when $\mathbf{y}^\nu \to \mathbf{y}^*$. Observe that when Γ is a closed correspondence $\mathop{Lim\,sup}_{y \to y^*} \Gamma(y) = \Gamma(\mathbf{y}^*)$, for each $\mathbf{y}^* \in Y$. When this is not so, the Limsup may be thought of as an operator which "closes the

---

[2]Sections 5.2 and 5.3 correspond to Alós & Villar (1995).

graph" of Γ. Observe that this does not mean that it coincides with $\Gamma(\mathbf{y}*)$ when Γ is closed-valued.

Remark 5.1.- If $\Gamma(\mathbf{y})$ is a cone, then $Lim \sup_{y \to y^*} \Gamma(y)$ is also a cone (that follows trivially from the definition).

Remark 5.2.- We shall use the abbreviated expression $LS(\mathbf{y}^*)$ instead of $Lim \sup_{y \to y^*} \Gamma(y)$ when no confusion is derived from that simpler notation.

Lemma 5.1.-
Let $\mathbf{Y} \subset \mathbb{R}^\ell$, $\Gamma{:}\mathbf{Y} \to \mathbb{R}^\ell$ be a set valued mapping. The correspondence $\varphi{:}\mathbf{Y} \to \mathbb{R}^\ell$ given by $\varphi(\mathbf{y}^*) = Lim \sup_{y \to y^*} \Gamma(y)$, has a closed graph.

Proof.-
Let two sequences

$$\{\mathbf{y}^r\} \subset Y \text{ with } \{\mathbf{y}^r\} \to \mathbf{y}^*$$

$$\{\mathbf{p}^r\} \subset \mathbb{R}^\ell \text{ with } \{\mathbf{p}^r\} \to \mathbf{p}^*$$

be such that $\mathbf{p}^r \in LS(\mathbf{y}^r)$. We have to show that $\mathbf{p}^* \in LS(\mathbf{y}^*)$ (see Remark 5.2). Now, for each r let $\{\mathbf{p}^r_\nu\}, \{\mathbf{y}^r_\nu\}$ be such that:

$$\{\mathbf{p}^r_\nu\} \to \mathbf{p}^r, \{\mathbf{y}^r_\nu\} \to \mathbf{y}^r, \mathbf{p}^r_\nu \in \Gamma(\mathbf{y}^r_\nu) \quad \forall \nu$$

Let $r \geq 1$. For each r there exists ν' such that:

$$\| \mathbf{p}^r_{\nu'} - \mathbf{p}^r \| < 1/r, \text{ and } \| \mathbf{y}^r_{\nu'} - \mathbf{y}^r \| < 1/r$$

Clearly $\{\mathbf{p}^r_{\nu'}\} \to \mathbf{p}^*, \{\mathbf{y}^r_{\nu'}\} \to \mathbf{y}^*$, and $\mathbf{p}^r_{\nu'} \in \Gamma(\mathbf{y}^r_{\nu'})$ so that, according to the definition above, $\mathbf{p}^* \in LS(\mathbf{y}^*)$. ♠

The next result may well be considered as the key for the upper hemicontinuity of the marginal pricing rule:

Proposition 5.1.-
Let $\mathbf{Y} \subset \mathbb{R}^\ell$ be a closed set, and $\Gamma{:}\mathbf{Y} \to \mathbb{R}^\ell_+$ a correspondence such that $\Gamma(\mathbf{y})$ is a cone, for each $\mathbf{y} \in \mathbf{Y}$. Define then a new correspondence $\mathbb{N}{:}\mathbf{Y} \to \mathbb{R}^\ell_+$ which associates to each $\mathbf{y}^* \in \mathbf{Y}$ the convex hull of $\mathbf{LS}(\mathbf{y}^*)$, that is, $\mathbb{N}(\mathbf{y}^*) = Co\mathbf{LS}(\mathbf{y})$. Then $\mathbb{N}$ has a closed graph (and, in particular, $\mathbb{N}(\mathbf{y}^*)$ is closed for every $\mathbf{y}^* \in \mathbf{Y}$).

Proof.-
Let $\{\mathbf{y}^\nu\} \to \mathbf{y}^*$ be a sequence in Y, and let $\{\mathbf{p}^\nu\} \to \mathbf{p}^*$ be a sequence in $\mathbb{R}^\ell$ such that $\mathbf{p}^\nu \in \mathbb{N}(\mathbf{y}^\nu) \ \forall \nu$. We want to show that $\mathbf{p}^* \in \mathbb{N}(\mathbf{y}^*)$.

Making use of Carathéodory's Theorem[3], we can write:

$$\mathbf{p}^{\nu} = \sum_{i=1}^{\ell+1} \lambda_i^{\nu} \mathbf{p}_i^{\nu}, \text{ with } \mathbf{p}_i^{\nu} \in LS(\mathbf{y}^{\nu}), \ \lambda_i^{\nu} \geq 0 \ \forall \nu, i, \ \sum_{i=1}^{\ell+1} \lambda_i^{\nu} = 1, \ \forall \nu$$

Now observe that $\Gamma(\mathbf{y}) \subset \mathbb{R}_+^{\ell} \ \forall \mathbf{y} \in Y$, and $\{\mathbf{p}^{\nu}\} \to \mathbf{p}^*$ implies that $\mathbf{p}^*$ is also in $\mathbb{R}_+^{\ell}$. Trivially $\mathbf{0} \in \mathbf{N}(\mathbf{y}^*)$ (since $\Gamma(\mathbf{y})$ is a cone for all $\mathbf{y} \in Y$). Then if $\mathbf{p}^* = \mathbf{0}$, the proof is done. Suppose then that $\mathbf{p}^* > \mathbf{0}$, and let $\mathbf{e}$ stand for the unit vector, $\mathbf{e} \equiv (1, 1, \ldots, 1)$. It follows that $\mathbf{p}^*\mathbf{e} > 0$, and that $\mathbf{p}^{\nu}\mathbf{e} > 0$ for ν big enough (for every $\nu > \nu'$, say).

Therefore, for $\nu > \nu'$ we have:

$$\mathbf{p}^{\nu} = \mathbf{p}^{\nu}\mathbf{e}\sum_{i=1}^{\ell+1} \pi_i^{\nu}, \text{ with } \pi_i^{\nu} = \frac{\lambda_i^{\nu}}{\mathbf{p}^{\nu}\mathbf{e}}\mathbf{p}_i^{\nu} \in \mathbb{R}_+^{\ell}$$

and

$$\pi_i^{\nu}\mathbf{e} = \frac{\lambda_i^{\nu}}{\mathbf{p}^{\nu}\mathbf{e}}\mathbf{p}_i^{\nu}\mathbf{e} \leq 1$$

that is, for every $i, \pi_i^{\nu} \in K \equiv \{\mathbf{p} \in \mathbb{R}_+^{\ell} \ / \ \mathbf{pe} \leq 1\}$, which is a compact set. This in turn implies that we can choose a convergent subsequence $\{\pi_i^{\nu}\} \to \pi_i \in K$.

We know from Lemma 5.1 that the mapping LS has a closed graph. Since $LS(\mathbf{y})$ is a cone for each $\mathbf{y} \in Y$ (see Remark 5.1 above), then $\pi_i^{\nu} \in LS(\mathbf{y}^{\nu})$. Hence: $\{\mathbf{y}^{\nu}\} \to \mathbf{y}^*, \{\pi_i^{\nu}\} \to \pi_i$ and $\pi_i^{\nu} \in LS(\mathbf{y}^{\nu})$ imply that π_i must be a point in $LS(\mathbf{y}^*)$. Taking limits when $\nu \to \infty$, we have:

$$\mathbf{p}^* = \mathbf{p}^*\mathbf{e}\sum_{i=1}^{\ell+1} \pi_i$$

that is, $\mathbf{p}^* \in CoLS(\mathbf{y}^*) \equiv \mathbf{N}(\mathbf{y}^*).\spadesuit$

Let $Y \subset \mathbb{R}^{\ell}$ be nonempty, and let $\mathbf{z}$ be a point in $\mathbb{R}^{\ell}$. The **distance** between $\mathbf{z}$ and Y is a function $d_Y : Y \to \mathbb{R}$ given by:

$$d_Y(\mathbf{z}) = \inf\{\|\mathbf{z} - \mathbf{y}\| \ / \ \mathbf{y} \in Y\}$$

---

[3] Carathéodory's Theorem: Let $S \subset \mathbb{R}^{\ell}$ and $\mathbf{x} \in CoS$ (the convex hull of S). Then, there exist $(\ell+1)$ points $\mathbf{x}^i \in S$ and $(\ell+1)$ nonnegative scalars λ_i $(i = 1, 2, ..., \ell+1)$, such that

$$\mathbf{x} = \sum_{i=1}^{\ell+1} \lambda_i \mathbf{x}^i, \text{ with } \sum_{i=1}^{\ell+1} \lambda_i = 1$$

We shall assume that $\|.\|$ stands for the Euclidean norm, that is,

$$\|\mathbf{z} - \mathbf{y}\| = [\sum_{i=1}^{\ell}(z_i - y_i)^2]^{1/2}$$

A vector $\mathbf{p} \in \mathbb{R}^{\ell}$ is *perpendicular* to a closed set Y at $\mathbf{y}$, if $\mathbf{y}$ is the point in Y at minimum distance of $\mathbf{p}$, that is, if $d_Y(\mathbf{p} + \mathbf{y}) =\| \mathbf{p} \|$ (i.e., if the distance between $(\mathbf{p} + \mathbf{y})$ and Y is precisely the norm of $\mathbf{p}$).

The following definition makes it precise the concept, when we concentrate on *directions*, rather than magnitudes:

Definition 5.2.-

Let $Y \subset \mathbb{R}^{\ell}$ be closed, and let $\mathbf{y} \in Y$. The cone of vectors which are **perpendicular** to Y at $\mathbf{y}$, denoted by $\perp_Y(\mathbf{y})$, is given by:

$$\perp_Y(\mathbf{y}) = \{\mathbf{p} = \lambda(\mathbf{y}' - \mathbf{y}), \lambda \geq 0, \mathbf{y}' \in \mathbb{R}^{\ell} \text{ and } d_Y(\mathbf{y}') =\| \mathbf{y}' - \mathbf{y} \|\}$$

Observe that if Y is not a convex set, there may be points $\mathbf{y}^* \in Y$ for which no perpendicular vector exists. One way of avoiding this problem is by making use of the limsup operator. Figure 5.1 illustrates the set $Lim \sup_{y \to y^*} \perp_Y(\mathbf{y})$. This correspondence associates two different vectors $\mathbf{p}, \mathbf{p}' \in \mathbb{R}^{\ell}$ as limits of sequences approaching $\mathbf{y}^*$ from the left and right hand side, respectively.

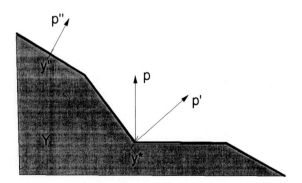

Figure 5.1

The following Proposition gives us a useful characterization of the sets of perpendicular vectors:

Proposition 5.2.-

Let $Y \subset \mathbb{R}^\ell$ be closed. Then, the set $\perp_Y(\mathbf{y})$ can equivalently be defined as:

$$\{\mathbf{p} \in \mathbb{R}^\ell \ / \ \mathbf{py} \geq \mathbf{py}' - (\lambda/2) \parallel \mathbf{y} - \mathbf{y}' \parallel^2, \ \forall \mathbf{y}' \in Y, \text{ some } \lambda \geq 0\}$$

Proof.-

$(\Rightarrow)$

Let $\mathbf{p} = \lambda(\mathbf{y}'' - \mathbf{y}) \in \perp_Y(\mathbf{y})$. By definition, $d_Y(\mathbf{y}'') = \parallel \mathbf{y}'' - \mathbf{y} \parallel$ and $\lambda \geq 0$. Let us call $\mathbf{x}^2$ to the scalar product $\mathbf{xx}$, for any $\mathbf{x}$ in $\mathbb{R}^\ell$, and let $\mathbf{y}' \in Y$ be such that $\parallel \mathbf{y}'' - \mathbf{y}' \parallel \geq \parallel \mathbf{y}'' - \mathbf{y} \parallel$. Then,

$\parallel \mathbf{p} \parallel^2 = [\lambda(\mathbf{y}'' - \mathbf{y})]^2 \leq [\lambda(\mathbf{y}'' - \mathbf{y}')]^2 = [\lambda(\mathbf{y}'' - \mathbf{y}) + \lambda(\mathbf{y} - \mathbf{y}')]^2$

$= \lambda^2(\mathbf{y}'' - \mathbf{y})^2 + \lambda^2(\mathbf{y} - \mathbf{y}')^2 + 2\lambda^2(\mathbf{y}'' - \mathbf{y})(\mathbf{y} - \mathbf{y}')$

$= \parallel \mathbf{p} \parallel^2 + \lambda^2 \parallel \mathbf{y} - \mathbf{y}' \parallel^2 + 2\lambda\mathbf{p}(\mathbf{y} - \mathbf{y}')$

Then, $2\lambda\mathbf{p}(\mathbf{y} - \mathbf{y}') \geq -\lambda^2 \parallel \mathbf{y} - \mathbf{y}' \parallel^2$. Trivially, $\lambda = 0$ implies $\mathbf{p} = \mathbf{0}$ and the result follows. For $\lambda > 0$ we have:

$$\mathbf{py} \geq \mathbf{py}' - (\lambda/2) \parallel \mathbf{y} - \mathbf{y}' \parallel^2, \forall \mathbf{y}' \in Y$$

$(\Leftarrow)$

Let $\mathbf{p} \in \mathbb{R}^\ell$, $\lambda \geq 0$, and suppose that $\mathbf{p}(\mathbf{y} - \mathbf{y}') \geq -(\lambda/2) \parallel \mathbf{y} - \mathbf{y}' \parallel^2$ for each $\mathbf{y}' \in Y$. If $\lambda = 0$, $\mathbf{p}(\mathbf{y} - \mathbf{y}') \geq 0 \ \forall \mathbf{y}' \in Y$ and therefore, for $\lambda' > 0$ we have: $\mathbf{p}(\mathbf{y} - \mathbf{y}') \geq -\lambda' \parallel \mathbf{y} - \mathbf{y}' \parallel^2$. Hence we can let $\lambda > 0$ without loss of generality.

Let then $\mathbf{y}'' = \mathbf{y} + (1/\lambda)\mathbf{p}$. It follows that:

(i) $\parallel \mathbf{y}'' - \mathbf{y} \parallel = (1/\lambda) \parallel \mathbf{p} \parallel$

(ii) $\forall \mathbf{y}' \in Y, \parallel \mathbf{y}'' - \mathbf{y}' \parallel^2 = \parallel \mathbf{y} - \mathbf{y}' + (1/\lambda)\mathbf{p} \parallel^2$

$= [\mathbf{y} - \mathbf{y}' + (1/\lambda)\mathbf{p}]^2 = \parallel \mathbf{y} - \mathbf{y}' \parallel^2 + (1/\lambda^2) \parallel \mathbf{p} \parallel^2 + (2/\lambda)\mathbf{p}(\mathbf{y} - \mathbf{y}')$

$\geq \parallel \mathbf{y} - \mathbf{y}' \parallel^2 + [(1/\lambda) \parallel \mathbf{p} \parallel]^2 - (2/\lambda)(\lambda/2) \parallel \mathbf{y} - \mathbf{y}' \parallel^2$

and therefore,

$$\parallel \mathbf{y} - \mathbf{y}' \parallel \geq (1/\lambda) \parallel \mathbf{p} \parallel = \parallel \mathbf{y}'' - \mathbf{y} \parallel$$

We conclude then that $dist[Y, \mathbf{y}] = \parallel \mathbf{y}'' - \mathbf{y} \parallel$ implies that

$$\mathbf{p} = \lambda(\mathbf{y}'' - \mathbf{y}) \in \perp_Y(\mathbf{y})$$

♠

The notion of Clarke cone is now easy to understand: it consists of the convex hull of this set $Lim \sup_{y \to y^*} \perp_y(\mathbf{y})$. Formally:

Definition 5.3.-

Let Y be a closed subset of $\mathbb{R}^\ell$ and $\mathbf{y}^* \in Y$. Then, the **Clarke Normal Cone** $\mathbb{N}_Y(\mathbf{y}^*)$ to Y at $\mathbf{y}^*$ is given by [4]

$$\mathbb{N}_Y(\mathbf{y}^*) \equiv Co\{\underset{y \to y^*}{Lim \sup \perp_y} (\mathbf{y})\}$$

By this definition the Clarke Normal Cone at a point $\mathbf{y}^*$ is the convex cone generated by the vectors perpendicular to Y at $\mathbf{y}^*$, and the limits of vectors which are perpendicular to Y in a neighbourhood of $\mathbf{y}^*$ [Cf. Quinzii (1992, p. 19)]. Figure 5.2 provides an illustration.

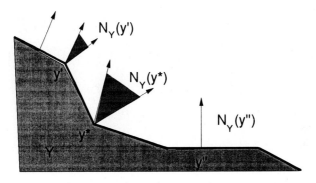

Figure 5.2

The following results give us the main properties of Clarke normal cones:

---

[4]Clarke (1975) defines this cone as the closed and convex hull of $\underset{y \to y^*}{Lim \sup \perp_Y} (\mathbf{y})$. Closedness is not required, since it is a derived property, as will be shown below.

Proposition 5.3.-

Let Y be a closed subset of $\mathbb{R}^\ell$, and $\mathbf{y} \in Y$. Then:

(i) **If $\mathbf{py} \geq \mathbf{py}'$ for all $\mathbf{y}' \in \mathbf{Y}$, then $\mathbf{p} \in \mathbb{N}_Y(\mathbf{y})$.**

(ii) **If Y is also convex, then,**

$$\mathbb{N}_Y(\mathbf{y}) = \perp_Y(\mathbf{y}) = \{\mathbf{p} \in \mathbb{R}^\ell \ / \ \mathbf{p}(\mathbf{y}' - \mathbf{y}) \leq \mathbf{0} \ \forall \mathbf{y}' \in \mathbf{Y}\}$$

Proof.-

(i) Follows directly from Proposition 5.2, by letting $\lambda = 0$.

(ii) Let us denote by $\nabla_Y(\mathbf{y})$ the set

$$\{\mathbf{p} \in \mathbb{R}^\ell \ / \ \mathbf{p}(\mathbf{y}' - \mathbf{y}) \leq \mathbf{0} \ \forall \mathbf{y}' \in \mathbf{Y}\}$$

We shall show first that $\perp_Y (\mathbf{y}) = \nabla_Y(\mathbf{y})$. It follows again from proposition 5.2 that $\nabla_Y(\mathbf{y}) \subseteq \perp_Y (\mathbf{y})$. To see that the other inclusion holds, note that $\forall \mathbf{y}' \in Y$ we have: $\mathbf{py} \geq \mathbf{py}' - (\lambda/2) \parallel \mathbf{y} - \mathbf{y}' \parallel^2$. Since Y is assumed to be convex, for each $t \in [0,1], \mathbf{y} + t(\mathbf{y}' - \mathbf{y}) \in Y$. Thus,

$$\mathbf{py} \geq \mathbf{p}[\mathbf{y} + t(\mathbf{y}' - \mathbf{y})] - (\lambda/2) \parallel t(\mathbf{y}' - \mathbf{y}) \parallel^2$$

which implies: $0 \geq t\mathbf{p}(\mathbf{y}' - \mathbf{y}) - (\lambda/2)t^2 \parallel \mathbf{y}' - \mathbf{y} \parallel^2$, and hence

$$t\mathbf{p}(\mathbf{y}' - \mathbf{y})] \leq (\lambda/2)t^2 \parallel \mathbf{y}' - \mathbf{y} \parallel^2$$

which, when $t > 0$ results

$$\mathbf{p}(\mathbf{y}' - \mathbf{y})] \leq (\lambda/2)t \parallel \mathbf{y}' - \mathbf{y} \parallel^2$$

Taking limits, when $t \to 0$, we get $\mathbf{p}(\mathbf{y}' - \mathbf{y}) \leq 0$, which is the desired result.

Let us see now that $\mathbb{N}_Y(\mathbf{y}) = \perp_Y (\mathbf{y})$. It follows from the definition that $\perp_Y (\mathbf{y}) \subset \mathbb{N}_Y(\mathbf{y})$. We shall prove then that the other inclusion also holds. Let $\{\mathbf{y}^\nu\} \to \mathbf{y}$ be a sequence in Y, and $\{\mathbf{p}^\nu\} \to \mathbf{p}$ a sequence in $\mathbb{R}^\ell$, such that $\mathbf{p}^\nu \in \perp_Y (\mathbf{y}^\nu) \ \forall \nu$. It follows from the previous inclusion that $\forall \nu, \forall \mathbf{y}' \in Y, \mathbf{p}^\nu(\mathbf{y}' - \mathbf{y}^\nu) \leq 0$. Taking limits we conclude:

$$\mathbf{p}(\mathbf{y}' - \mathbf{y}) \leq 0, \forall \mathbf{y}' \in Y$$

Since $\nabla_Y(\mathbf{y})$ is a closed and convex set, the inclusion follows.♠

Theorem 5.1.-

Let Y be a nonempty and closed subset in $\mathbb{R}^\ell$, and suppose that $Y - \mathbb{R}^\ell_+ \subset Y$. Then:

(i) $\mathbb{N}_Y(\mathbf{y})$ is a cone in $\mathbb{R}^\ell_+$ with vertex zero, $\forall \mathbf{y} \in Y$

(ii) The correspondence $\mathbb{N}_Y : Y \to \mathbb{R}^\ell$ which associates $\mathbb{N}_Y(\mathbf{y})$ to each $\mathbf{y} \in Y$, is closed.

(iii) $\mathbb{N}_Y(\mathbf{y}) = \{0\}$ if and only if $\mathbf{y} \in intY$.

Proof.-

(i) Let $\mathbf{p} \in \perp_Y(\mathbf{y})$. Proposition 5.2 implies that there is $\lambda \geq 0$ such that

$$\mathbf{py} \geq \mathbf{py}' - (\lambda/2) \parallel \mathbf{y} - \mathbf{y}' \parallel^2, \forall \mathbf{y}' \in Y$$

Take an arbitrary point $\mathbf{v} \in \mathbb{R}^\ell_+$, and let $t > 0$. We can pick a point $\mathbf{y}'$ in Y which is given by: $\mathbf{y}' = \mathbf{y} - t\mathbf{v}$ (this is possible, since $Y - \mathbb{R}^\ell_+ \subset Y$, by assumption). Then, $\mathbf{py} \geq \mathbf{p}(\mathbf{y} - t\mathbf{v}) - (\lambda/2) \parallel t\mathbf{v} \parallel^2$, and hence:

$$0 \geq -t\mathbf{pv} - (\lambda/2)t^2 \parallel \mathbf{v} \parallel^2$$

that is, $\mathbf{pv} \geq -(\lambda/2)t \parallel \mathbf{v} \parallel^2$. Taking limits when t goes to zero, we conclude: $\mathbf{pv} \geq 0$ for every $\mathbf{v} \in \mathbb{R}^\ell_+$ which is true if and only if $\mathbf{p} \in \mathbb{R}^\ell_+$.

(ii) It follows directly from proposition 5.1 and definition 5.3.

(iii $\Rightarrow$) Let $\{\mathbf{y}^\nu\} \to \mathbf{y} \in intY$. Then, for ν big enough ($\nu > \nu'$,say), $\mathbf{y}^\nu \in intY$, so that $\perp_Y(\mathbf{y}^\nu) = \{0\}$ by definition. Therefore, $\{\mathbf{p}^\nu\}$ converges to $\mathbf{p}$ and $\mathbf{p}^\nu \in \perp_Y(\mathbf{y}^\nu)$ imply that $\mathbf{p} = 0$.

(iii $\Leftarrow$) Let $\mathbb{N}_Y(\mathbf{y}) = \{0\}$, and suppose $\mathbf{y} \in \partial Y$. Then there exists a sequence $\{\mathbf{z}^\nu\} \to \mathbf{y}$, such that $\mathbf{z}^\nu \notin Y$ for all ν. As Y is closed, choose $\mathbf{y}^\nu \in Y$ such that $0 < d_Y(\mathbf{z}^\nu) = dist[\mathbf{y}^\nu, \mathbf{z}^\nu]$ (i.e., we choose $\mathbf{y}^\nu$ so that for each $\mathbf{z}^\nu$ is a point in Y at minimum distance). Then,

$$\mathbf{p}^\nu \equiv \mathbf{z}^\nu - \mathbf{y}^\nu \in \perp_Y(\mathbf{y}^\nu)$$

with $\mathbf{p}^\nu \in \mathbb{R}^\ell_+$ [as shown in part (i) above], and $\mathbf{p}^\nu \neq 0$. Being $\perp_Y(.)$ a cone, it follows that $\hat{\mathbf{p}}^\nu = \mathbf{p}^\nu/\mathbf{p}^\nu\mathbf{e} \in \perp_Y(\mathbf{y}^\nu) \cap \mathbb{P}$ (where $\mathbb{P}$ stands for the unit simplex). Thus $\{\hat{\mathbf{p}}^\nu\}$ is a sequence in a compact set. There is a convergent subsequence such that $\{\hat{\mathbf{p}}^\nu\} \to \mathbf{p}$ (a point in $\mathbb{P}$). Since, by construction, $\{\mathbf{y}^\nu\} \to \mathbf{y}$, and the graph of $\mathbb{N}_Y(.)$ is closed [see (ii) above], it follows that $\mathbf{p} \notin \mathbb{N}_Y(\mathbf{y}) = \{0\}$.♠

5.3   THE MARGINAL PRICING RULE

It is time now to present the definition and main properties of the marginal pricing rule (let us recall here Remark 4.3):

Definition 5.4.-
   Let Y be a production set, and $\mathbf{y}$ a boundary point. The **Marginal Pricing Rule** is a correspondence $\phi^{MP} : \partial Y \to \mathbb{P}$ given by:

$$\phi^{MP}(\mathbf{y}) \equiv \mathbb{N}_Y(\mathbf{y}) \bigcap \mathbb{P}$$

The following result summarizes the main properties of this pricing rule:

Proposition 5.4.-
   Let Y be a closed subset of $\mathbb{R}^\ell$, such that $\mathbf{Y} - \mathbb{R}^\ell_+ \subset \mathbf{Y}$, and let $\phi^{MP}{:}\partial\mathbf{Y} \to \mathbb{P}$ be the Marginal Pricing correspondence. Then, ϕ^{MP} is a regular mapping.
   Proof.-
   According to (ii) of theorem 5.1, $\mathbb{N}_Y$ has a closed graph. Being ϕ^{MP} the intersection of $\mathbb{N}_Y$ with $\mathbb{P}$, its values are compact, and hence ϕ^{MP} is upper hemicontinuous [Border (1985,Ch.11)]. Part (i) of the theorem tells us that $\mathbb{N}_Y$ is a convex cone, so that $\mathbb{N}_Y(\mathbf{y}) \bigcap \mathbb{P}$ is also convex. Finally, part (iii) of theorem 5.1 establishes that $\mathbb{N}_Y(\mathbf{y})$ is a non-degenerate cone if $\mathbf{y} \in \partial Y$, so that $\mathbb{N}_Y(\mathbf{y}) \bigcap \mathbb{P}$ is nonempty. ♠

   Consider now the following assumptions:

<u>A.5.1.</u>- For each $i = 1, 2, \ldots, m$:(a) X_i is a nonempty, closed and convex subset of $\mathbb{R}^\ell$, bounded from below; (b) $u_i : X_i \to \mathbb{R}$ is a continuous and quasi-concave function, which satisfies local non-satiation.

<u>A.5.2.</u>- For all $j, Y_j = C_j - \mathbb{R}^\ell_+$, where C_j is non-empty, compact and there exists $k > 0$ such that $\mathbf{c} \geq -k\mathbf{e}$ for all $\mathbf{c} \in C_j$.

<u>A.5.3.</u>- Let **PE** denote the set of production equilibria. Then, the restriction of r_i on **PE** is continuous, with $r_i(\mathbf{p}, \tilde{\mathbf{y}}) > b_i(\mathbf{p})$, and $\sum\limits_{i=1}^{m} r_i(\mathbf{p}, \tilde{\mathbf{y}}) = \mathbf{p}(\omega + \sum\limits_{i=1}^{m} \mathbf{y}_j)$.

   Assumptions (A.5.1) and (A.5.3) correspond to assumptions (A.4.1) and (A.4.2) in previous chapter. Assumption (A.5.2) is a strengthening of (A.4.2) which postulates a precise structure of production sets (they become "flat" if one goes beyond some values of the production plans).

We shall present now an existence result for marginal pricing which derives from theorem 4.1. The following lemma will facilitate its proof:

Lemma 5.2.-
Under assumption (A.5.2), if $\mathbf{y}_j \in \mathbb{F}_j$ and $y_{jh}=-k'$, then $q_h=0$ for any $\mathbf{q} \in \phi_j^{MP}(\mathbf{y}_j)$, any $k' > k$.
Proof.-
Let $\delta > 0$ be a positive scalar, and let $\mathbf{y}_j^\delta$ be a point in $\mathbb{R}^\ell$ given by $y_{jt}^\delta = y_{jt}$ for all $t \neq h$, and $y_{jh}^\delta = y_{jh} + \delta$. By construction, $\mathbf{y}_j^\delta$ will be in $\mathbb{F}_j$, for δ small enough.
Suppose first that $\mathbf{q} \in \perp_Y (\mathbf{y}_j)$ (i.e., $\mathbf{q}$ is perpendicular to $\mathbb{F}_j$ at $\mathbf{y}_j$). According to proposition 5.2, we know that:

$$\mathbf{q}(\mathbf{y}_j - \mathbf{y}_j') \geq -(\lambda/2) \|\mathbf{y}_j - \mathbf{y}\|^2 \, \forall \mathbf{y} \in Y_j, \quad some \; \lambda \geq 0$$

For $\mathbf{y}_j^\delta$ we have:

$$\mathbf{q}(\mathbf{y}_j - \mathbf{y}_j^\delta) = -q_h\delta, \left\|\mathbf{y}_j - \mathbf{y}_j^\delta\right\|^2 = \delta^2$$

Hence, $q_h\delta \leq (\lambda/2)\delta^2$, that is:

$$q_h \leq \lambda\delta/2 \qquad [1]$$

If $\lambda = 0$ the conclusion follows. Suppose that $\lambda > 0$. Take now a sequence of points $\mathbf{y}^\delta$ with $\delta \to 0$. The right hand side goes to zero and q_j cannot be greater than $\lambda\delta/2$. As Y_j is closed, this implies that $q_h = 0$.
Finally, suppose that $\mathbf{q} \notin \perp_Y (\mathbf{y}_j)$, but is a point in $\phi_j^{MP}(\mathbf{y}_j)$. By definition, $\mathbf{q}$ belongs to the convex hull of the limits of those points which are perpendicular to $\mathbf{y}_j$, and hence take on value zero at q_h^ν for all ν. It follows that $q_h = 0$ also in this case. ♠

We can present now the existence result for marginal pricing:

Proposition 5.5.-
Under assumptions (A.5.1) to (A.5.3), a marginal pricing equilibrium exists.
Proof.-
It suffices to show that assumption (A.5.2) implies assumption (A.4.5), and then apply theorem 4.1.

Choose $k' > k$ where k' is big enough so that $K' = \{\mathbf{z} \in \mathbb{R}^\ell$ such that $\mid z_h \mid \leq k'$, for all $h = 1, 2, \ldots, \ell\}$ contains in its interior all attainable sets. Let $\mathbf{y}_j \in \mathbb{F}_j \cap K'_+$ and suppose that $\mathbf{p} \notin \phi_j^{MP}(\mathbf{y}_j)$. Then, for some commodity h it must be the case that $q_{jh} > p_h$. Lemma 5.2 shows that, under assumption (A.5.2), it cannot be the case that $y_{jh} = -k$, i.e., $y_{jh} > -k > -k'$ and hence (A.4.5) is trivially satisfied.

Then, the result follows.♠

There are two properties of marginal pricing worth considering:

(i) This pricing rule satisfies the necessary conditions for optimality, and it coincides with profit maximization when production sets are convex (proposition 5.3). Yet, when production sets are not convex, these necessary conditions may well not be sufficient (we shall elaborate on this later on).

(ii) When there are increasing returns to scale, marginal pricing implies losses ("marginal costs" are smaller than "average costs"). This entails that this pricing rule requires the design of a system of transfers (embodied in consumers' wealth functions, say), so that these firms can cover their losses. Letting aside the informational problem [see Calsamiglia (1977)], this can be seen as an additional complication of the regulation policy, which requires taking decisions about its distributional impact.

5.4 FINAL COMMENTS

The first results on the existence of equilibria with nonconvex firms refer to marginal pricing (with the exception of Scarf's (1986) paper, which was written in 1963, and some of those referred to in Chapter 8). The idea of regulating nonconvex firms by setting prices equal to marginal costs is an old wisdom (which, in the context of partial analysis, can be associated to the names of Dupuit, Marshall, Pigou, Lange, Lerner, Allais and Hotelling among others). It derives from the observation that a necessary condition for Pareto optimality is that all agents equate prices to their marginal rates of transformation. The distortion introduced by the necessity of covering the firms' losses was the subject of an interesting discussion which is reviewed in Ruggles (1949),(1950).

From a general equilibrium standpoint, Mantel (1979) and Beato (1982) independently showed the existence of equilibrium in an economy with a single firm whose production set has a smooth boundary, but need not be convex. They realized that, under the free disposal assumption, the set of efficient and attainable production plans can be made homeomorphic to a simplex, and hence the nonconvexities can be handled in the convex "mirror's image" (see lemma 4.3).

Cornet (1990) (a paper written in 1982) provides a first existence theorem for marginal pricing in an economy with a single firm but dispensing with the smoothness assumption. For that he introduces Clarke's normal cones as the proper way of defining marginal pricing in the general case.

Brown & Heal (1982) gave an index-theoretic proof of existence for Mantel's model. Beato & Mas-Colell (1985) extend the existence result for the case of several non-convex firms, and Brown, Heal, Khan & Vohra (1986) analyze the case of a private ownership economy with a single non-convex firm and several convex firms. More general results on this specific pricing rule appear in Bonnisseau & Cornet (1990a,b), and Vohra (1992). See also the problem raised in Jouini's (1988) paper.

5.5   APPENDIX

Marginal Pricing and Bounded Losses

It was mentioned in section 3.4 that the assumption of bounded-losses imposes structure on production sets for particular pricing rules. Bonnisseau & Cornet (1988a) show that, under assumption (A.4.2), marginal pricing yields bounded losses if and only if Y is star-shaped. We shall show here one of these implications, using the analytics developed in sections 5.2 and 5.3.

Consider now the following definition:

Definition 5.5.-

A production set $Y \subset \mathbb{R}^\ell$ is called **Star-Shaped**, if there is a scalar α such that, for every $\mathbf{y} \in \partial Y$, the segment $[\alpha e, \mathbf{y}]$ is contained in Y.

The next result provides a sufficient condition, established on the production set, for marginal pricing to yield bounded losses:

Proposition 5.6.-

Let Y be a nonempty and closed subset of $\mathbb{R}^\ell$. If Y is Star-Shaped, then Marginal Pricing is a pricing rule with bounded losses (in particular, for each $\mathbf{p} \in \mathbb{N}_Y(\mathbf{y}) \cap \mathbb{P}$, every $\mathbf{y} \in \partial Y$, we have: $\mathbf{py} \geq \alpha$).

Proof.-

We shall divide the proof into three steps.

(Step 1: : $[\mathbf{y} \in \partial Y \ \& \ \mathbf{p} \in \perp_Y (\mathbf{y})] \Rightarrow \mathbf{py} \geq \alpha]$

Let $\{t^\nu\} \to 0$ be a sequence in $(0,1]$. Then, $\mathbf{y} + t^\nu(\alpha \mathbf{e} - \mathbf{y})$ is a point in the segment $[\alpha \mathbf{e}, \mathbf{y}] \subset Y$. It follows from proposition 5.2 that

$$\mathbf{py} \geq \mathbf{p}[\mathbf{y} + t^\nu(\alpha \mathbf{e} - \mathbf{y})] - (\lambda/2) \parallel \mathbf{y} + t^\nu(\alpha \mathbf{e} - \mathbf{y}) - \mathbf{y} \parallel^2$$

and hence,

$$t^\nu \mathbf{p}(\alpha \mathbf{e} - \mathbf{y}) \leq (\lambda/2)(t^\nu)^2 \parallel \alpha \mathbf{e} - \mathbf{y} \parallel^2$$

and, since $t^\nu > 0$, $\mathbf{p}(\alpha \mathbf{e} - \mathbf{y}) \leq (\lambda/2)t^\nu \parallel \alpha \mathbf{e} - \mathbf{y} \parallel^2$. Taking limits when t goes to zero, it follows that: $\mathbf{p}(\alpha \mathbf{e} - \mathbf{y}) \leq 0$ so that $\mathbf{py} \geq \alpha \mathbf{pe} = \alpha$ (since $\mathbf{p} \in \mathbb{P}$).

(Step 2: $\left[y \in \partial Y \ \& \ \mathbf{p} \in \left[\underset{y' \to y}{Lim \sup \perp_y} (y')\right] \cap \mathbb{P}\right] \Rightarrow \mathbf{py} \geq \alpha)$

Let $\mathbf{p} \in [\underset{y' \to y}{Lim \sup \perp_Y} (\mathbf{y})] \cap \mathbb{P}$. By definition, $\mathbf{p} = \lim .\mathbf{p}^\nu$, where $\mathbf{p}^\nu$ is a point in $\perp_Y (\mathbf{y}^\nu)$, and $\{\mathbf{y}^\nu\} \to \mathbf{y}$ is a sequence in Y. Since $\mathbf{p} \neq \mathbf{0}, \mathbf{y}$ must be a point in the boundary of Y (see Theorem 5.2). Let

$$\hat{\mathbf{p}}^\nu = \frac{\mathbf{p}^\nu}{\mathbf{p}^\nu \mathbf{e}} \in \perp_Y (\mathbf{y}^\nu) \cap \mathbb{P}$$

From Step 1 it follows that, for all ν, $\hat{\mathbf{p}}^\nu \mathbf{y}^\nu = (\mathbf{p}^\nu/\mathbf{p}^\nu \mathbf{e})\mathbf{y}^\nu \geq \alpha$, that is, $\mathbf{p}^\nu \mathbf{y}^\nu \geq \alpha \mathbf{p}^\nu \mathbf{e}$. Taking limits when $\nu \to \infty$, we get: $\mathbf{py} \geq \alpha \mathbf{pe} = \alpha$.

(Step 3 $\left[y \in \partial Y \& \mathbf{p} \in Co\left[\underset{y' \to y}{Lim \sup \perp_Y} (y')\right] \cap \mathbb{P}\right] \Rightarrow \mathbf{py} \geq \alpha)$

Let $\mathbf{p} \in Co[\underset{y' \to y}{Lim \sup \perp_Y} (\mathbf{y}')] \cap \mathbb{P}$, and suppose that $\mathbf{p}$ is not a point in $[\underset{y' \to y}{Lim \sup \perp_Y} (\mathbf{y}')] \cap \mathbb{P}$. By Caratheodory's Theorem, we can write:

$$\mathbf{p} = \sum_{i=1}^{\ell+1} \lambda_i \mathbf{p}_i$$

for some $\lambda_i \geq 0$ such that $\sum_{i=1}^{\ell+1} \lambda_i = 1$, some $\mathbf{p}_i \in \underset{y' \to y}{Lim \sup \perp_Y} (\mathbf{y}')$. Without loss of generality, suppose that $\mathbf{p}_i \neq \mathbf{0}$ for all i (otherwise delete those points $\mathbf{p}_i = \mathbf{0}$). Define then

$$\hat{\mathbf{p}}_i = \mathbf{p}_i/\mathbf{p}_i \mathbf{e} \in \perp_Y (\mathbf{y}^\nu) \cap \mathbb{P}$$

From Step 2 it follows that: $\hat{\mathbf{p}}_i \mathbf{y} = (\mathbf{p}_i/\mathbf{p}_i \mathbf{e})\mathbf{y} \geq \alpha$, that is, $\mathbf{p}_i \mathbf{y} \geq \alpha \mathbf{p}_i \mathbf{e} \forall i$. Then,

$$\mathbf{py} = \left(\sum_{i=1}^{\ell+1} \lambda_i \mathbf{p}_i\right) \mathbf{y} \geq \alpha \left(\sum_{i=1}^{\ell+1} \lambda_i \mathbf{p}_i\right) \mathbf{e} = \alpha \mathbf{pe} = \alpha \qquad \spadesuit$$

Remark 5.3.- Bonnisseau & Cornet (1988a, Lemma 4.2)], prove that, if one also assumes that $Y - \mathbb{R}_+^\ell \subset Y$, then the converse is also true. Yet one has to go through the characterization of Clarke cones as polar of Clarke tangent cones. They also show that these conditions are satisfied if there exists a non-empty, compact subset K_j of $\mathbb{R}^\ell$, if

$$\alpha_j = \inf_h \{y_{jh} \ / \ y_j = (y_{jh}) \in K_j\}$$

and if one of the following conditions holds: (C.1) $Y_j = K_j - \mathbb{R}_+^\ell$; or (C.2) $Y_j \backslash K_j$ is convex. Observe that our assumption (A.5.2) implies then bounded losses.

Chapter 6

TWO-PART MARGINAL PRICING

6.1 INTRODUCTION

The *marginal pricing rule* has deserved special attention, because it satisfies the necessary conditions for optimality, and coincides with profit maximization when production sets are convex. Hence it describes competitive behaviour in the convex case, and defines a specific regulation policy when there are increasing returns to scale (even though its efficiency properties are far from satisfactory).

When there are increasing returns to scale marginal pricing implies losses, so it asks for the simultaneous design of a system of taxes and transfers to balance the budget. This can be seen as a complication of this regulation policy, which requires taking decisions about its distributional impact. In particular, a marginal pricing equilibrium may not be individually rational, and even if it is individually rational, some consumers may feel that they are paying "too much" (so there is little hope for social stability). See Guesnerie (1990), Vohra (1991) and Quinzii (1992), for a detailed discussion.

These distributional problems induced the consideration of regulation policies which satisfy a break-even constraint. *Two-part marginal pricing* is a case in point. The chief idea is that those consumers who buy positive amounts of the goods produced by non-convex firms are charged an entrance fee plus a proportional one (which corresponds to marginal pricing). Therefore, by using a (personalized) system of non-linear prices one can meet both the necessary conditions for optimality and the break-even constraint.

Even though the optimality of two-part marginal pricing also fails (see chapter 7), one can think of a number of reasons to argue in favour of this regulation policy: (i) It always offers the consumer the possibility of not paying the hook-up by abstaining from buying the monopoly good; (ii) It does not require the design of an explicit redistribution policy, since it establishes limits on agents' liability (no one is taxed while someone else is subsidized); and (iii) Even though it is not a lump-sum transfer mechanism (which would allow to achieve efficient allocations), it may provide more flexibility than the fixed rules of income distribution [see Edlin & Epelbaum (1993)].

Observe that wealth functions are not continuous in a two-part tariffs model (they typically jump when the consumption of those goods produced by nonconvex firms becomes zero).

Brown, Heller & Starr (1992) analyze the existence (and decentralizability) of a particular form of two-part marginal pricing, in a full fledged general equilibrium model. They propose a hook-up system which relies on the notion of "willingness to pay", and develop a careful analysis of their implications. This model is presented in section 3, whereas section 2 analyzes a more general case.

Remark 6.1.- Those readers who are not familiar with the standard competitive model are kindly invited to read first chapter 8.

6.2   TWO PART MARGINAL PRICING

Consider now a general equilibrium model which is a particular case of that in chapter 5: a market economy with h non-convex firms, indexed as $1, 2, \ldots, h$ (to be interpreted as regulated monopolies), and $n - h$ competitive convex firms. As before, there are ℓ perfectly divisible commodities, m consumers and n firms, and $\omega \in \mathbb{R}^\ell$ denotes the vector of initial endowments.

Remark 6.2.- Even though it is not necessary from an analytical viewpoint, it is convenient to interpret non-convex firms as exhibiting increasing returns to scale on their attainable production sets, and monopoly goods as consumption goods.

Convex firms maximize profits at given prices, that is, the jth firm's *supply* is given by a mapping $\eta_j : \mathbb{P} \to Y_j$ such that:

$$\eta_j(\mathbf{p}) \equiv \{\mathbf{y}_j \in Y_j \ / \ \mathbf{p}\mathbf{y}_j \geq \mathbf{p}\mathbf{y}'_j \ \forall \ \mathbf{y}'_j \in Y_j\}$$

The profit function $\pi_j : \mathbb{P} \to \mathbb{R}$ is given by $\mathbf{p}\mathbf{y}_j$, for $\mathbf{y}_j \in \eta_j(\mathbf{p})$.

Every non-convex firm produces *a single output*, good j, for $j = 1, 2, .., h$ (the *jth* monopoly good), which is not produced by any other firm, and the initial endowments of these goods are taken to be zero. Regulation takes the form of marginal pricing with personalized "hook-up" fees charged for the right to consume the monopoly goods. The hook-up fees are intended to recover the losses incurred by the monopolies when using marginal pricing. Hence in equilibrium monopolies make zero profits.

This pricing policy implies that the *ith* consumer's budget constraint will exhibit the following structure:

$$r_i(\mathbf{p}, \tilde{\mathbf{y}}) = \mathbf{p}\omega_i + \sum_{j=h+1}^{n} \theta_{ij}\pi_j(\mathbf{p}) - \sum_{j=1}^{h} q_{ij}(\mathbf{p}, \tilde{\mathbf{y}})$$

where θ_{ij} stands for the *ith* consumer's share in the *jth* firm's profits (with $\sum_{i=1}^{m} \theta_{ij} = 1$, for $j = h+1, \ldots, n$), and $q_{ij}(.)$ represents the *ith* consumer's *jth* hook-up fee, that she only pays when consuming positive amounts of the *jth* monopoly good $(j = 1, 2, \ldots, h)$.

Consider the following definitions,

Definition 6.1.-

A **Hook-up System** is a family of mh functions q_{ij} from $\mathbb{P} \times \mathbb{F}$ into $\mathbb{R}$ such that, for each $j = 1, 2, \ldots, h$:

(i) $q_{ij}(\mathbf{p}, \tilde{\mathbf{y}}) = 0$, if $x_{ij}^* = 0$, $i = 1, 2, \ldots, m$ (where x_{ij}^* stands for the *ith* consumer's demand of the *jth* commodity).

(ii) $\sum_{i=1}^{m} q_{ij}(\mathbf{p}, \tilde{\mathbf{y}}) = -\mathbf{p}y_j$.

(iii) Either $q_{ij}(\mathbf{p}, \tilde{\mathbf{y}}) \geq 0$, or $q_{ij}(\mathbf{p}, \tilde{\mathbf{y}}) \leq 0, \forall i$.

A Hook-up System is thus a collection of mh mappings such that: (a) Every q_{ij} takes on the value zero if the *ith* consumer does not consume the *jth* monopoly good; (b) The aggregate hook-up fees offset the losses (resp. distribute the profits) derived from the production of the monopoly goods; and (c) All hook-ups referring to a given firm have the same sign (positive for the case of losses and negative for the case of profits).

Definition 6.2.-

A **Two-Part Marginal Pricing Equilibrium relative to a Hook-up System** (q_{ij}) is a price vector $\mathbf{p}^* \in \mathbb{P}$ and an allocation $[(\mathbf{x}_i^*), \tilde{\mathbf{y}}^*]$ such that:

(α) For all $i = 1, 2, \ldots, m$, $u_i(\mathbf{x}_i^*) \geq u_i(\mathbf{x}_i)$, for every $\mathbf{x}_i$ such that

$$\mathbf{p}_i^* \mathbf{x}_i \leq \mathbf{p}_i^* \omega_i + \sum_{j=h+1}^{n} \theta_{ij}\pi_j(\mathbf{p}^*) - \sum_{j=1}^{h} q_{ij}(\mathbf{p}^*, \tilde{\mathbf{y}}^*).$$

(β) $\mathbf{p}^* \in \bigcap\limits_{j=1}^{n} \phi_j^{MP}(\mathbf{y}_j^*)$

(γ) $\sum\limits_{i=1}^{m} \mathbf{x}_i^* - \sum\limits_{j=1}^{n} \mathbf{y}_j^* - \omega \leq \mathbf{0}$, and $p_k^* = 0$ if the kth inequality is strict.

A Two-Part Marginal Pricing Equilibrium relative to (q_{ij}) is thus a price vector and an allocation such that: (i) Every consumer maximizes utility at given prices within her budget set (which includes the hook-up fees); (ii) Convex firms maximize profits at given prices; (iii) Non-convex firms follow the marginal pricing rule; and (iv) All markets clear.

Consider now the following assumptions:

<u>A.6.1.-</u> For all $i = 1, 2, \ldots, m$,
    (i) X_i is a closed convex subset of $\mathbb{R}^{\ell}$, bounded from below.
    (ii) $u_i : X_i \to \mathbb{R}$ is a continuous and quasi-concave utility function which satisfies local non-satiation.
    (iii) $\omega_i \in X_i$ and $\omega_{ig} = 0$ when g is a monopoly good.
    (iv) $r_i(\mathbf{p}, \tilde{\mathbf{y}}) > b_i(\mathbf{p})$ for $(\mathbf{p}, \tilde{\mathbf{y}}) \in \mathbf{PE}$.

<u>A.6.2.-</u> For each firm $j = 1, 2, \ldots, h$,
    (i) $Y_j = C_j - \mathbb{R}_+^{\ell}$, where C_j is non-empty, compact and there exists $k > 0$ such that $\mathbf{c} \geq -k\mathbf{e}$ for all $\mathbf{c} \in C_j$.
    (ii) For $j = 1, 2, \ldots, h$, the jth firm is the only producer of good j, which is produced as a single output.

<u>A.6.3.-</u> For $j = h+1, h+2, \ldots, n, Y_j$ is a convex and closed subset of $\mathbb{R}^{\ell}$, such that $\mathbf{0} \in Y_j$, and $Y_j - \mathbb{R}_+^{\ell} \subset Y_j$.

<u>A.6.4.-</u> $\forall \, \omega' \geq \omega, \; A(\omega')$ is compact.

Assumptions (A.6.1) to (A.6.3) specialize the model in chapter 5, and require no additional comment. Assumption (A.6.4) is introduced because convex firms are not assumed to have the structure postulated in (A.6.2) (let us recall here the discussion in section 3.3).

The next result follows:

Proposition 6.1.-
Let E be an economy satisfying assumptions (A.6.1), to (A.6.4), and let $(\mathbf{q}_{ij})$ be a Hook-up system such that every $\mathbf{q}_{ij}$ is continuous on PE. Then there exists a Two-Part marginal pricing equilibrium relative to $(\mathbf{q}_{ij})$.

Proof.-

First note that all firms follow the marginal pricing rule (which corresponds to profit maximization when Y_j is a convex set). The assumptions of the theorem clearly imply (A.4.1), (A.4.2), (A.4.3) and (A.4.4). It is easy to check that (A.4.5) is also satisfied (see lemma 5.2 and the proof of proposition 8.1 below). Then, theorem 4.1 gives us the desired result.♠

Let us conclude this section by presenting a specific hook-up system which is economically meaningful, and based on observable variables: agents' wealth. Here again it is worth interpreting monopolies as firms with increasing returns to scale (otherwise the ethical content of this proposal evaporates).

Let now (q_{ij}) be a Hook-up System defined as follows: For each $j = 1, 2, \ldots, h,$

(a) $q_{ij}(\mathbf{p}, \tilde{\mathbf{y}}) = 0$, if the *ith* consumer does not consume the *jth* monopoly good .

(b) Otherwise we have:

$$q_{ij}(\mathbf{p}, \tilde{\mathbf{y}}) = \frac{\mathbf{p}\omega_i + \sum\limits_{j=h+1}^{n} \theta_{ij}\mathbf{p}\mathbf{y}_j}{\mathbf{p}\omega + \sum\limits_{j=h+1}^{n} \mathbf{p}\mathbf{y}_j}\mathbf{p}\mathbf{y}_j$$

that is, q_{ij} distributes $\mathbf{p}\mathbf{y}_j$ proportionally to the *ith* consumers's net wealth.

If we assume that $\mathbf{p}\omega + \sum\limits_{j=h+1}^{n} \mathbf{p}\mathbf{y}_j > 0$ over the set of production equilibria, then q_{ij} turns out to be continuous on **PE**, and the existence result (proposition 6.1) applies.

6.3   THE BROWN-HELLER-STARR MODEL

Brown, Heller & Starr (1992) develop a Two-Part Marginal Pricing model with a specific Hook-up System, based on consumers' willingness to pay. Let us present here this model, as a particular case of the one above.

Suppose that there is now a single nonconvex firm, indexed as firm 1, and let X_i^* denote a convex compact subset of $\mathbb{R}^\ell$ containing in its (relative) interior the *ith* consumer's set of attainable consumptions. Assume that utilities are *strictly* quasi-concave. Calculate then each household's "reservation level of utility", i.e., the maximum utility level she could obtain if the monopoly good were not available $V_i(\mathbf{p})$, as the solution to the following program:

$$Max\ \ u_i(\mathbf{x}_i)$$

subject to:

$$\mathbf{p}\mathbf{x}_i \leq \mathbf{p}\omega_i + \sum_{j=2}^{n} \theta_{ij}\pi_j(\mathbf{p}), x_{i1} = 0,\ \text{and}\ \mathbf{x}_i \in X_i^*$$

The expenditure function can be used to calculate the income which is necessary to reach the reservation utility level, when the monopoly good is available. This income, $E_i[\mathbf{p}, V_i(\mathbf{p})]$, is given by the solution to:

$$Min\ \mathbf{p}\mathbf{x}_i$$

subject to:

$$u_i(\mathbf{x}_i) \geq V_i(\mathbf{p})\ \text{and}\ \mathbf{x}_i \in X_i^*$$

Then, each consumer's willingness to pay for the monopolist's output, at $\mathbf{p}$ is given by:

$$s_i(\mathbf{p}) = \mathbf{p}\omega_i + \sum_{j=2}^{n} \theta_{ij}\pi_j(\mathbf{p}) - E_i[\mathbf{p}, V_i(\mathbf{p})]$$

that is, "it is the amount at current prices that must be subtracted from current income to reduce utility to what it was when the monopoly good was unavailable... Of course, s_i is an ordinal concept, i.e., it is independent of the utility representation" [Cf. Brown, Heller & Starr (1992, p. 62)].

Consider the following assumptions:

A.6.1'.- For each $i = 1, 2, \ldots, m$, (i) and (iii) as in (A.6.1). Furthermore:

(ii') $u_i : X_i \to \mathbb{R}$ is a continuous and strictly quasi-concave function, which satisfies non-satiation.

A.6.2'.- Same as (A.6.2) except in that $h = 1$.

A.6.5.- Let $(\mathbf{p}, \tilde{\mathbf{y}})$ be a production equilibrium. Then,

$$\sum_{i=1}^{m} s_i(\mathbf{p}) > -\mathbf{p}y_1$$

Note that assumption (A.6.1') coincides with (A.6.1) except in that it includes the strict quasi-concavity of utilities, and excludes the restriction on the wealth function (it is implied by (A.6.5) and the hook-up system). Assumption (A.6.5) says that the aggregate willingness to pay exceeds the monopoly losses.

In order to define the **Brown-Heller-Starr** (BHS, for short) **Hook-up System**, let $s(\mathbf{p}) = \sum_{i=1}^{m} s_i(\mathbf{p})$, and

$$\tau(\mathbf{p}, \mathbf{y}_1) = \frac{-\mathbf{p}\mathbf{y}_i}{s(\mathbf{p})}$$

Observe that, under (A.6.5), τ is well defined over production equilibria. The *BHS hook-up system* is given by:

$$q_i^{BHS}(\mathbf{p}, \mathbf{y}_1) \equiv \tau(\mathbf{p}, \mathbf{y}_1)s_i(\mathbf{p})$$

that is, the proportional hook-up charge for the ith consumer is a fraction of her willingness to pay.

The assumptions of the model imply that q_i^{BHS} is a continuous function of $(\mathbf{p}, \mathbf{y}_1)$ over the set of production equilibria, such that: a) It is always non-negative and smaller than $s_i(\mathbf{p})$ when this is a positive number; and b) It is equal to zero if $s_i = 0$.

The next corollary follows immediately (simply note that (iv) of (A.6.1) is implied by (A.6.4) and the specific form of the Brown-Heller-Starr hook-up system):

Corollary 6.1.-
Under assumptions (A.6.1'), (A.6.2'), (A.6.3), (A.6.4) and (A.6.5), there exists a Two-Part Marginal Pricing Equilibrium relative to $\left(q_i^{BHS}\right)$.

6.4 FINAL COMMENTS

Two-part marginal pricing may be understood as a regulation policy which satisfies two principles: the necessary conditions for optimality, and budget balance. The compatibility between these principles is obtained by means of a non-linear pricing schedule, which allows for different ways of covering the monopoly losses (i.e., for alternative pricing policies). *Linear pricing under break-even constraints* is an alternative regulation policy, which avoids the use of personalized prices but shares the idea of budget balance. Since marginal pricing is abandoned in this approach, prices become policy variables: when there are multiple outputs (the case of joint production), the budget balance condition does not determine the relative output prices.

There is an extensive literature on the theory of linear pricing in public enterprises subject to a break-even constraint [mostly in terms of partial equilibrium analysis, as described for instance in Sharkey (1982) or Bös (1987)].

We shall conclude this chapter by briefly referring to two basic results in this context: Boiteaux-Ramsey pricing and cost-allocation schemes.

Ramsey (1927) (for a single agent economy) and Boiteaux (1956) analyzed the necessary conditions for optimality subject to a break-even constraint and linear pricing. The prices which satisfy these conditions are called Boiteaux-Ramsey prices. In the simplest version, where there is a single non-convex firm producing two outputs b_1, b_2 (whose cross elasticities of demand can be neglected), the firm is required to balance its budget and price the outputs at q_1, q_2 according to the "inverse of elasticity" formula:

$$q_1 - c_1 = \Omega \frac{b_1}{\partial x_1/\partial p_1} \qquad q_2 - c_2 = \Omega \frac{b_2}{\partial x_2/\partial p_2}$$

where c_1, c_2 represent the marginal cost of producing goods 1 and 2, respectively, and $\partial x_1/\partial p_1$, $\partial x_2/\partial p_2$ are the partial derivatives of compensated demand of the two goods. The number Ω is determined by the budget equation:

$$C(\mathbf{b}) = q_1 b_1 + q_2 b_2 = c_1 b_1 + c_2 b_2 + \Omega b_1^2 (\partial x_1/\partial p_1)^{-1} + \Omega b_2^2 (\partial x_2/\partial p_2)^{-1}$$

where $C(\mathbf{b})$ is the given total cost of producing output $\mathbf{b}$ [Cf. Dierker, Guesnerie & Neuefeind (1985,pp.1381-1382)].

The intuition behind this rule is that one has to charge relatively higher prices over those products whose demand is relatively more inelastic. It is worth noticing that these prices are obtained from conditions over the maximization of the aggregate surplus, and that their distributive effects may well run in any direction [Cf. Mas-Colell (1987, p. 55)].

A different pricing principle emerges from an axiomatization of cost allocation schemes inspired by the Shapley Value for non-atomic games [first analyzed in Aumann & Shapley (1974), and used in Billera, Heath & Raanan (1978) for telephone billing rates which share the cost of a telephone system]. As in the case of marginal pricing (and unlike Boiteaux-Ramsey pricing), these prices only depend on the cost of production, and take advantage of the fact that the Shapley Value can be defined by an explicit formula. Interestingly enough, they can be characterized by a set of axioms on the cost functions and the quantities produced [see for instance Billera & Heath (1982), Mirman & Tauman (1982), Samet & Tauman (1982)].

In order to sketch these ideas, we shall follow closely the work in Mirman & Tauman (1982). Think of a firm producing r outputs, and let $\mathbf{M}$ be a family of functions f defined on a full dimensional comprehensive subset $C^M \subset \mathbb{R}_+^r$, and such that $f(\mathbf{0}) = (0)$ (no fixed cost), and f is continuously differentiable on C^M. We define a *price mechanism* as a function

$P : \mathbf{M} \times C^M \to \mathbb{R}^r$ that, for each $f \in \mathbf{M}$, and for every $\mathbf{b} \in C^M$, assigns a vector of prices:

$$P(f, \mathbf{b}) = [P_1(f, \mathbf{b}), P_2(f, \mathbf{b}), \ldots, P_r(f, \mathbf{b})]$$

Here f is to be interpreted as the cost function, and $\mathbf{b}$ as the output vector. A price mechanism is then a way of pricing the outputs as a function of quantities and costs.

Consider now the following axioms:

(CS) (COST-SHARING) For every $g \in \mathbb{F}$ and every $\mathbf{b} \in C^M$: $\mathbf{b}P(f, \mathbf{b}) = f(\mathbf{b})$ (that is, total cost equals total revenue).

(A) (ADDITIVITY) Let $f, g, h \in \mathbf{M}$ be defined over the same domain, and such that $f = g + h$. Then: $P(f, \mathbf{b}) = P(g, \mathbf{b}) + P(h, \mathbf{b})$ (i.e., if the cost f can be broken into two components, g and h , then calculating the price determined by the cost function f can be accomplished by adding the prices determined by g and h separately).

(P) (POSITIVITY) If f is non-decreasing on C^M, then $P(f, \mathbf{b}) \geq 0$

(C) (CONSISTENCY) For $f \in \mathbf{M}$, Let $C = \{z \in_+ | z = \sum_{t=1}^{r} b_t, \text{ for } \mathbf{b} \in C^M\}$. If there is a function G defined on C such that $f(\mathbf{b}) = G(\sum_{t=1}^{r} b_t)$, then:

$$P_i(f, \mathbf{b}) = P(G, \sum_{t=1}^{r} b_t)$$

(i.e., splitting commodities in irrelevant classifications -that is, in a way that does not affect costs-, has no effect on prices).

(R) (RESCALING) Let $f \in \mathbf{M}$, and let $\lambda = (\lambda_1, \lambda_2, \ldots, \lambda_r)$ be a vector of r positive real numbers. Define $C^M(\lambda) = \{z \in \mathbb{R}^r_+ \mid z_t = b_t/\lambda_t,$ for $\mathbf{b} \in C^M\}$, and let $g \in \mathbf{M}$ be a function on $C^M(\lambda)$ defined by $g(\mathbf{b}) = \mathbb{F}(\lambda_1 b_1, \ldots, \lambda_r b_r)$. Then: $P_i(g, \mathbf{b}) = \lambda_i P[f, (\lambda_1 b_1, \ldots, \lambda_r b_r)]$ (i.e., changing the scale of a commodity yields an equivalent change in prices).

Mirman & Tauman show that there exists one and only one price mechanism P satisfying the above five axioms, and that this mechanism is the Aumann-Shapley price mechanism, that is, the one defined through the formula:

$$P_i(f, \mathbf{b}) = \int_0^1 \frac{\partial f}{\partial b_i}(t\mathbf{b})dt$$

The apparent connection between Aumann-Shapley values and marginal pricing is analyzed in Samet & Tauman (1982). They show that dropping the cost-sharing assumption (CS), and substituting axiom (P) by the following:

(P^*) If f is non-decreasing in a neighbourghood of $\mathbf{b}$, then $P(f, \mathbf{b}) \geq 0$.

Then, axioms $(A), (P^*), (C)$ and (R) actually characterize the Marginal Pricing rule.

Dierker, Guesnerie & Neuefeind (1985) provide an existence result for a family of Average Cost Pricing rules which includes Boiteaux-Ramsey and Aumann-Shapley pricing. Indeed, it can be shown that, under reasonable conditions, these pricing rules are regular, so that theorem 4.1 applies.

There is a large number of contributions which analyze different pricing policies in terms of the properties of the associated cost-functions. Besides those already referred to, let us mention the works of Mirman, Samet & Tauman (1983), Ten Raa (1983), Greenberg & Shitovitz (1984), Mirman, Tauman & Zang (1985),(1986), Reichert (1986 Part I), Dehez & Drèze (1988b), Mas-Colell & Silvestre (1989) and Hart & Mas-Colell (1990) [see also Sharkey (1989, Section 3)]. Moulin's (1988) excellent monograph is highly recommended for those willing to establish links between these models and more general collective decision mechanisms.

Chapter 7

EFFICIENCY

7.1 THE SECOND WELFARE THEOREM

Let $E = \{(X_i, u_i), (Y_j), \omega\}$ describe our economy of reference, that is, an economy with ℓ commodities, m consumers (characterized by their consumption sets and utility functions), n firms (characterized by their production sets), and a vector of initial endowments $\omega \in \mathbb{R}^\ell$. It will be shown here (theorem 7.1) that every efficient allocation can be decentralized as a marginal pricing equilibrium, provided we are free to make arbitrary transfers. This result extends the standard second welfare theorem since, according to proposition 5.3, when production sets are convex, marginal pricing corresponds to profit maximization.

Consider now the following assumption (which is a weakening of the assumptions established in chapter 4):

A.7.1.- (i) For every $j = 1, 2, \ldots, n$, Y_j is a closed subset of $\mathbb{R}^\ell$ such that $Y_j - \mathbb{R}_+^\ell \subset Y_j$.

(ii) For every $i = 1, 2, \ldots, m$, $X_i \subset \mathbb{R}^\ell$ is a nonempty, closed and convex, and $u_i : X_i \to \mathbb{R}$ is a continuous and quasi-concave function, which satisfies local non-satiation.

Next definition makes it precise the concept of efficient (or Pareto optimal) allocations:

Definition 7.1.-

An attainable allocation $[(\mathbf{x}_i^*), \tilde{\mathbf{y}}^*] \in A(\omega)$ is said to be **Pareto Optimal** if there is no other attainable allocation $[(\mathbf{x}_i), \tilde{\mathbf{y}}]$ such that $u_i(\mathbf{x}_i) \geq u_i(\mathbf{x}_i^*)$ for all i, with $u_k(\mathbf{x}_k) > u_k(\mathbf{x}_k^*)$ for some k.

An allocation is called Pareto optimal when it is attainable, and there is
no other attainable allocation at which everybody is better-off. This is to
be interpreted as an efficiency requirement concerning the performance of a
resource allocation mechanism (that is why Pareto optimality and efficiency
are used as equivalent notions in this context). The absence of Pareto optimality indicates that the organization of economic activity can be improved
upon. Yet, this notion is devoid of any trace of economic justice. As Sen
puts it, "an economy can be Pareto optimal and still be perfectly disgusting"
[Cf. Sen (1970, p.22)].

The following lemma (which is stated without proof), gives us a key
instrumental result for the general proof for the extension of the second
welfare theorem:

Lemma 7.1.- [Clarke (1983, Th. 2.4.5)]

**Let Y be a closed subset of $\mathbb{R}^\ell$, and let $\mathbb{T}_Y(y)$ denote the polar
cone of $\mathbb{N}_Y(y)$ (also called Tangent Cone). A point v belongs to
$\mathbb{T}_Y(y)$ if and only if, for every sequence $\{y^\nu\} \to y$ in Y,$\{t^\nu\} \to 0$ in
$(0,\infty)$, there is a sequence $\{v^\nu\} \to v$ in $\mathbb{R}^\ell$ such that $(y^\nu + t^\nu v^\nu) \in Y$,
for all ν.**

Remark 7.1.- The proof of this result is not particularly difficult, but
it takes a rather long excursion through Clarke's "Generalized Gradients"
(chapter 2 of his book).

The following result [due originally to Guesnerie (1975)] is an extension of
the Second Welfare Theorem to economies with nonconvex production sets
[see also Vohra (1991, th.1), Quinzii (1992, th.2.6)]:

Theorem 7.1.-

**Let $\mathbf{E} = \{(X_i, u_i), (Y_j), \omega\}$ be an economy satisfying assumption
(A.7.1), and let $[(x_i^*), \tilde{y}^*]$ be a Pareto Optimal allocation. Then,
there exists $\mathbf{p} \in \mathbb{P}$, such that:**

(a) For all $i, u_i(x_i) \geq u_i(x_i^*) \Rightarrow px_i \geq px_i^*$.

(b) $\mathbf{p} \in \phi_j^{MP}(\mathbf{p}, \tilde{y}^*)$, for all j.

Proof.-

Let us define the following sets:

$$BE_i(\mathbf{x}_i^*) \equiv \{\mathbf{x}_i \in X_i / u_i(\mathbf{x}_i) \geq u_i(\mathbf{x}_i^*)\}$$
$$B_i(\mathbf{x}_i^*) \equiv \{\mathbf{x}_i \in X_i / u_i(\mathbf{x}_i) > u_i(\mathbf{x}_i^*)\}$$

and, by letting $\mathbf{x}^* \equiv \sum_{i=1}^{m} \mathbf{x}_i^*$, write: $BE(\mathbf{x}^*) \equiv \sum_{i=1}^{m} BE_i(\mathbf{x}_i^*)$. Define now:

$$G \equiv \sum_{j=1}^{n} [\mathbb{T}_{Y_j}(\mathbf{y}_j^*) + \{\mathbf{y}_j^*\}] + \{\omega\}$$

By construction, under assumption (A.7.1) the sets G and $BE(\mathbf{x}^*)$ are convex. Moreover, since $\mathbf{0} \in \mathbb{T}_{Y_j}(\mathbf{y}_j^*)$ and $\omega = \sum_{i=1}^{m} \mathbf{x}_i^* - \sum_{j=1}^{n} \mathbf{y}_j^*$ (because $[(\mathbf{x}_i^*),(\mathbf{y}_j^*)]$ is a feasible allocation), we deduce that $G \cap BE(\mathbf{x}^*) \neq \emptyset$.

Let us show now that $G \cap int BE(\mathbf{x}^*) = \emptyset$ (where $int BE(\mathbf{x}^*)$ denotes the interior of $BE(\mathbf{x}^*)$, i.e., the set of points which can be expressed as the sum of points $\mathbf{x}_i$ such that $\mathbf{x}_i \in BE_i(\mathbf{x}_i^*) \forall i$, and $\mathbf{x}_h \in B_h(\mathbf{x}_h^*)$ for some h). To do that suppose that there exists $\mathbf{x}_i \in BE_i(\mathbf{x}_i^*), i = 1, 2, \dots, m$, with $\mathbf{x}_h \in B_h(\mathbf{x}_h^*)$, for some h, and $\mathbf{z}_j \in \mathbb{T}_{Y_j}(\mathbf{y}_j^*), j = 1, 2, \dots, n$, such that:

$$\sum_{i=1}^{m} \mathbf{x}_i - \sum_{j=1}^{n} (\mathbf{z}_j + \mathbf{y}_j^*) = \omega$$

Since $\omega = \sum_{i=1}^{m} \mathbf{x}_i^* - \sum_{j=1}^{n} \mathbf{y}_j^*$, we have:

$$\sum_{i=1}^{m} \mathbf{x}_i - \sum_{j=1}^{n} (\mathbf{z}_j + \mathbf{y}_j^*) = \sum_{i=1}^{m} \mathbf{x}_i^* - \sum_{j=1}^{n} \mathbf{y}_j^*$$

and hence

$$\sum_{j=1}^{n} \mathbf{z}_j = \sum_{i=1}^{m} (\mathbf{x}_i - \mathbf{x}_i^*) \qquad [1]$$

Part (ii) of (A.7.1) implies that, for every $t \in (0,1)$, we have:

$$t\mathbf{x}_i + (1-t)\mathbf{x}_i^* = \mathbf{x}_i^* + t(\mathbf{x}_i - \mathbf{x}_i^*) \in BE_i(\mathbf{x}_i^*), \forall i$$
$$t\mathbf{x}_h + (1-t)\mathbf{x}_h^* = \mathbf{x}_h^* + t(\mathbf{x}_h - \mathbf{x}_h^*) \in B_h(\mathbf{x}_h^*), \text{ some } h$$

Then, from [1] we have:

$$\sum_{i=1}^{m} \mathbf{x}_i^* + t \sum_{j=1}^{n} \mathbf{z}_j \in int BE(\mathbf{x}^*), \forall t \in (0,1) \qquad [2]$$

As $\mathbf{z}_j \in \mathbb{T}_{Y_j}(\mathbf{y}_j^*)$ for all j, from lemma 7.1 we know that for any sequence of positive real numbers $\{t^q\} \to 0$, there exists, for each j, a sequence $\{\mathbf{z}_j^q\} \to \mathbf{z}_j$ such that $\mathbf{y}_j^* + t^q \mathbf{z}_j^q \in Y_j$. For q large enough, $\sum_{j=1}^{n} \mathbf{z}_j^q$ becomes arbitrarily close to $\sum_{j=1}^{n} \mathbf{z}_j$. By the continuity of utilities and [2], it follows that there exists q large enough such that:

$$\sum_{i=1}^{m} \mathbf{x}_i^* + t^q \sum_{j=1}^{n} \mathbf{z}_j^q \in int BE(\mathbf{x}^*) \qquad [3]$$

Because $\omega = \sum_{i=1}^{m} \mathbf{x}_i^* - \sum_{j=1}^{n} \mathbf{y}_j^*$, we can write:

$$\sum_{i=1}^{m} \mathbf{x}_i^* + t^q \sum_{j=1}^{n} \mathbf{z}_j^q - \sum_{j=1}^{n}(t^q \mathbf{z}_j^q + \mathbf{y}_j^*) = \omega$$

with $\sum_{j=1}^{n}(t^q \mathbf{z}_j^q + \mathbf{y}_j^*) \in \sum_{j=1}^{n} Y_j$. But this along with [3] contradicts the Pareto optimality of $[(\mathbf{x}_i^*), (y_j^*)]$ Therefore, $G \cap int BE(\mathbf{x}^*) = \emptyset$.

Thus we can apply now the separating hyperplane theorem to assert that there exists $\mathbf{p} \in \mathbb{R}^\ell, \mathbf{p} \neq \mathbf{0}$, such that for each $\mathbf{x} \in BE(\mathbf{x}^*)$, and every $\mathbf{q}$ in G,

$$\mathbf{px} \geq \mathbf{pq} \qquad [4]$$

In particular, since $\omega = \sum_{i=1}^{m} \mathbf{x}_i^* - \sum_{j=1}^{n} \mathbf{y}_j^*$, and $\{\omega\} + \sum_{j=1}^{n} \mathbf{y}_j^* \in G$, we get: $\mathbf{px}^* = \mathbf{p}\omega + \mathbf{p} \sum_{j=1}^{n} \mathbf{y}_j^* \leq \mathbf{px}, \forall \mathbf{x} \in BE(\mathbf{x}^*)$, that is, $\mathbf{px} \geq \mathbf{px}^*$ for all points in $BE(\mathbf{x}^*)$. It is easy to deduce that this happens if and only if $\mathbf{px}_i^*$ minimizes $\mathbf{px}_i$ over $BE_i(\mathbf{x}_i^*)$ for every i.

Applying the same reasoning, we deduce that for every $\mathbf{q}$ in G, we have: $\mathbf{pq} \leq \mathbf{p}\omega + \mathbf{p} \sum_{j=1}^{n} \mathbf{y}_j^*$, i.e., $\mathbf{p}\omega + \mathbf{p} \sum_{j=1}^{n} \mathbf{y}_j^*$ maximizes the value of points $\sum_{j=1}^{n} \mathbf{z}_j + \sum_{j=1}^{n} \mathbf{y}_j^* + \{\omega\}$ over G, which happens to be true if and only if it maximizes $\mathbf{z}_j + \mathbf{y}_j^*$ over $\{\mathbb{T}_{Y_j}(\mathbf{y}_j^*) + \{\mathbf{y}_j^*\}\}$ for each j. Now, since $\mathbf{y}_j^* \in \mathbb{T}_{Y_j}(\mathbf{y}_j^*) + \{\mathbf{y}_j^*\}$ for every j, it follows that $\mathbf{py}_j^* \geq \mathbf{p}(\mathbf{z}_j + \mathbf{y}_j^*)$, for every $\mathbf{z}_j \in \mathbb{T}_{Y_j}(\mathbf{y}_j^*)$, that is, $\mathbf{pz}_j \leq 0 \ \forall \mathbf{z}_j \in \mathbb{T}_{Y_j}(\mathbf{y}_j^*)$, and hence $\mathbf{p}$ is in $\mathbb{N}_{Y_j}(\mathbf{y}_j^*), \forall j$.

Finally, since $Y_j - \mathbb{R}_+^\ell \subset Y_j$ by assumption, theorem 5.1 ensures that $\mathbb{N}_{Y_j}(\mathbf{y}_j^*) \subset \mathbb{R}_+^\ell$ for all j, and hence, $\mathbf{p} > \mathbf{0}$.♠

The next figure illustrates the situation:

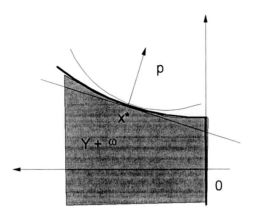

Figure 7.1

Remark 7.2.- Let $[(\mathbf{x}_i^*), \tilde{\mathbf{y}}]$ be a Pareto Optimal allocation, and suppose that for some consumer u_i is differentiable at $\mathbf{x}_i^* \in intX_i$. Then, for this consumer, the (normalized) vector of marginal rates of substitution is unique. Thus the price vector supporting that allocation turns out to be unique. Let us also recall here that, according to proposition 2.4, cost minimization implies utility maximization if $\mathbf{p}^*\mathbf{x}_i^* > b_i(\mathbf{p}^*)$.

Theorem 7.1 provides an extension of the second welfare theorem allowing for nonconvex production sets. It tells us that any efficient allocation can be decentralized as a marginal pricing equilibrium, provided we are free to carry out any feasible lump-sum transfer which may be required. This suggests that the way of interpreting marginal rates of transformation as Clarke normal cones is appropriate. The remark above reinforces such an idea: it says that (under very mild regularity conditions) *marginal pricing is a necessary condition for achieving Pareto optimality through a price mechanism.*

Thus, in the context of a regulated economy where arbitrary lump-sum transfers are possible, efficiency can be obtained by instructing firms to follow marginal pricing. Notice that when production sets are convex, marginal pricing corresponds to profit maximization. Therefore we can interpret this result in terms of a mixed economy with a competitive sector (convex firms) and a regulated one, where all firms follow marginal pricing, and efficiency is obtained by suitably redistributing wealth.

7.2   THE EFFICIENCY PROBLEM

It is not true, however, that Marginal Pricing implies optimality, that is, Marginal Pricing is a necessary but not a sufficient condition for optimality (a general problem for nonconvex programming). To see this we shall briefly report on some key examples. First, we shall observe that production efficiency may fail in a marginal pricing equilibrium, due to the fact that there is an inadequate number of active firms (example 1). In order to avoid this type of complication, we shall concentrate on economies with a single firm. The second example shows a single-firm economy in which no marginal pricing equilibrium is Pareto efficient [the example is developed in Brown & Heal (1979), after Guesnerie's (1975) previous one]. The third example [Vohra (1988b)] presents a situation of a single-firm economy in which marginal pricing is Pareto dominated by average cost pricing (and thus is not even second best efficient). Each of these examples illustrates different aspects of the problem. Finally, we shall address the efficiency problem en the context of two-part tariffs, and show that the negative results obtained extend to this framework (example 4).

Example 1.- Let us start by considering a constant returns to scale economy with two identical firms, two identical consumers and two goods (good 1 is an input whereas good 2 is an output). Each firm's efficient production plan takes the form $\lambda(-1, 1)$. At equilibrium prices $\mathbf{p'} = (0.5, 0.5)$, each consumer supplies one unit of input and demands one unit of output). Consumer 1 trades with firm 1, and consumer 2 trades with firm 2.

Suppose now that firm's 1 technology changes, so that the slope of the boundary becomes steeper for those production plans involving more than 1.5 units of input (i.e., firm 1 becomes more productive for higher levels of output). It is clear that efficiency requires closing down firm 2, and operate only the most efficient firm. Yet $\mathbf{p'}$ still gives us a marginal pricing equilibrium in which each consumer trades one unit of input against one unit of output in each firm. This implies that marginal pricing equilibria do not ensure production efficiency when there are several firms [see Beato & Mas-Colell (1983), (1985) for a more detailed example].

The simple economy described above illustrates an extremely serious problem: when there are increasing returns to scale, the necessary conditions for optimality may yield equilibrium allocations in which aggregate production belongs to the interior of the aggregate production set. Is this the only source of concern?. The answer is no. The next examples consider economies with a single firm in which marginal pricing still fails to achieve Pareto optimality.

Example 2.- [see Brown & Heal (1979), Quinzii (1992,Ch.4)]

Consider an economy with two goods, a single non-convex firm and two consumers. The production set, which presents an extreme form of indivisibility, is given by:

$$Y \equiv \left(\mathbf{y} \in \mathbb{R}^2 \mid \begin{cases} y_1 > -7, y_2 \le 0 \\ y_1 \le -7, y_2 \le 7 \end{cases} \right)$$

that is, no output can be produced with less than 7 units of input and seven units of output can be produced with 7 or more units of input. The only efficient production plans are thus $\mathbf{y}^o = (0,0)$, and $\mathbf{y}' = (-7,7)$. Moreover, $N_Y(\mathbf{y}^o) = N_Y(\mathbf{y}') = \mathbb{R}_+^2$ (that is, marginal pricing imposes no restriction on equilibrium prices). Consumers' preferences are described by the following utilities:

$$u_1(\mathbf{x}_1) = \begin{cases} x_{12} + \frac{4}{3}x_{11} & \text{if } x_{12} \ge x_{11} \\ \frac{700}{312}\left(x_{12} + \frac{4}{100}x_{11}\right) & \text{if } x_{12} \le x_{11} \end{cases}$$

$$u_2(\mathbf{x}_2) = \begin{cases} \frac{3x_{22}+5x_{21}}{18} & \text{if } x_{22} \ge \frac{1}{3}x_{21} \\ x_{22} & \text{if } x_{22} \le \frac{1}{3}x_{21} \end{cases}$$

Initial endowments and shares are given by:

$$\omega_1 = (0,5), \omega_2 = (15,0), \theta_1 = 1, \theta_2 = 0$$

There are two equilibria in this economy which are candidates to efficient marginal pricing equilibria. The structure of the model implies that both of them may well be regarded as pure exchange equilibria, the first one because it does not involve production, and the second one because it can be viewed as an equilibrium of an economy with no production and initial endowments given by:

$$\omega_1' = (-7,12), \omega_2' = (15,0)$$

The first equilibrium is given by:

$$\mathbf{p}^o = (4,100), \ \mathbf{y}^o = (0,0), \ \mathbf{x}_1^o = (13.393, 4.464), \ \mathbf{x}_2^o = (1.607, 0.536)$$

with utilities

$$u_1(\mathbf{x}_1^o) = 11.216, \qquad u_2(\mathbf{x}_2^o) = 0.536$$

The second equilibrium is given by:

$$\mathbf{p}' = (5,3), \mathbf{y}' = (-7,7), \mathbf{x}_1' = (0,1/3), \mathbf{x}_2' = (8,35/3)$$

with utilities

$$u_1(\mathbf{x}_1') = 1/3, \quad u_2(\mathbf{x}_2') = 4.166$$

Consider now the allocation $\mathbf{x}_1 = (1.5,\ 0.5)$, $\mathbf{x}_2 = (13.5,\ 4.5)$ which is feasible for the economy when no production takes place. The utilities associated with this allocation are:

$$u_1(\mathbf{x}_1) = 1.256, \quad u_2(\mathbf{x}_2) = 4.5$$

which are strictly greater than those associated with the equilibrium involving production.

Take now the allocation $\mathbf{x}_1'' = (1.2,\ 9.8), \mathbf{x}_2'' = (6.8,\ 2.2)$, which is feasible for the economy producing $\mathbf{y}' = (-7,7)$. The utilities associated with this allocation are:

$$u_1(\mathbf{x}_1'') = 11.4, \quad u_2(\mathbf{x}_2'') = 2.2$$

which Pareto dominate the first equilibrium allocation.

Therefore, no marginal pricing equilibrium is Pareto optimal.

Example 3.- [Vohra (1988b)]
Consider a private ownership economy with two goods, two consumers and a single non-convex firm, whose data are summarized as follows:

$$X_1 = \mathbb{R}_+^2, u_1(x_1) = x_{12}, \omega_1 = (0,10), \theta_1 = 1$$

$$X_2 = \mathbb{R}_+^2, u_2(x_2) = 4\log.x_{21} + x_{22}, \omega_2 = (20,0), \theta_2 = 0$$

$Y = \{\mathbf{y} \in \mathbb{R}^2 \mid y_1 \le 0; y_1 + y_2 \le 0 \text{ if } y_1 \ge -16 \text{ and } 10y_1 + y_2 + 144 \le 0 \text{ if } y_1 \le -16\}$

In view of u_1 we can take $p_2 = 1$. It can be shown that the only marginal pricing equilibrium of this economy corresponds to:

$$\mathbf{p}^* = (1,1), \mathbf{y}^* = (-16,16), \mathbf{x}_1^* = (0,10), \mathbf{x}_2^* = (4,16)$$

Let us think now of the situation corresponding to an average cost pricing equilibrium (see the next chapter for details). It can be checked that

$$\mathbf{p}' = (2,1), \mathbf{y}' = (-18,36), \mathbf{x}_1' = (0,10), \mathbf{x}_2' = (2,36)$$

is an average cost pricing equilibrium. Notice that the first consumer's utility is the same as in the marginal pricing equilibrium $(u_1' = 10)$, while the second consumer is now better-off (since $u_2' = 4\log.2 + 36$ is greater than $u_2^* = 4\log.4 + 16$).

The analysis developed so far points out that there are two factors which can be considered "responsible" of this asymmetry between the validity of the second welfare theorem and the failure of the first one:

(i) There may well be a wrong number of active firms in a marginal pricing equilibrium: decentralization with increasing returns may result in production inefficiency.

(ii) There are single-firm economies for which the rules of income distribution are inherently incompatible with efficiency. The reason is that, contrary to the convex case, the mapping associating efficient allocations to income distributions is *not onto*. Thus, for fixed income distribution schemes, we can find non-convex economies such that the agents' characteristics (technology and preferences) are such that marginal pricing generates an income distribution which has an empty intersection with the subset of efficient income distributions. Examples 2 and 3 show this feature. The third one also indicates that there may be better alternatives than marginal pricing in specific contexts where Pareto optimality fails.

A natural question is then whether there is some possibility of obtaining efficiency in the case of fixed distribution rules which are supplemented by some limited transfers, in he case of single-firm economies. Vohra's (1990),(1991) papers address this point, by considering the case where transfers can only be used in order to finance the possible losses of nonconvex firms, and not for redistribution purposes. Thus these transfers will be taxes if nonconvex firms have losses, and subsidies otherwise, so that "no consumer is subsidized if some other consumer is taxed". This idea corresponds to the notion of a hook-up system, so that the question can be formulated as follows: Can we find hook-up systems, depending on each specific economy, so that the associated two-part marginal pricing equilibrium be efficient?

The following example, tells us the bad news: The answer is no in general.

Example 4.- [Vohra (1990, Example 4.1)[1]]
Consider a private ownership economy with 3 commodities, 2 consumers and 2 firms, whose data are summarized as follows:

$$X_1 = X_2 = \mathbb{R}^3_+; \omega_1 = \omega_2 = (20, 0, 0); \theta_{11} = 0, \theta_{21} = 1$$

$$u_1(\mathbf{x}_1) = \begin{cases} 0.5x_{11} + x_{12} + x_{13} & \text{if } x_{12} + x_{13} \leq 12 \\ 0.5x_{11} + 12 & \text{otherwise} \end{cases}$$

---

[1]This is a mere reproduction of Vohra's example. Helpful drawings of the situation involved can be found in Vohra's paper.

$$u_2(\mathbf{x}_2) \;=\; \begin{cases} 3x_{21} + x_{22} + x_{23} & \text{if } x_{21} \le 19.5 \\ 58.5 + x_{22} + x_{23} & \text{otherwise} \end{cases}$$

$$Y_1 = \begin{cases} \{y_1 \in \mathbb{R}^3 / y_{11} \le 0;\, 1.5y_{13} + y_{12} \le 0\} & \text{if } y_{11} \ge -4 \\ \{y_1 \in \mathbb{R}^3 / y_{11} \le 0;\, y_{13} + y_{12} - 2 \le 0\} & \text{otherwise} \end{cases}$$

$$Y_2 = \begin{cases} \{y_2 \in \mathbb{R}^3 / y_{21} \le 0,\, y_{22} \le 0,\, y_{23} \le 0\} & \text{if } y_{21} \ge -5 \\ \{y_2 \in \mathbb{R}^3 / y_{21} \le 0,\, y_{22} \le 0,\, 2y_{23} + 10 \le 0\} & \text{otherwise} \end{cases}$$

Since commodities 2 and 3 are perfect substitutes in consumption, efficiency requires that only firm 1 is active when producing low levels of aggregate output, and only firm 2 be used for producing high levels. In particular, efficiency demands that either

(a) $y_{23} = 0$ and $y_{12} \le 14$; or

(b) $y_{12} = 0$ and $y_{23} \ge 14$.

Suppose first that we are in case (a). We can take $p_2 = 1$ (in view of consumer's 2 preferences). From technology, it follows that marginal pricing implies for firm 1 that $p_1 \ge 1$. Since firm 2 is not active, there are no losses, and hence consumer's 1 income is greater or equal than 20. As $y_{23} = 0$, it follows that consumer 1 will consume at least 12 units of commodity 2. Thus in equilibrium, $y_{12} \ge 12$. Given the technology of firm 1, this implies that in equilibrium, $p_1 = 1$ and $y_{12} = 12$. Since $y_{12} > 6$, the profit of firm 1 is 2 and consumer's 2 income is 22. This implies that $x_{22} = 2.5$. Thus $y_{12} = 14.5 > 14$ which is a contradiction.

Take now case (b). We can let $p_3 = 1$. Since $y_{23} > 0$ the marginal pricing rule implies that $p_1 = 2$. The total loss of the firm is 10 and $q_1 + q_2 = 10$. We know that $x_{13} \le 12$. Consumer 2 will consume 19.5 units of commodity 1 since $(20, 0, 0)$ is feasible. Any remaining income is spent in commodity 3. Since income cannot be greater than 40, and 19.5 units of commodity 1 cost $39, x_{23} \le 1$. Thus, $x_{13} + x_{23} \le 13$, and $y_{23} \le 13$, a contradiction.

Example 4 shows that the partial equilibrium intuition about the efficiency of two-part marginal pricing equilibrium actually fails. Note that we have not imposed any specific structure on the hook-up system, that is, for the economy in the example, there is no way of achieving efficient outcomes by means of two-part marginal pricing equilibrium. Again the same conclusion follows: There is no general way of ensuring Pareto optimality by instructing non-convex firms to follow marginal pricing, if we are not ready to perform an explicit redistribution policy.

Remark 7.3.- This result also points out that the second welfare theorem does not ensure that efficient allocations can be decentralized as two-part marginal pricing equilibria. It turns out that the "willingness to pay" condition (see section 5.4), is necessary and sufficient for the decentralizability of efficient allocations as two-part marginal equilibria. On this see Vohra (1990), Quinzii (1992,Ch.3) and Brown, Heller & Starr (1992).

7.3 THE CORE

The idea behind the core is that of social stability: if an allocation is in the core of an economy, there is no group of agents who can do better on their own. Let us present more formally this notion.

Let an economy $E = \{(X_i, u_i), (Y_j), \omega\}$, and call $\mathcal{M}$ the set of indices identifying the m consumers (i.e., $\mathcal{M} = \{1, 2, \ldots, m\}$). A subset of $\mathcal{M}$ is called a **coalition**. Let $[(\mathbf{x}_i'), \mathbf{y}'] \in \prod_{i=1}^{m} X_i \times \sum_{j=1}^{n} Y_j$ be a given allocation (in which production plans are taken in aggregate), and denote by $[(\mathbf{x}_i), \mathbf{y}]^S \in \prod_{i \in S} X_i \times \sum_{j=1}^{n} Y_j$ an allocation relative to a coalition $S \subset \mathcal{M}$. We say that a coalition S can *improve upon* the allocation $[(\mathbf{x}_i'), \mathbf{y}']$, if there exists an allocation $[(\mathbf{x}_i), \mathbf{y}]^S$ relative to the coalition S, such that:

a) $\sum_{i \in S} \mathbf{x}_i \leq \sum_{i \in S} \omega_i + \mathbf{y}$.

b) $u_i(\mathbf{x}_i) \geq u_i(\mathbf{x}_i')$ for all $i \in S$, and $u_h(\mathbf{x}_h) > u_h(\mathbf{x}_h')$ for some $h \in S$.

That is, a coalition can improve upon an allocation if there is another allocation which is feasible for that coalition [condition a)], and their members are better-off [condition b)].

Definition 7.2.-

The **Core** of an economy $E = \{(X_i, u_i), (Y_j), \omega\}$ is the set of feasible allocations which cannot be improved upon by any coalition.

Observe that if an allocation is in the core, then it is Pareto optimal. Note also that no reference to prices or markets appears in the definition of the core.

At first glance, one would expect that the presence of increasing returns may facilitate the nonemptyness of the core: bigger coalitions are more likely to get higher productivity. This intuition, however, is far from reality. Scarf (1986) (a paper written in 1963) provides the following result [see the proof in Quinzii (1992, Th. 6.2)]:

Theorem 7.2.-

Let Y be a closed subset of $\mathbb{R}^\ell$ (to be interpreted as the aggregate production set), such that $0 \in Y, Y - \mathbb{R}^\ell_+ \subset Y$, and $\{\omega\} + Y$ is bounded from above, for all $\omega \in \mathbb{R}^\ell$. Consider the class of economies:

$$E(Y) \equiv \{[(X_i, u_i, \omega_i), Y]\}$$

where, for each i=1,2,...,m: **(a)** $X_i = \mathbb{R}^\ell_+$; **(b)** $u_i : X_i \to \mathbb{R}$ is a continuous and quasi-concave function, which satisfies local non-satiation; and **(c)** $\omega_i >> 0$. Then, each economy in $E(Y)$ has a nonempty core if and only if Y is a convex cone.

This result says that, with the degree of generality given by the assumptions of the theorem, we can always construct economies with increasing returns and empty cores. Hence, the difficulties between increasing returns and efficiency are somehow more substantial than the way of pricing commodities.

In spite of this discouraging result, Scarf (1986) also identifies a particular family of economies with nonempty cores. Chapter 9 takes up Scarf's approach.

7.4   FINAL COMMENTS

In a remarkable paper, Guesnerie (1975) showed that marginal pricing is a necessary condition for optimality. He did that by extending the second welfare theorem to economies with non-convex production sets, and using the Dubovickii-Miljutin cones of interior displacements as the main tool to extend the notion of marginal pricing to non-smooth, non-convex sets. After Cornet's introduction of the Clarke normal cones for this type of analysis, Khan & Vohra (1987) extended this result to economies with public goods, and Bonnisseau & Cornet (1988b) to economies with an infinite dimensional commodity space [see also Cornet (1986)]. Vohra (1991) and Quinzii (1992, Ch. 2) provide elegant and easy proofs of this result.

The failure of Marginal Pricing equilibria to achieve Pareto optimality was also shown in Guesnerie (1975) (he gave the first example of an economy in which *all* marginal pricing equilibria were inefficient). Additional examples of this phenomenon appeared in Brown & Heal (1979). Beato & Mas-Colell (1983) provided a first example in which marginal pricing equilibria were not in the set of efficient aggregate productions. Vohra (1988b), (1990) develops a systematic analysis of the inefficiency of marginal pricing for fixed rules of income distribution, and of the inefficiency of two-part tariffs, respectively. An excellent exposition of the efficiency problems in this context appears in Vohra (1991). Brown, Heller & Starr (1992) prove that efficient allocations can be decentralized as two-part marginal equilibria, provided there is sufficient willingness to pay.

Some positive results are available for the case of a single non-convex firm. Brown & Heal (1983) showed that assuming homothetic preferences (which implies that Scitovsky's community indifference curves do not intersect), there exists at least a Pareto optimal marginal pricing equilibrium. Sufficient conditions for the optimality of marginal pricing in a more general context are analyzed in Dierker (1986) and Quinzii (1991). These conditions refer to the relative curvature of the production frontier and of the community indifference curves, so that when the social indifference curve is tangent to the feasible set it never cuts inside it. See also the special cases analyzed in Vohra (1991). See Quinzii (1992) for an exposition of these results. Vohra (1990) shows that when there are two goods, and a single nonconvex firm (whose nonconvexity derives from the existence of set-up costs), two-part marginal pricing are efficient. Edlin & Epelbaum (1993) present a model with many firms and efficient two-part marginal pricing equilibrium.

On the validity of the two welfare theorems in economies with nonconvex production sets, see the illuminating discussions in Guesnerie (1990), Vohra (1991) and Quinzii (1992 Chs. 1 - 4).

An excellent and very detailed discussion of the nonemptyness of the core of an economy with nonconvex technologies can be found in Quinzii (1992, Ch.6). Sharkey's (1989) survey is also highly recommended. Besides Scarf's (1986) paper, it is worth mentioning the contributions of Sharkey (1979) (for the case of a single input), Quinzii (1982), Ichiischi & Quinzii (1983) (dispensing with the requirement of "inputs which are not consumed"), and Reichert (1986) (who uses a nonlinear single-production input-output model, to allow for the presence of many nonconvex firms).

Part III

LOSS-FREE PRICING RULES AND PRIVATE OWNERSHIP MARKET ECONOMIES

By "loss-free" we refer to that family of pricing rules in which firms' equilibrium profits are nonnegative. This family covers most of the ways of modelling the behaviour of non-convex firms in a context of unregulated markets (but also those regulation policies satisfying a break-even constraint, as two-part marginal pricing). We shall concentrate here on private ownership market economies, that is, economies in which both initial endowments and firms belong to the consumers, and there is no regulation policy.

It is worth pointing out from the very beginning that there are few existence results for positive models with increasing returns which are both general and interesting. One may well consider that monopolistic (or oligopolistic) competition arises as a natural framework to deal with non-convex firms: if there are increasing returns to scale firms will not be negligible and thus will not behave as price-takers. Alas, the possibility of extending partial equilibrium results to a general equilibrium framework, in the realm of imperfect competition, faces enormous difficulties even with convex production sets. To make it precise: there is still no satisfactory answer to the basic positive problem of general equilibrium with increasing returns: how to model the strategic interaction among firms with market power.

Chapter 8 presents some general results about loss-free pricing rules, and focuses on the case of profit maximization. It will be shown that, when production sets are convex (or when nonconvexities are due to external economies), we can recover the standard result about the existence of competitive equilibrium, as a corollary of theorem 4.1. Chapter 9 deals with the analysis of constrained profit maximization: the case in which firms maximize profits at given prices, subject to quantity restrictions (both input and output constraints). The compatibility between constrained profit maximization and average cost-pricing, via the notion of distributive production sets, will also be discussed. Finally, chapter 10 presents a positive model with increasing returns in which consumers create firms (by supplying the required inputs) in those sectors of the economy with the highest profitability. An equilibrium is defined as a situation in which supply equals demand and all firms are equally profitable.

Chapter 8

BASIC RESULTS

8.1 GENERALITIES

Loss-free is a family of pricing rules in which firms' admissible profits are always nonnegative. The discussion of these pricing rules is carried out focusing on the case of *private ownership market* economies.

A **private ownership** economy is one in which consumers own the initial endowments and firms. Thus every consumer is now characterized by a collection

$$[X_i, u_i, \omega_i, (\theta_{ij})]$$

where X_i, u_i stand for the *ith* consumer's consumption set and utility function, respectively, ω_i is a point in $\mathbb{R}^\ell$ which describes her initial endowments (with $\sum_{i=1}^m \omega_i = \omega$), and θ_{ij} denotes the *ith* consumer's participation in the *jth* firm (with $\sum_{i=1}^m \theta_{ij} = 1$, for all j). The *ith* consumer's share in the *jth* firm is to be interpreted as an entitlement to a share θ_{ij} of the *jth* firm's profits.

In a **market economy** with private ownership (that is, when there is no intervention of the public sector, apart from ensuring property rights), the *ith* consumer's wealth mapping is given by:

$$r_i(\mathbf{p}, \tilde{\mathbf{y}}) = \mathbf{p}\omega_i + \sum_{j=1}^n \theta_{ij}\mathbf{p}\mathbf{y}_j$$

that is, the *ith* consumer's wealth, relative to a pair $(\mathbf{p}, \tilde{\mathbf{y}}) \in \mathbb{P} \times \mathbb{F}$, consists of the value of her initial endowments plus the sum of her shares in the profits. Observe that r_i is continuous in $(\mathbf{p}, \tilde{\mathbf{y}})$, and that total wealth equals the aggregate worth of initial endowments plus total profits.

Let us start by formally introducing the family of loss-free pricing rules:

Definition 8.1.-

$\phi_j : \mathbb{P} \times \mathbb{F} \to \mathbb{P}$ is a **Loss-Free Pricing Rule**, if for each $(\mathbf{p}, \tilde{\mathbf{y}})$ in $\mathbb{P} \times \mathbb{F}$, all $\mathbf{q}$ in $\phi_j(\mathbf{p}, \tilde{\mathbf{y}})$, we have: $\mathbf{q}\mathbf{y}_j \geq 0$.

Thus, a firm is said to follow a loss-free pricing rule whenever it does not find "acceptable" any prices-production combination yielding negative profits.

Consider now the following assumptions, which specialize the model of chapter 4:

A.8.1.- For each $i = 1, 2, \ldots, m$:

(a) X_i is a closed and convex subset of $\mathbb{R}^\ell$, bounded from below.

(b) $u_i : X_i \to \mathbb{R}$ is a continuous and quasi-concave function, which satisfies local non-satiation.

(c) $\omega_i \in X_i$ and there exists $\mathbf{x}_i^o \in X_i$ such that $\mathbf{x}_i^o << \omega_i$.

A.8.2.- For each firm $j = 1, 2, \ldots, n$:

(i) Y_j is a closed subset of $\mathbb{R}^\ell$, with $\mathbf{0} \in Y_j$.

(ii) $Y_j - \mathbb{R}_+^\ell \subset Y_j$.

(iii) For every $\omega' \geq \omega$, the set $A(\omega')$ is bounded.

Assumption (A.8.1) differs from (A.4.1) in that we have introduced the requirements $\omega_i \in X_i$ (i.e., the ith consumer can always survive by eating up her endowments), and $\mathbf{x}_i^o << \omega_i$ for some $\mathbf{x}_i^o \in X_i$. This is a strengthening of the survival assumption which ensures the continuity of the budget set whenever profits are nonnegative. In particular, in the case of a private ownership market economy in which firms follow loss-free pricing rules, it follows that $r_i(\mathbf{p}, \tilde{\mathbf{y}}) > b_i(\mathbf{p})$ over the set of production equilibria.

Assumption (A.8.2) differs from (A.4.2) in that it postulates the feasibility of inaction (i.e., $\mathbf{0} \in Y_j$ for all j). This permits firms to close down when market conditions get bad, so that nonnegative profits can always be guaranteed in equilibrium.

The following result turns out to be an immediate consequence of theorem 4.1:

Proposition 8.1.-

Let E stand for a private ownership market economy satisfying assumptions (A.8.1) and (A.8.2). An Equilibrium exists when firms follow regular and loss-free pricing rules.

Proof.-

First note that assumption (A.4.4) is automatically satisfied, because r_i is continuous on $(\mathbf{p},\tilde{\mathbf{y}})$ and (c) of (A.8.1) directly implies that $r_i(\mathbf{p},\tilde{\mathbf{y}}) > b_i(\mathbf{p})$ over the set of production equilibria.

Let us show now that (A.4.5) also holds[1]. For suppose $r_i(\mathbf{p},\tilde{\mathbf{y}}) < b_i(\mathbf{p})$ for some i, some $\tilde{\mathbf{y}} \in \mathbb{F} \cap K_+^n$. That means that there is some firm j for which $\mathbf{p}\mathbf{y}_j < 0$. This along with the fact that ϕ_j is a loss-free pricing rule, means that for all $\mathbf{q}_j$ in $\phi_j(\mathbf{p},\tilde{\mathbf{y}})$ one has $(\mathbf{q}_j - \mathbf{p})\mathbf{y}_j > 0$. Since $\mathbf{q}_j$ and $\mathbf{p}$ are points in the unit simplex, it follows that $(\mathbf{q}_j - \mathbf{p})k\mathbf{e} = \mathbf{0}$, and we get $(\mathbf{q}_j - \mathbf{p})(\mathbf{y}_j - k\mathbf{e}) > 0$. Certainly, for all $h = 1, 2, ..., l$, $\mathbf{y}_{jh} \geq -k$. But this must imply that there exists a commodity h such that $\mathbf{y}_{jh} > -k$ and $q_{jh} > p_h$. Since this holds for all $\mathbf{q}_j \in \phi_j(\mathbf{p},\tilde{\mathbf{y}})$, it completes the proof that (A.4.5) is satisfied.

Now theorem 4.1 gives us the desired result.♠

Thus, in the context of private ownership market economies which satisfy (A.8.1) and (A.8.2), loss-free pricing rules constitute a special case in which the *wealth structure is always compatible with firms' behaviour*. Note that, since equilibrium profits are always nonnegative, equilibrium allocations always satisfy: $u_i(\mathbf{x}_i^*) \geq u_i(\omega_i) \ \forall i$.

We shall now consider two prominent examples of regular and loss-free pricing rules: *Profit Maximization* and *Average Cost Pricing*.

8.2 COMPETITIVE EQUILIBRIUM

The standard notion of competition identifies competitive behaviour with profit maximization at given prices. This amounts to saying that, with the only restriction of trading at market prices, firms can buy inputs and sell outputs at will. Therefore, the *jth* firm's choice set can be identified with its production set, since the firm does not experience any quantity constraint.

The story which justifies this way of modelling competition is that each firm is individually "insignificant" (negligible) with respect to the size of the market, so that it cannot affect market prices by its individual policy. This of course is not really true as far as the number of firms is finite, but let us take it as an approximate truth (indeed in a competitive equilibrium firms will be selling and buying whatever amounts they decide, so that this "competitive conjecture" is actually fulfilled).

---

[1] Borrowed from Vohra (1988b, Corollary 1)

This implicitly rules out the presence of technologies with increasing returns to scale (otherwise firms would increase indefinitely their scale of operations whenever profits were positive). With this motivation (although with wider implications), let us consider the following assumption:

<u>A.8.2*.-</u> For every $j = 1, 2, \ldots, n$:
   (i), (ii) and (iii) as in (A.8.2).
   (iv) Y_j is a convex set.

The inclusion of (iv) in (A.8.2) excludes the presence of increasing returns. In particular, it discards the presence of "fixed costs" or indivisible commodities.

The usual formulation of competitive firms' behaviour [e.g. Debreu (1959, ch.3)] is as follows: $\mathbf{y}'_j$ is said to be an *equilibrium production plan* for the *jth* firm, at prices $\mathbf{p}$, if:

$$\mathbf{p}\mathbf{y}'_j \geq \mathbf{p}\mathbf{y}_j, \quad \forall \mathbf{y}_j \in Y_j$$

Then, one defines the jth firm's supply correspondence as a mapping $\eta_j :\to Y_j$ given by:

$$\eta_j(\mathbf{p}) \equiv \{\mathbf{y}'_j \in Y_j \ / \ \mathbf{p}\mathbf{y}'_j \geq \mathbf{p}\mathbf{y}_j \ \forall \mathbf{y}_j \in Y_j\}$$

(which need not be defined for every $\mathbf{p}$ in $\mathbb{P}$). Notice that, according to proposition 3.1, this implies that competitive firms will always select efficient production plans. It is easy to see that $\eta_j(\mathbf{p})$ is closed and convex valued for all $\mathbf{p}$. As $\mathbf{p}\mathbf{y}_j$ is a continuous mapping, it follows from the Maximum Theorem (Lemma 2.1) that η_j is an upper hemicontinuous correspondence over any compact subset of Y_j.

Let us now proceed to formally model the behaviour of competitive firms according to the pricing rule approach. When Y_j is a convex set, this can be done as follows:

<u>Definition 8.2.-</u>
The **Profit Maximization** pricing rule for the *jth* firm is a mapping $\phi_j^{PM} : \mathbb{F}_j \to \mathbb{P}$, given by:

$$\phi_j^{PM}(\mathbf{y}_j) \equiv \{\mathbf{q} \in \mathbb{P} \mid \mathbf{q}\mathbf{y}_j \geq \mathbf{q}\mathbf{y}'_j, \forall \mathbf{y}'_j \in Y_j\}$$

This pricing rule associates with every efficient production plan, the set of prices which support it as the most profitable one (that is, in this case

ϕ_j coincides with the *inverse supply mapping*). Figure 8.1 illustrates this pricing rule.

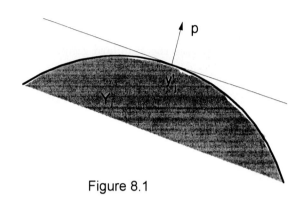

Figure 8.1

The following result tells us the main properties of this pricing rule:

Proposition 8.2.-
     Under assumption (A.8.2*) ϕ_j^{PM} is a regular and loss-free pricing rule.
     Proof.-
     Since Y_j is convex, we can define ϕ_j^{PM} as $\mathbb{N}_Y(\mathbf{y}_j) \cap \mathbb{P}$, where $\mathbb{N}_Y(\mathbf{y}_j)$ is the normal cone of Y_j at $\mathbf{y}_j$ (see proposition 5.3). Therefore, it follows from Theorem 5.1 that ϕ_j^{PM} is a regular pricing rule. Moreover, as $\mathbf{0} \in Y_j$, it cannot be the case that, for some $\mathbf{y}_j \in \mathbb{F}_j$, one has: $\mathbf{q} \in \phi_j^{PM}(\mathbf{y}_j)$ and $\mathbf{qy}_j < 0$.♠

     Consider now the following definition:

Definition 8.3.-
     A **competitive equilibrium** is an equilibrium for a private ownership market economy in which firms follow the profit maximization pricing rule.

     The following result is obtained as an immediate consequence of propositions 8.1 and 8.2:

Corollary 8.1.-

Let E be a private ownership market economy satisfying assumptions (A.8.1) and (A.8.2*). Then, a competitive equilibrium exists.

This result is relevant because it ensures that the model developed in chapter 4 actually encompasses the standard general equilibrium model of a competitive economy.

Remark 8.1.- It can be shown that, under assumption (A.8.2*), the aggregate production set $Y \equiv \sum_{j=1}^{n} Y_j$, satisfies the following properties: (a) Y is closed[2] ; (b) $-\mathbb{R}_+^\ell \subset Y$; (c) Y is convex. See also Section 3.3 for a discussion of (iii) in (A.8.2).

In order to show that competitive equilibria are Pareto efficient, let us prove first a simple result which says that aggregate profits are maximized at prices $\mathbf{p}^*$ if all individual firms are maximizing profits at $\mathbf{p}^*$.

Lemma 8.1.-

Let $\mathbf{Y} \equiv \sum_{j=1}^{n} Y_j$, and call $\mathbf{y}$ to a typical element of $\mathbf{Y}$ (that is, $\mathbf{y} = \sum_{j=1}^{n} \mathbf{y}_j$, for $\mathbf{y}_j \in Y_j$ for all j). Then, $\mathbf{p}^* \in \bigcap_{j=1}^{n} \phi_j^{PM}(\mathbf{y}_j^*)$ if and only if $\mathbf{p}^*\mathbf{y}^* \geq \mathbf{p}^*\mathbf{y}$, for all $\mathbf{y} \in \mathbf{Y}$.

Proof.-

(i) It follows trivially from the definition that $\mathbf{p}^* \in \bigcap_{j=1}^{n} \phi_j^{PM}(\mathbf{y}_j^*)$ implies that $\mathbf{p}^*\mathbf{y}^* \geq \mathbf{p}^*\mathbf{y}$, for all $\mathbf{y} \in \mathbf{Y}$.

(ii) Suppose now that $\mathbf{p}^*\mathbf{y}^* \geq \mathbf{p}^*\mathbf{y}$ for all $\mathbf{y} \in \mathbf{Y}$, but $\mathbf{p}^*$ is not a point in $\bigcap_{j=1}^{n} \phi_j^{PM}(\mathbf{y}_j^*)$. Thus we can find some $\mathbf{y}_k' \in Y_k$ such that $\mathbf{p}^*\mathbf{y}_k' > \mathbf{p}^*\mathbf{y}_k^*$, for some k. But then substituting $\mathbf{y}_k^*$ by $\mathbf{y}_k'$ in the aggregate vector $\mathbf{y}^*$ we would get:

$$\mathbf{p}^* \left(\sum_{j \neq k} \mathbf{y}_j^* + \mathbf{y}_k' \right) > \mathbf{p}^*\mathbf{y}^*$$

with $\left(\sum_{j \neq k} \mathbf{y}_j^* + \mathbf{y}_k' \right) \in \mathbf{Y}$, against the assumption. ♠

Observe that the result is very general, but that it becomes operational only when production sets are convex (because in this case $\phi_j^{PM}(\mathbf{y}_j)$ is well

---

[2]This is a difficult outcome having to do with the properties of asymptotic cones, that will not be discussed here.

defined).

Proposition 8.3.-
Let E be a private ownership market economy in which every consumer has a continuous and locally non-satiated utility function. And let $(\mathbf{p}^*, [(\mathbf{x}_i^*), \tilde{\mathbf{y}}^*])$ be a competitive equilibrium. Then the allocation $[(\mathbf{x}_i^*), \tilde{\mathbf{y}}^*]$ is Pareto efficient.
Proof.-
Suppose that this is not true, that is, there exists a feasible allocation $[(\mathbf{x}_i'), \tilde{\mathbf{y}}']$ such that:

$$u_i(\mathbf{x}_i^*) \geq u_i(\mathbf{x}_i^*), \forall i, \quad \& \quad u_k(\mathbf{x}_k') > u_k(\mathbf{x}_k^*), \text{ some } k.$$

According to proposition 2.5, that implies $\mathbf{p}^* \mathbf{x}_i' \geq \mathbf{p}^* \mathbf{x}_i^*$ for all i, with $\mathbf{p}^* \mathbf{x}_k' > \mathbf{p}^* \mathbf{x}_k^*$ for those consumers with $u_k(\mathbf{x}_k') > u_k(\mathbf{x}_k^*)$. It then follows that $\mathbf{p}^* \sum_{i=1}^m \mathbf{x}_i' > \mathbf{p}^* \sum_{i=1}^m \mathbf{x}_i^*$. As $\mathbf{p}^* \mathbf{x}_i^* = \mathbf{p}^* \omega_i + \sum_{j=1}^m \theta_{ij} \mathbf{p}^* \mathbf{y}_j^*$, this in turn implies:

$$\mathbf{p}^* \mathbf{x}' > \mathbf{p}^* \omega + \mathbf{p}^* \mathbf{y}^*$$

Moreover, $\sum_{j=1}^n \mathbf{y}_j' \geq \sum_{i=1}^m \mathbf{x}_i' - \omega$, because $[(\mathbf{x}_i'), \tilde{\mathbf{y}}']$ is a feasible allocation. Hence,

$$\mathbf{p}^* \sum_{j=1}^n \mathbf{y}_j' \geq \mathbf{p}^*(\sum_{i=1}^m \mathbf{x}_i' - \omega) > \mathbf{p}^* \sum_{j=1}^n \mathbf{y}_j^*$$

But this contradicts the assumption that $(\mathbf{p}^*, [(\mathbf{x}_i^*), \tilde{\mathbf{y}}^*])$ is a competitive equilibrium, according to lemma 8.1. ♠

Observe that this result ensures that competitive equilibria are Pareto optimal (but not that a competitive equilibrium exists).

As for the second welfare theorem, it is an immediate application of theorem 7.1 that any Pareto efficient allocation can be decentralized as a competitive equilibrium.

Let us conclude this section by considering the case of Profit Maximization, when there may be *nonconvexities due to external effects in production* [an idea first introduced by Marshall (1890)].
Let $Y_j(\tilde{\mathbf{y}})$ denote the production set of the jth firm, when all other firms' production plans are described by the vector

$$\tilde{\mathbf{y}}_{-j} = (\mathbf{y}_1, \ldots, \mathbf{y}_{j-1}, \mathbf{y}_{j+1}, \ldots, \mathbf{y}_n)$$

When $Y_j(\tilde{\mathbf{y}})$ is a convex set for all $\tilde{\mathbf{y}}$, *Profit Maximization* can be defined in terms of a pricing rule $\psi_j^{PM} : \mathbb{F} \to \mathbb{P}$, given by:

$$\psi_j^{PM}(\tilde{\mathbf{y}}) \equiv \{\mathbf{q} \in \mathbb{P} \ / \ \mathbf{q}\mathbf{y}_j \geq \mathbf{q}\mathbf{y}_j', \forall \mathbf{y}_j' \in Y_j(\tilde{\mathbf{y}})\}$$

If $Y_j(\tilde{\mathbf{y}})$ satisfies (A.8.2*) for all $\tilde{\mathbf{y}}$, this is obviously a *loss-free* pricing rule (since $\mathbf{0} \in Y_j(\tilde{\mathbf{y}})$ for each j). It can be shown that ψ_j^{PM} is *regular*, when Y_j varies continuously with $\tilde{\mathbf{y}}$. Thus,

Corollary 8.2.-
  Let E be an economy satisfying assumptions (A.8.1) and (A.8.2), and suppose that, for each $\tilde{\mathbf{y}} \in \mathbb{F}$, all j, $\mathbf{Y}_j(\tilde{\mathbf{y}})$ is a continuous correspondence, with closed and convex values, and such that $\mathbf{0} \in \mathbf{Y}_j(\tilde{\mathbf{y}})$ and $-\mathbb{R}_+^\ell \subset \mathbf{Y}_j(\tilde{\mathbf{y}})$. Then a competitive equilibrium does exist.

The reader should understand that the optimality result in proposition 8.3 does not apply to this more general context: individual maximization and global maximization are not equivalent any more.

8.3   AVERAGE COST PRICING

Average cost-pricing is a pricing rule with a long tradition in economics, both in positive and normative analysis. It is associated with some regulation policies under a break even constraint (e.g. Boiteaux-Ramsey or two-part marginal pricing), and it is the basic idea behind mark-up pricing models.
  The next definition formalizes this pricing rule:

Definition 8.4.-
  The **Average Cost Pricing Rule** can be formulated as a mapping ϕ_j^{AC} from $\mathbb{F}_j$ into $\mathbb{P}$ which is given by:
  (a) If $\mathbf{y}_j \neq \mathbf{0}$
$$\phi_j^{AC}(\mathbf{y}_j) \equiv \{\mathbf{q} \in \mathbb{P} \ / \ \mathbf{q}\mathbf{y}_j = 0\}$$
  (b) $\phi_j^{AC}(\mathbf{0})$ is the closed convex hull of the following set:

$$\{\mathbf{q} \in \mathbb{P} \ / \ \exists \{\mathbf{q}^\nu, \mathbf{y}_j^\nu\} \subset \mathbb{P} \times [\mathbb{F}_j \backslash \mathbf{0}], \text{ such that,}$$

$$\{\mathbf{q}^\nu, \mathbf{y}_j^\nu\} \to (\mathbf{q}, \mathbf{0}), \text{ with } \mathbf{q}^\nu \mathbf{y}_j^\nu = 0\}$$

Therefore, this rule associates with every efficient production plan for the *jth* firm, those prices yielding zero profits. Since this way of defining the average cost pricing rule places no restriction at the origin (i.e., for $\mathbf{y}_j = \mathbf{0}$, one would have $\phi_j^{AC}(\mathbf{0}) \equiv \mathbb{P}$), the definition has to be completed with part (b), in order to make non-vacuous the associated equilibrium concept. Indeed, if one admits $\phi_j^{AC}(\mathbf{0}) \equiv \mathbb{P}$, the fixpoint argument which gives us the existence of equilibrium might simply correspond to the pure exchange equilibrium [that is known to exist under assumption (A.8.1)]. In order to prevent this trivial equilibrium, part (b) of the definition requires taking $\phi_j(\mathbf{0})$ as the closed convex hull of the limit points of those prices associated to sequences of points $\mathbf{y}_j \neq \mathbf{0}$ which converge to zero.

The next figure gives us an illustration of this pricing rule.

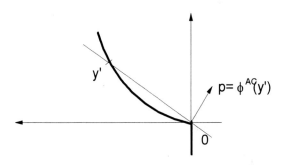

Figure 8.2

Under assumption (A.8.2), ϕ_j^{AC} is a loss-free and regular pricing rule (the upper hemicontinuity is left as an exercise). Hence, proposition 8.1 provides an implicit existence result for those economies in which firms are instructed to obtain zero profits. Formally:

Proposition 8.4.-
Let E be an economy satisfying assumptions (A.8.1) and (A.8.2). Then an equilibrium relative to ϕ^{AC} (i.e., an Average Cost Pricing Equilibrium) does exist.

8.4   FINAL COMMENTS

There are two special cases in which nonconvexities are compatible, at least partially, with the standard competitive model. The first one is that in which increasing returns to scale are due to external economies, shortly discussed in section 8.3 [an idea, due to Marshall (1890) and much criticized by Sraffa (1920)]. The second one corresponds to the case in which nonconvexities are "small in relation to the size of the economy"; in this case one can still get an upper-hemicontinuous aggregate supply mapping. For a discussion of these cases see also Debreu (1954), Chipman (1970), Arrow & Hahn (1971, Ch.6), Mas-Colell (1987, Ch. VI).

Existence results for average cost pricing (or, more generally, mark-up pricing) abound. Apart from those presented above, let us recall here that Dierker, Guesnerie & Neuefeind (1985) prove the existence of equilibrium when firms follow several forms of average cost pricing. Böhm (1986) and Corchón (1988) develop models where firms set prices by adding a mark-up over average costs. Herrero & Villar (1988), and Villar (1991) provide average cost pricing models where the production side is formulated as a nonlinear Leontief (resp. a nonlinear von Neumann) model.

Chapter 9

CONSTRAINED PROFIT MAXIMIZATION

9.1 INTRODUCTION

The presence of increasing returns to scale is in most cases incompatible with the competitive behaviour of firms (i.e., profit maximization at given prices). Imperfect competition arises then as a natural framework to analyze market economies with increasing returns: the behaviour of individual firms may well have an impact on prices. Unfortunately, such an analysis is still pending in the context of a general equilibrium model of this type: the difficulties seem extraordinary even in the convex case.

An alternative way of modelling market economies with increasing returns is that in which firms maximize profits at given prices, subject to quantity constraints. This is the subject of this chapter. We consider here two different pricing rules which can be regarded as extensions of the profit maximization principle to nonconvex production sets. They correspond to profit maximization under quantity constraints, and will be referred to as input- and output-constrained profit maximization, respectively. The input-constrained profit maximization model is based in Scarf's (1986) work on the analysis of nonempty cores, while the output-constrained one adapts the ideas in Dehez & Drèze (1988a).

The models presented below differ from those in Scarf (1986) and Dehez & Drèze (1988a,b) in what follows. Input-constrained profit maximization is defined for an economy with many firms, without excluding the possibility that inputs on which constraints exist may be consumed. Scarf considers a single firm, and limiting inputs are not consumed. Output-constrained profit maximization is defined with respect to a fixed subset of those commodities which can appear as outputs. This, contrary to the model of Dehez & Drèze, requires introducing an assumption of "convex sections".

The type of formulation used in this chapter tries to emphasize the symmetry between both kind of models.

9.2   INPUT-CONSTRAINED PROFIT MAXIMIZATION

Consider a private ownership market economy as that in chapter 8, made of m consumers, n firms and ℓ commodities. The key difference is that now there is a group of commodities that can be identified *a priori* as inputs to production. The following assumption, used throughout sections 9.2 and 9.3, makes this precise:

<u>A.9.0.-</u> Let $\mathcal{L} \equiv \{1, 2, \ldots, \ell\}$ stand for the set of commodity indices. For each $j = 1, 2, \ldots, n, \mathcal{L}$ can be partitioned into two disjoint subsets, I_j, I_j^c, so that, if $\mathbf{y}_j \in Y_j : t \in I_j \Rightarrow y_{jt} \leq 0$.

Assumption (A.9.0) says that, for each firm $j = 1, 2, \ldots, n$, we can distinguish a priori a group of commodities which defines the $j th$ firm's restrictions on the input side. Thus, we shall refer to goods in I_j as *limiting inputs* (or *factors*). The way of presenting this idea tries to emphasize that there is flexibility in the way of taking the partition. In particular, commodities in I_j^c can be both inputs and outputs.

Under (A.9.0) it is convenient to write production plans in the form: $\mathbf{y}_j = (\mathbf{a}_j, \mathbf{b}_j)$, with $\mathbf{a}_j \leq \mathbf{0}$, in the understanding that $\mathbf{a}_j$ is a point in the $j th$ firm's subspace of limiting inputs.

Consider now the following definition:

<u>Definition 9.1.-</u>

The **Input-Constrained Profit Maximization** pricing rule for the $j th$ firm, is a mapping $\phi_j^{IC} : \mathbb{F}_j \rightarrow \mathbb{P}$ given by:

$$\phi_j^{IC}(\mathbf{y}_j) \equiv \{\mathbf{q} \in \mathbb{P} \ / \ \mathbf{q}\mathbf{y}_j \geq \mathbf{q}\mathbf{y}_j', \forall \mathbf{y}_j' \in Y_j \text{ with } \mathbf{a}_j' \geq \mathbf{a}_j\}$$

Thus, ϕ_j^{IC} pictures the $j th$ firm as selecting, for each given efficient production plan $\mathbf{y}_j$, prices such that it is not possible to obtain higher profits within the set of production plans which make use of equal or fewer factors.

We may interpret this situation as a case in which the jth firm faces (variable) input constraints so that it chooses a profit maximizing production within its attainable set.

Without loss of generality, let $I_j = \{1, 2, \ldots, k\}$, for some integer $k < \ell$, and consider the following assumptions:

<u>A.9.1.-</u> For each $i = 1, 2, \ldots, m$:
    (a) X_i is a closed and convex subset of $\mathbb{R}^\ell$, bounded from below.
    (b) $u_i : X_i \to \mathbb{R}$ is a continuous and quasi-concave function, which satisfies local non-satiation.
    (c) $\omega_i \in X_i$ and there exists $\mathbf{x}_i^o \in X_i$ such that $\mathbf{x}_i^o \ll \omega_i$.

<u>A.9.2.-</u> For each firm $j = 1, 2, \ldots, n$:
    (i) Y_j is a closed subset of $\mathbb{R}^\ell$, with $\mathbf{0} \in Y_j$.
    (ii) $Y_j - \mathbb{R}_+^\ell \subset Y_j$.
    (iii) For every $\omega' \geq \omega$, the set $A(\omega')$ is bounded. In particular, $\mathbf{a}_j = \mathbf{0} \Rightarrow \mathbf{b}_j \leq \mathbf{0}$.

<u>A.9.3.-</u> For all $j = 1, 2, \ldots, n$, every $\mathbf{a}_j' \in -\mathbb{R}_+^k$ the set

$$B_j(\mathbf{a}_j') \equiv \{\mathbf{b}_j \in \mathbb{R}^{\ell-k} / (\mathbf{a}_j, \mathbf{b}_j) \in Y_j \text{ for some } \mathbf{a}_j \geq \mathbf{a}_j'\}$$

is convex.

Assumptions (A.9.1) and (A.9.2) are identical to (A.8.1) and (A.8.2) in chapter 8 except in that it is assumed that limiting inputs are necessary for production (i.e., $\mathbf{b}_j \leq \mathbf{0}$ whenever $\mathbf{a}_j = \mathbf{0}$). Assumption (A.9.3) says that, for any given vector of limiting inputs $\mathbf{a}_j'$, the projection on $\mathbb{R}^{\ell-k}$ of those production plans not using more limiting inputs than those in $\mathbf{a}_j'$ is a convex set. This suggests that we can think of these inputs as those elements of fixed capital which give raise to non-convexities. Observe that this assumption is compatible with the presence of firms with constant, increasing or decreasing returns to scale, set-up costs or S-shaped cost curves. Note that the bigger the cardinal of I_j the less restrictive this assumption becomes (in particular, if $k = \ell - 1$, as in non-linear input-output models, this is not a restriction, while $k = 0$ implies that Y_j is a convex set).

The following result tells us that this is a regular pricing rule, under the assumptions established:

Proposition 9.1.-

Under assumptions (A.9.2) and (A.9.3), ϕ_j^{IC} is a regular and loss-free pricing rule.

Proof.-

Under assumption (A.9.2), for every $\mathbf{y}_j' \in \mathbb{F}_j, \phi_j^{IC}(\mathbf{y}_j')$ is clearly convex. Let us show that it is nonempty. By (A.9.2) and (A.9.3) , $B_j(\mathbf{a}_j')$ is a convex and comprehensive set; hence, the standard separation argument ensures that there is a point $\mathbf{v} \in \mathbb{R}_+^{\ell-k}, \mathbf{v} \neq \mathbf{0}$, which supports $\mathbf{b}_j'$. Call λ to the inverse of $\sum_{h=k+1}^{\ell} v_h$. Then, any vector $\mathbf{q}$ in $\mathbb{P}$ such that $\mathbf{q} = (\mathbf{0}, \lambda \mathbf{v})$ will be in $\phi_j^{IC}(\mathbf{y}_j')$.

To see that the graph is closed, let $[(\mathbf{a}^o, \mathbf{b}^o), \mathbf{p}^o]$ be an arbitrary point in $\mathbb{F}_j \times \mathbb{P}$, and let $\{(\mathbf{a}^\nu, \mathbf{b}^\nu), \mathbf{p}^\nu\}$ be a sequence converging to $[(\mathbf{a}^o, \mathbf{b}^o), \mathbf{p}^o]$, such that $[(\mathbf{a}^\nu, \mathbf{b}^\nu), \mathbf{p}^\nu] \in \mathbb{F}_j \times \mathbb{P}$, and $\mathbf{p}^\nu$ belongs to $\phi_j^{IC}(\mathbf{a}^\nu, \mathbf{b}^\nu)$, for all ν. Suppose, by way of contradiction, that $\mathbf{p}^o$ is not in $\phi_j^{IC}(\mathbf{a}^o, \mathbf{b}^o)$. Then there exists $(\mathbf{a}', \mathbf{b}') \in Y_j$, with $\mathbf{a}' \geq \mathbf{a}^o$, such that $\mathbf{p}^o(\mathbf{a}', \mathbf{b}') > \mathbf{p}^o(\mathbf{a}^o, \mathbf{b}^o)$. This implies that, for ν big enough ($\nu > \nu'$, say), we also have:

$$\mathbf{p}^\nu(\mathbf{a}', \mathbf{b}') > \mathbf{p}^\nu(\mathbf{a}^\nu, \mathbf{b}^\nu)$$

If $\mathbf{a}' \geq \mathbf{a}^\nu$ and $\nu > \nu'$, this contradicts the assumption that $\mathbf{p}^\nu$ belongs to $\phi_j^{IC}(\mathbf{a}^\nu, \mathbf{b}^\nu)$. Suppose that this is not the case. We have now two possibilities. First, $\mathbf{a}^o = \mathbf{0}$, and consequently $\mathbf{a}' = \mathbf{0}$. Then it follows that $\mathbf{b}^o = \mathbf{0} \geq \mathbf{b}'$, and hence the inequality above cannot hold. Suppose then that $\mathbf{a}^o < \mathbf{0}$, and construct a new point $(\mathbf{a}", \mathbf{b}")$ in Y_j as follows:

(i) $\mathbf{a}_t^{''} = \mathbf{a}_t' + \varepsilon$, if $\mathbf{a}_t' < 0$ (where $\varepsilon > 0$ is a scalar arbitrarily small), and $\mathbf{a}_t^{''} = 0$, otherwise; and

(ii) $\mathbf{b}_t^{''} = \mathbf{b}_t' - \delta_t$ (where $\delta_t \geq 0$ is a scalar arbitrarily small).

Since Y_j is a closed and comprehensive set, these scalars can always be chosen so that $(\mathbf{a}", \mathbf{b}")$ lies in Y_j, and $\mathbf{p}^o(\mathbf{a}", \mathbf{b}") > \mathbf{p}^o(\mathbf{a}^o, \mathbf{b}^o)$. Note that, by construction, $\mathbf{a}" > \mathbf{a}' \geq \mathbf{a}^o$.

Now observe that for ν big enough, there will be points $(\mathbf{a}^\nu, \mathbf{b}^\nu)$ close to $(\mathbf{a}^o, \mathbf{b}^o)$ such that $\mathbf{a}" \geq \mathbf{a}^\nu$. For these points we have:

$$\mathbf{p}^\nu(\mathbf{a}^{''}, \mathbf{b}^{''}) > \mathbf{p}^\nu(\mathbf{a}^\nu, \mathbf{b}^\nu)$$

while $\mathbf{p}^\nu \in \phi_j^{IC}(\mathbf{a}^\nu, \mathbf{b}^\nu)$, contradicting the hypothesis.

Finally, since $\mathbf{0} \in Y_j, \mathbf{q}\mathbf{y}_j \geq 0$, for all $\mathbf{q} \in \phi_j^{IC}(\mathbf{y}_j)$.♠

The next result follows immediately from propositions 9.1 and 8.1:

Proposition 9.2.-

Let E be a private ownership market economy satisfying assumptions (A.9.0) to (A.9.3). Then, there is an equilibrium where firms follow input-constrained profit maximization.

This Equilibrium consists of a price vector and a feasible allocation (involving an allocation of limiting inputs) in which all agents are maximizing their payoff functions within their feasible sets. These feasible sets correspond to budget sets, for the case of consumers, and production sets subject to an input constraint, for the case of firms. Note that if all firms are convex, a standard competitive equilibrium is an input-constrained profit maximization equilibrium (although the converse may not be true).

Remark 9.1.- Observe that those input restrictions faced by firms refer to a fixed subset of commodities, which typically does not include all inputs (think of the case of labour). This implies that producing nothing will not generally be an equilibrium, so that the equilibrium concept is non-vacuous.

9.3 INPUT-DISTRIBUTIVE SETS

When production sets are convex cones (constant returns to scale), average cost pricing coincides with profit maximization. Yet in general average cost pricing may well be inconsistent with profit maximization (either constrained or unconstrained). This implies that average cost pricing is a loss-free and regular pricing rule whose associated equilibria may be difficult to sustain, because some firms may find it profitable to deviate from the equilibrium production plans. This may happen both for the case of convex and for the case of non-convex production sets. One may thus consider whether there exists some restriction on production sets that makes average cost pricing compatible with constrained profit maximization (this would extend the properties of convex cones to a more general setting).

Scarf (1986) introduces the notion of *input distributive sets* (he speaks of distributive sets), as a class of production sets with non-decreasing returns to scale for which the average cost and the input-constrained profit maximization pricing rules do intersect. Let us define the notion of input-distributive sets, in the understanding that assumption (A.9.0) holds:

<u>Definition 9.2.-</u>

A production set Y_j is said to be **input-distributive**, if for any collection of points $(\mathbf{y}^t, \lambda^t), t = 1, 2, \ldots, s$, with $\mathbf{y}^t = (\mathbf{a}^t, \mathbf{b}^t) \in Y_j, \lambda^t \in \mathbb{R}_+$, the following condition holds:

$$\sum_{h=1}^{s} \lambda^h \mathbf{a}^h \leq \mathbf{a}^t, t = 1, 2, \ldots, s \Rightarrow \sum_{h=1}^{s} \lambda^h \mathbf{y}^h \in Y_j$$

In words: A production set is input-distributive when any nonnegative weighted sum of feasible production plans is feasible, if it does not use fewer inputs than any of the original plans. From a geometrical standpoint, this amounts to saying that a straight line connecting any point $\mathbf{y}'_j$ in the boundary of Y_j with the origin, does not cut the interior of the set $\{\mathbf{y}_j \in Y_j / \mathbf{a}_j \geq \mathbf{a}'_j\}$. It can be seen that if a production set is distributive, then it exhibits non-decreasing returns to scale, and has convex iso-inputs sets [i.e., the set $B(\mathbf{a}_j) \equiv \{\mathbf{b}_j \in \mathbb{R}^{\ell-k} / (\mathbf{a}_j, \mathbf{b}_j) \in Y_j\}$ is convex, so that assumption (A.9.3) is automatically satisfied]. Input-distributivity ensures not only the additivity of production sets, but also that the constrained profit maximization process which characterizes the behaviour of firms, is well defined and compatible with zero profits (indeed this property practically characterizes those production sets for which average cost pricing and input-constrained profit maximization are compatible). See the discussion in Scarf (1986), Dehez & Drèze (1988b) and Quinzii (1992, Ch. 6).

The next Proposition [due to Scarf (1986, Th. 1)], gives us the essential property which allows for the compatibility of input-constrained profit maximization and average cost pricing. The proof illuminates about the nature of the requirements involved in the notion of input-distributivity.

Proposition 9.3.-

Let Y_j be an input-distributive set satisfying assumptions (A.9.0) and (A.9.2). Then for every $\mathbf{y}'_j \in \mathbb{F}_j$ there exists $\mathbf{p}' \in \mathbb{P}$ such that:

$$0 = \mathbf{p}' \mathbf{y}'_j \geq \mathbf{p}' \mathbf{y}_j, \ \forall \ \mathbf{y} \in Y_j(\mathbf{a}'_j) = \{\mathbf{y}_j \in Y_j \ / \ \mathbf{a}_j \geq \mathbf{a}'_j\}.$$

<u>*Proof.-*</u>

Let us drop the firm's subscript, for the sake of simplicity in notation. Three different cases will be considered:

(a) Let us suppose first that $\mathbf{y}' = (\mathbf{a}', \mathbf{b}') \in \mathbb{F}$ is such that $\mathbf{a}' << \mathbf{0}$ (i.e., all factors are used at $\mathbf{y}'$). Define then:

$$T(\mathbf{y}') \equiv \{\mathbf{y} = \sum \alpha^t \mathbf{y}^t / \alpha^t \geq 0, \mathbf{y}^t = (\mathbf{a}^t, \mathbf{b}^t) \in Y, \mathbf{a}^t \geq \mathbf{a}'\}$$

the smallest convex cone with vertex 0 containing $Y(\mathbf{a}')$. $T(\mathbf{y}')$ is comprehensive (since it is a convex cone and Y is itself comprehensive). By letting $\alpha^1 = 1, \alpha^t = 0, \forall t \neq 1$, it follows that $\mathbf{y}' \in T(\mathbf{y}')$. Furthermore, $\mathbf{y}' \in \partial T(\mathbf{y}')$. To see this, suppose that there exists $\mathbf{y}''$ in $T(\mathbf{y}')$ such that $\mathbf{y}'' >> \mathbf{y}'$; then $\mathbf{y}'' = \sum \alpha^t \mathbf{y}^t$ for some $(\alpha^t, \mathbf{y}^t)$ such that for all $t, \mathbf{y}^t \in Y$ and $\alpha^t \geq 0$ and $\mathbf{a}^t \geq$ a'. But then Input-distributivity implies that $\mathbf{y}'' \in Y$, which is not possible because under (A.9.2) $\mathbf{y} \in \mathbb{F}$ if and only if it is weakly efficient.

Therefore, since $\mathbf{y}'$ is a point on the boundary of a convex cone with vertex 0, there exists a supporting hyperplane to $T(\mathbf{y}')$ passing through $\mathbf{0}$ and $\mathbf{y}'$, that is, there exists $\mathbf{p}' \in \mathbb{R}^\ell_+, \mathbf{p}' \neq \mathbf{0}$, such that $0 = \mathbf{p}'\mathbf{y}' \geq \mathbf{p}'\mathbf{y}$ for all $\mathbf{y}$ in $T(\mathbf{y}')$ [and hence, in particular, for all $\mathbf{y} \in Y(\mathbf{a}')$].

(b) Consider now the case where $a'_i < 0$ for some indices, while $a'_j = 0$ for some others. Without loss of generality assume that $I = \{1, \ldots, s\}$, and that $y'_1, y'_2, \ldots, y'_h = 0$, while $y'_{h+1}, y'_{h+2}, \ldots, y'_\ell < 0$, for some h. Then, let Z denote the projection of Y on the $\mathbb{R}^{\ell-h}$ space, and call $\mathbf{z}'$ the corresponding projection of $\mathbf{y}'$. It is easy to see that Z is an Input-Distributive production set, and by applying the reasoning in (a), there exists $\mathbf{q} \in \mathbb{R}^{\ell-h}_+, \mathbf{q} \neq \mathbf{0}$, such that $0 = \mathbf{q}\mathbf{z}' \geq \mathbf{q}\mathbf{z}$, for every $\mathbf{z}$ in $Z(\mathbf{z}')$. Choose then $\mathbf{p}' = (\mathbf{0}, \mathbf{q})$ (where $\mathbf{0}$ is the vector all whose components are zero in $\mathbb{R}^h$), and the result follows.

(c) Finally, suppose $\mathbf{a}' = \mathbf{0}$. Then, $Y(\mathbf{a}')$ consists of points of the form $(\mathbf{0}, \mathbf{b})$, and any vector $(\mathbf{q}, \mathbf{0}) \in \mathbb{R}^\ell_+$, with $\mathbf{q} \neq \mathbf{0}$ will do.♠

Scarf (1986) proposes the following refinement of the input-constrained profit maximization pricing rule:

$$\phi^S_j(\mathbf{y}_j) \equiv \{\mathbf{q} \in \mathbb{P} \mid \mathbf{q} \in \phi^{IC}_j(\mathbf{y}_j) \ \& \ \mathbf{q}\mathbf{y}_j = 0\}$$

that is, ϕ^S_j selects those price vectors which satisfy input-constrained profit maximization, and yield null profits. Let us call a *Scarf equilibrium* to one in which firms behave according to the ϕ^S_j pricing rule. Observe that ϕ^S_j can be equivalently defined as the intersection of two regular and loss-free pricing rules: input-constrained profit maximization, and average cost pricing. This implies that ϕ^S_j is an upper hemicontinuous correspondence, with compact and convex values. Proposition 9.3 shows that it is also non-empty valued. As a consequence:

Corollary 9.1.-

Let E be a private ownership market economy satisfying assumptions (A.9.0), (A.9.1) and (A.9.2). If, for all j, Y_j is an input-distributive set, then a Scarf Equilibrium exists.

It was pointed out in chapter 7 that, under the general assumptions of chapter 4, one can always find economies with empty cores unless all production sets are convex cones. A key element in that result is the possibility that all commodities are consumed. Scarf (1986) identifies a family of economies in which this negative result does not hold, by assuming that limiting inputs do not enter utility functions. Let us introduce this assumption and present the positive result on the nonemptyness of the core.

A.9.4.- Limiting inputs $h = 1, 2, \ldots, k$, are pure inputs, so that they do not enter the preferences of consumers.

The following result gives us another relevant implication of input distributivity:

Theorem 9.1.-

Let E be an economy satisfying assumptions (A.9.0), (A.9.1), (A.9.2), and (A.9.4). Suppose furthermore that $Y_0 = \sum_{j=1}^n Y_j$ is an input-distributive set. Then there exists a Scarf equilibrium which is in the core.

Proof.-

The proof will be divided into two steps.

(i) Consider an economy E_0 identical to E in all respects except in that we substitute all individual firms by a single aggregate one Y_0. Clearly, Y_0 satisfies (A.9.2).

Now, for each $y_0 \in \mathbb{F}_0$, denote by $\phi_0^S(y_0)$ Scarf's pricing rule for the aggregate firm. We know that this mapping is an upper hemicontinuous correspondence, with nonempty, convex and compact values. Hence, corollary 9.1 ensures the existence of a Scarf equilibrium for the E_0 economy.

Let us show now that this equilibrium for E_0 actually corresponds to a Scarf equilibrium for the original economy. First notice that, by construction, y_0^* can be expressed as $\sum_{j=1}^n y_j^*$ with $y_j^* \in Y_j$ for all j. It follows that if y_0^* maximizes profits at prices p^* within the set $\{y_0 \in Y_0$ such that $a_0 \geq a_0^*\}$, it must be the case that *every* y_j^* maximizes profits at p^* in the set $\{y_j \in Y_j / a_j \geq a_j^*\}, j = 1, 2, \ldots, n$. For suppose not, that is, suppose that there exists $\mathbf{y}'_k$ with $\mathbf{a}'_k \geq \mathbf{a}^*_k$ such that $\mathbf{p}^*\mathbf{y}'_k > \mathbf{p}^*\mathbf{y}^*_k$; then, substituting $\mathbf{y}^*_k$ by $\mathbf{y}'_k$ in $\mathbf{y}^*_0$ we would get:

$$\mathbf{p}^*\left[\sum_{j \neq k} y^*_j + y'_k\right] > \mathbf{p}^*y^*_0$$

with $\left[\sum_{j \neq k} y^*_j + y'_k\right] \in \{y_0 \in Y_0 \,/\, \mathbf{a}_0 \geq \mathbf{a}^*_0\}$, contradicting the hypothesis.

Now observe that, since $\mathbf{p}^*\mathbf{y}^*_0 = 0$, and $0 \in Y_j$ for all j, it follows that $\mathbf{p}^*\mathbf{y}^*_j = 0$ for all j. Then, the aggregation of individual firms into a single one does not affect consumers' wealth functions. This implies that the allocation $[(\mathbf{x}^*_i), \mathbf{y}^*_0]$ can be dis-aggregated into an allocation of the original economy $[(\mathbf{x}^*_i), \tilde{\mathbf{y}}^*]$ such that $[\mathbf{p}^*, (\mathbf{x}^*_i), \tilde{\mathbf{y}}^*]$ is a Scarf equilibrium.

(ii) Let $[(\mathbf{x}^*_i)\tilde{\mathbf{y}}^*]$ be the allocation constructed in part (i), and suppose that there is an allocation $[(\mathbf{x}'_i), \tilde{\mathbf{y}}']$ and a coalition S of consumers such that: (a) $u_i(\mathbf{x}'_i) \geq u_i(\mathbf{x}^*_i)$ for every $i \in S$, with a strict inequality for some consumer; and (b) $\sum_{i \in S} \mathbf{x}'_i - \sum_{i \in S} \omega_i = \sum_{j=1}^{n} \mathbf{y}'_j$. Now notice that non-satiation implies that

$$\mathbf{p}^*\sum_{i \in S} \mathbf{x}'_i > \mathbf{p}^*\sum_{i \in S} \mathbf{x}^*_i = \mathbf{p}^*\sum_{i \in S} \omega_i$$

Therefore substituting we get $\sum_{j=1}^{n} \mathbf{p}^*\mathbf{y}'_j > 0$.

But this is not possible, since: (a) Feasibility and assumption (A.9.4) imply that $\sum_{j=1}^{n} \mathbf{a}'_j \geq -\omega^K$ (the aggregate endowment of limiting inputs); and

(b) $\sum_{j=1}^{n} \mathbf{y}^*_j$ is a profit maximizing combination of production plans, subject to the restriction $\sum_{j=1}^{n} \mathbf{a}'_j \geq \sum_{j=1}^{n} \mathbf{a}^*_j = -\omega^K$, with $\mathbf{p}^*\sum_{j=1}^{n} \mathbf{y}^*_j = 0$ [in view of (A.9.4), the definition of Scarf equilibrium, and the way in which $\tilde{\mathbf{y}}^*$ has been chosen].

The proof is in this way completed.♠

This theorem provides us with sufficient conditions for the efficiency and social stability of some equilibrium allocations. Note that the theorem says that there exists a Scarf equilibrium which is in the core, not that every equilibrium allocation is a core allocation. Yet, the possibility that agents coordinate on an inefficient equilibrium lacks of social stability. Also observe that we have assumed that the aggregate production set is input-distributive (rather than each individual production set). This is due to the fact that the input-distributivity property is not preserved by summation.

Remark 9.2.- Observe that there is no inconsistency between the optimality of the equilibrium (implied by the core property), and the use of Scarf's pricing rule instead of marginal pricing. The reason is that since there is a group of commodities which do not enter the preferences of consumers, optimality imposes no restriction on them. Indeed, Scarf's prices are marginal with respect to the production sets truncated by the equilibrium allocation of limiting inputs.

The next result is then immediate:[1]

Corollary 9.2.- [Scarf (1986)]
   Under the assumptions of Theorem 9.1, suppose that the economy consists of a single input-distributive firm. Then Scarf equilibria do exist and every equilibrium allocation is in the core.

9.4   OUTPUT-CONSTRAINED PROFIT MAXIMIZATION

The pricing rule to be considered here is an adaptation of the notion of *voluntary trading*, introduced by Dehez &Drèze (1988a) as a way of extending the notion of competitive equilibria to a context whereby firms behave as quantity takers, and there may be increasing returns to scale [see also Dierker & Neuefeind (1988)]. The model in this section is symmetric with respect to that in sections 9.2 and 9.3, so the exposition will be shorter.

Consider now the following assumption and definition:

A.9.0'.- Let $\mathcal{L} \equiv \{1, 2, \ldots, \ell\}$ stand for the set of commodity indices. For each $j = 1, 2, \ldots, n, \mathcal{L}$ can be partitioned into two disjoint subsets, O_j and O_j^c, so that, for every j, if $\mathbf{y}_j \in Y_j$ and $t \in O_j$ then $y_{jt} \geq 0$

Assumption (A.9.0') simply says that, for each firm $j = 1, 2, \ldots, n$, we can identify a priori a group of commodities which defines the jth firm's restrictions on the output side. Commodities in O_j^c have no sign restriction (i.e., they may be inputs or outputs). Production plans will now be written as $\mathbf{y}_j = (\mathbf{a}_j, \mathbf{b}_j)$, with $\mathbf{b}_j \geq 0$, in the understanding that $\mathbf{b}_j$ a point in the jth firm's subspace of outputs.

---

[1]Scarf speaks in this case of a *social equilibrium*.

Definition 9.3.-

The **Output-Constrained Profit Maximization** pricing rule for the *jth* firm, is a mapping $\phi_j^{OC} : \mathbb{F}_j \to \mathbb{P}$ given by:

$$\phi_j^{OC}(\mathbf{y}_j) \equiv \{\mathbf{q} \in \mathbb{P} \,/\, \mathbf{qy}_j \geq \mathbf{qy}_j' \; \forall \; \mathbf{y}_j' \in Y_j \text{ with } \mathbf{b}_j' \leq \mathbf{b}_j\}$$

The main feature of this pricing rule is that at those prices "it is not more profitable for the producers to produce less. Thus at an equilibrium, producers maximize profits subject to a sales constraint" [Cf. Dehez & Drèze (1988a, p. 210)].

Without loss of generality, let $O_j^C = \{1, 2, \dots, h\}$, for some $h < \ell$ and consider now the following assumption:

A.9.3'.- For every $\mathbf{b}_j' \in \mathbb{R}_+^{\ell-h}$, the set

$$A_j(\mathbf{b}_j') \equiv \{\mathbf{a}_j \in \mathbb{R}^h /(\mathbf{a}_j, \mathbf{b}_j) \in Y_j \text{ and } \mathbf{b}_j \leq \mathbf{b}_j'\}$$

is convex.

Assumption (A.9.3') says that for any given vector of limiting outputs $\mathbf{b}_j'$, the projection on $\mathbb{R}^h$ of those production plans involving fewer limiting outputs is a convex set (this is related to the notion of "convex isoquants"). Again, this assumption is compatible with the presence of firms with constant, increasing or decreasing returns to scale, and becomes less restrictive the bigger the cardinal of O_j [indeed, if O_j includes all potential outputs, this assumption is not required, as shown in Dehez & Drèze (1988a)].

The following result, which can be obtained following the same procedure as in section 9.2, holds:

Proposition 9.4.-

Let E be a private ownership market economy satisfying assumptions (A.9.0'), (A.9.1), (A.9.2) and (A.9.3'). Then, there is an equilibrium where firms follow output-constrained profit maximization.

Proof.-

It suffices to show that ϕ_j^{OC} is a regular and loss-free pricing rule, and apply proposition 8.1. That ϕ_j^{OC} is loss-free is immediate, since $\mathbf{0}$ belongs to Y_j for all j. Finally, to see that ϕ_j^{OC} is regular one can apply the same reasoning as in the proof of proposition 9.1.♠

It is easy to see that if production sets are convex, a competitive equilibrium is an output-constrained profit maximization equilibrium, but the converse is not generally true. Dehez & Drèze (1988a) suggest a refinement of output-constrained profit maximization, so that it coincides with profit maximization when production sets are convex. This refinement can informally be explained as follows: for every $\mathbf{y}_j \in \mathbb{F}_j$, choose those prices $\mathbf{q}' \in \phi_j^{OC}(\mathbf{y}_j)$ such that $\mathbf{q}'\mathbf{y}_j \leq \mathbf{q}\mathbf{y}_j$ for all $\mathbf{q} \in \phi_j^{OC}(\mathbf{y}_j)$. The idea behind is the search for minimal output prices, that is, for prices such that lower output prices cannot sustain the same output quantities. We refer to Dehez & Drèze's paper for details.

A particular case of this refined model is that in which profits are zero. Let us call ϕ_j^{DD} to a pricing rule given by:

$$\phi_j^{DD}(\mathbf{y}_j) \equiv \{\mathbf{q} \in \phi_j^{OC}(\mathbf{y}_j) \; / \; \mathbf{q}\mathbf{y}_j = 0\}$$

This pricing rule corresponds to the intersection of two regular pricing rules: output-constrained profit maximization and average cost pricing. As it was the case before, there is a restriction on the class of production sets which ensures the nonemptyness of this new pricing rule. Dehez & Drèze (1988b) define the notion of *output distributive sets* for that purpose. Formally:

Definition 9.4.-

A production set Y_j is said to be **output-distributive**, if for any collection of points $(\mathbf{y}^t, \lambda^t), t = 1, 2, \ldots, s$, with $\mathbf{y}^t = (\mathbf{a}^t, \mathbf{b}^t) \in Y_j, \lambda^t \in \mathbb{R}_+$, the following condition holds:

$$\sum_{h=1}^{s} \lambda^h \mathbf{b}^h \geq \mathbf{b}^t, t = 1, 2, \ldots, s \Rightarrow \sum_{h=1}^{s} \lambda^h \mathbf{y}^h \in Y_j$$

In words: Any (nonnegative) weighted sum of feasible production plans is feasible if it involves more limiting outputs than any of the original plans. It can be shown that output-distributivity implies (A.9.3').

The next result is obtained:

Proposition 9.5.-

Let E be a private ownership market economy satisfying assumptions (A.9.0'), (A.9.1) and (A.9.2). Suppose furthermore that every Y_j is an output-distributive production set. Then an equilibrium where firms follow the ϕ_j^{DD} pricing rule does exist.

The proof of this result simply requires to show that the analog to proposition 9.3 holds (that is, under (A.9.0) and (A.9.2), output distributivity implies that for each $\mathbf{y}_j \in \mathbb{F}_j$ there exists $\mathbf{p} \in \mathbb{P}$ such that $0 = \mathbf{p}\mathbf{y}_j \geq \mathbf{p}\mathbf{y}'_j$, for all $\mathbf{y}'_j$ with $\mathbf{b}'_j \leq \mathbf{b}_j$). This can be done following the same steps as in proposition 9.3, and hence the proof of proposition 9.5 is left as an exercise.

Observe that, similar to the Scarf equilibrium, this equilibrium exhibits some competitive features. ϕ^{DD} is a pricing rule for which output-constrained profit maximization and average cost pricing coincide. Then in an equilibrium firms are maximizing profits subject to an output constraint, and maximum profits are actually null. Furthermore, when production sets are convex cones, it coincides with the standard competitive one.

9.5 FINAL COMMENTS

As mentioned before, imperfect competition might be thought of as a natural framework for the analysis of market economies with increasing returns. Following Negishi's (1961) work, Arrow & Hahn (1971, 6.4) present a model of monopolistic competition in which no assumption is made about the convexity of production sets. Silvestre (1977), (1978) criticizes this model and offers alternatives with better foundations. Nevertheless, these models are still restrictive. A related line of research (using "objective" rather than "subjective" demand curves) was developed by Gabsewicz & Vial (1972) and Fitzroy (1974); these models turn out to be even more restrictive (since objective demands impose much more structure than subjective ones). Indeed, the difficulties of building an imperfectly competitive general equilibrium model are enormous, even in the convex case [see the analysis in Roberts & Sonnenschein (1977), and the recent survey in Benassy (1991)].

We have developed here a positive approach to the modelling of nonconvex firms, which consists of allowing for the presence of quantity constraints (due to input or demand restrictions). In this context (constrained) profit maximization may be well defined. The existence of general equilibrium with quantity constraints was first dealt with in the classic paper by Scarf (1986) (where he analyzed the non-emptiness of the core in an economy with increasing returns). Besides the model by Dehez & Drèze (1988a) already discussed, let us also refer here to that one by Dierker & Neuefeind (1988) which extends the results in Dierker, Guesnerie & Neuefeind (1985), allowing for the presence of quantity targets.

Chapter 10

CLASSICAL EQUILIBRIUM

10.1 INTRODUCTION

This chapter presents a positive model of a static market economy with competitive features, in spite of the presence of increasing returns to scale. The key concept in the analysis will be that of a *classical equilibrium*. A classical equilibrium consists of a price vector and an allocation such that supply equals demand, and all active firms are equally profitable (where the common rate of return is the highest one attainable at these prices).

The idea that competition is a process which implies the equalization of firms' profitability is an old one. It played a central role in the modelling of markets by classical economists, such as Smith, Ricardo or Marx (but also Walras, Wicksell or Hayek). This is an appealing concept which reflects the combination of three key attributes of competitive markets: (1) Technology is freely available (that is, there are no "barriers to entry"); (2) Production and exchange are voluntary (that is, no agent can be forced to participate into production and exchange); and (3) Prices are outside the control of individual agents (which can be identified with price-taking behaviour). As a consequence, in a private ownership competitive economy, no agent will willingly accept a smaller return from her "investment" than the highest one attainable at given prices, so that firms will only become active in those activities which yield such a profitability. Note that these ideas are relatively independent of the nature of technology: no matter the kind of returns to scale prevailing, as far as the aforementioned properties hold, the classical notion of competition can be applied. The model presented here will be based on this fact.

The main features of the single-period private ownership market economy we shall be referring to are the following:

(i) Commodities will be divided into two groups: (a) *Produced commodities*, which correspond to those natural resources (to be interpreted as "produced by nature"), factors of production and consumption goods produced "yesterday" and/or inherited from the past; they constitute the initial endowments of today's economy. And (b) *New goods*, which include both consumption goods, and other inputs which can be produced today.

(ii) The technology will be modelled in terms of a finite number of production sets, which describe different production activities or economic sectors. These activities exhibit non-decreasing returns to scale; in particular, it will be assumed that production sets are *input-distributive*. There is free access to the technology.

(iii) Consumers are characterized by their consumption sets, their utility functions and their initial endowments, and are standard concerning these respects. They choose consumption vectors in order to maximize utility at given prices, subject to their budget constraints. Consumers' decisions also refer to the use of their initial holdings for production purposes (they contribute to the creation of firms by making available their endowments, looking for the highest profitability of their "investment").

(iv) Firms are not given a priori, but appear as part of consumers' optimal decisions. A firm is created when a set of consumers coordinate on the use of some of the technological possibilities, by providing the factors that might be required. Firms maximize profits at given prices, subject to their feasible sets (i.e., subject to the amounts of inputs provided by consumers at market prices).

Observe that a key characteristic of the way of modelling the economy is the distinction between *technology* (which belongs to the data of the model) and *firms* (which are dependent on consumers' decisions). The underlying idea is that *factors have to be made available before production takes place*. This implies, on the one hand, that a firm does not exist unless consumers provide some factors. And, on the other, that firms will be characterized by both the nature of production activities they carry out, and their feasible sets. Note also that consumers' shares in the firms' profits become now equilibrium variables, rather than parameters.

The model may well be interpreted as a two-stage process. In the first stage consumers take investment decisions and firms are created. In the second stage production takes place, consumers get paid and demand is realized. Yet, for the sake of simplicity in exposition, the model refers to a single-period economy. This feature also permits one to discuss the role of profits independently of the "interest rate" (or "discount factor").

10.2   THE MODEL

Consider a single-period, private ownership market economy, with ℓ commodities. Commodities $1, 2, \ldots, k$ are *produced commodities*, while commodities $k+1, k+2, \ldots, \ell$ are *new goods*. New goods are consumption goods and inputs that can be produced today. Produced commodities are consumption goods and inputs to production (factors) which are inherited from the past. These commodities cannot be produced again[1], and hence limit today's production possibilities. A point $\omega \in \mathbb{R}^{\ell}$ denotes the aggregate vector of initial endowments. According to the previous classification, this vector takes the form $\omega = (\sigma, \mathbf{0})$, where $\sigma \in \mathbb{R}^{k}$ denotes the aggregate endowment of produced commodities (that is, commodities which are available before production takes place), and $\mathbf{0} \in \mathbb{R}^{\ell-k}$.

Production possibilities are described by means of n production sets. Each of these sets summarizes the technical knowledge of a specific production activity. Production activities differ in the kind of inputs they use and/or the type of outputs they obtain. One may well interpret these activities as the "industries" or "sectors" of an economy. Thus, for $j = 1, 2, \ldots, n, Y_j \subset \mathbb{R}^{\ell}$ stands for the jth production set, while a point $\mathbf{y}_j \in Y_j$ denotes a production plan which is feasible for the jth activity. $\mathbb{F}_j$ stands for the jth set of weakly efficient production plans. A point $\tilde{\mathbf{y}} = (\mathbf{y}_1, \mathbf{y}_2, \ldots, \mathbf{y}_n)$ denotes an element of $\mathbb{F} \equiv \prod_{j=1}^{n} \mathbb{F}_j$.

According to the classification of commodities above, a production plan for the jth activity can be written as: $\mathbf{y}_j = (\mathbf{a}_j, \mathbf{b}_j)$, with $\mathbf{b}_j \in \mathbb{R}^{\ell-k}$ and $\mathbf{a}_j \in -\mathbb{R}_+^k$. No sign restriction is established on $\mathbf{b}_j$, so that there may be new goods used as inputs in today's production. The *technology* (which encompasses all activities) is publicly known and freely accessible.

A point $\mathbf{p} \in \mathbb{P}$ denotes a price vector (where $\mathbb{P}$ is the price simplex in $\mathbb{R}_+^{\ell}$). The scalar product $\mathbf{p}\mathbf{y}_j$ for $\mathbf{y}_j$ in Y_j gives us the profits associated with $\mathbf{y}_j$ at prices $\mathbf{p}$.

For a given pair $(\mathbf{p}, \mathbf{y}_j)$ the ratio $\mathbf{p}\mathbf{y}_j / \mathbf{p}(-\mathbf{a}_j, \mathbf{0})$ gives the profitability that can be obtained in the jth activity when prices are $\mathbf{p}$ and production is $\mathbf{y}_j$ (that is, the relation between profits and the cost of produced commodities). More formally, let $\rho_j : \mathbb{P} \times \mathbb{F}_j \to \mathbb{R}$ be a mapping given by:

$$\rho_j(\mathbf{p}, \mathbf{y}_j) \equiv \begin{cases} \mathbf{p}\mathbf{y}_j / \mathbf{p}(-\mathbf{a}_j, \mathbf{0}), & \text{if } \mathbf{y}_j \neq 0 \\ 0, & \text{otherwise} \end{cases}$$

(ρ_j is left undefined when $\mathbf{p}(-\mathbf{a}_j, \mathbf{0}) = 0$ and $\mathbf{y}_j \neq \mathbf{0}$). Then, call $\rho(\mathbf{p}, \tilde{\mathbf{y}})$ to

---

[1]Let us recall here that two commodities which are identical physically will be considered as different commodities if they are produced at two different periods.

the maximum profitability attainable (whenever defined), that is:

$$\rho(\mathbf{p}, \widetilde{\mathbf{y}}) \equiv \underset{j}{Max} \ \{\rho_j(\mathbf{p}, \mathbf{y}_j)\}$$

Hence, $\rho(\mathbf{p}, \widetilde{\mathbf{y}})$ tells us the biggest return one can get per dollar invested, when prices are $\mathbf{p}$ and production is evaluated at $\widetilde{\mathbf{y}}$.

There are m consumers, which are supposed to behave *competitively*. Each consumer $i = 1, 2, \ldots, m$, is characterized by a collection

$$[X_i, u_i, \omega_i, r_i]$$

where $X_i \subset \mathbb{R}^\ell, u_i : X_i \to \mathbb{R}$, and $\omega_i = (\sigma_i, 0) \in \mathbb{R}^\ell$ stand for the *ith* consumer's consumption set, utility function and initial endowments, and $r_i : \mathbb{P} \times \mathbb{F} \to \mathbb{R}$ denotes the *ith* consumer's wealth function.

Consumers own the initial endowments and maximize utility at given prices, by suitably choosing consumption bundles under the restriction of their available wealth. Wealth is given by the exchange value of their initial endowments, which depends upon prices and the profits that can be obtained by applying their resources of produced commodities to production activities. By construction, consumers are not interested in the nature of production activities they support, but just in the profitability they can obtain. Thus, whenever any two activities yield the highest profitability attainable, they will be indifferent in applying their resources to any of them. Moreover, the supply of inputs will only be directed to those activities yielding a return equal to $\rho(\mathbf{p}, \widetilde{\mathbf{y}}) \geq 0$.

This can formally be expressed as follows. Let $\alpha_{ij}(\mathbf{p}, \widetilde{\mathbf{y}}) \in \mathbb{R}^k$ denote the *ith* consumer's investment in the *jth* sector, and let $\alpha_i(\mathbf{p}, \widetilde{\mathbf{y}})$ in $\mathbb{R}^{kn}$ stand for the *ith* consumer's overall investment distribution. For any given pair $(\mathbf{p}, \widetilde{\mathbf{y}}), \alpha_i(\mathbf{p}, \widetilde{\mathbf{y}})$ solves the program:

$$Max \ r_i(\mathbf{p}, \widetilde{\mathbf{y}}) \equiv \sum_{j=1}^{n} \mathbf{p}(\alpha_{ij}, \mathbf{0})[1 + \rho_j(\mathbf{p}, \mathbf{y}_j)] + \mathbf{p}[(\sigma_i, \mathbf{0}) - (\sum_{j=1}^{n} \alpha_{ij}, \mathbf{0})]$$

The first term on this sum expresses the gross revenue derived from investing α_{ij} in sectors $j = 1, 2, ..., n$. The second, which gives us the worth of her remaining wealth, incorporates the restriction derived from the available produced commodities[2]. For a given $(\mathbf{p}, \widetilde{\mathbf{y}})$, let $I_i(\mathbf{p}, \widetilde{\mathbf{y}})$ stand for the *ith* consumer's aggregate supply of inputs, that is, the set of points $\mathbf{t} \in \mathbb{R}^k$ such

---

[2]Note that this form of writing the wealth function implicitly assumes that no trade is possible with the worth of those goods which have yet to be produced.

that $\mathbf{t} = \sum_{j=1}^{n} \alpha_{ij}(\mathbf{p},\tilde{\mathbf{y}})$. Note that this supply of inputs can be thought of as a correspondence I_i from $\mathbb{P} \times \mathbb{F}$ into $\mathbb{R}^k$, such that:

$$I_i(\mathbf{p},\tilde{\mathbf{y}}) = \{\mathbf{0}\}, \text{ if } \rho(\mathbf{p},\tilde{\mathbf{y}}) < 0$$

$$I_i(\mathbf{p},\tilde{\mathbf{y}}) = [\mathbf{0},\sigma_i], \text{ if } \rho(\mathbf{p},\tilde{\mathbf{y}}) = 0$$

$$I_i(\mathbf{p},\tilde{\mathbf{y}}) = \{\sigma_i\}, \text{ if } \rho(\mathbf{p},\tilde{\mathbf{y}}) > 0$$

Consumers will not develop production activities if $\rho(\mathbf{p},\tilde{\mathbf{y}})$ is negative, because no agent can be forced to participate into production. When $\rho(\mathbf{p},\tilde{\mathbf{y}}) = 0$ the *ith* consumer's wealth is given by $\mathbf{p}(\sigma_i,\mathbf{0})$, no matter how she allocates her initial endowments; hence the supply of inputs can be taken as the whole interval $[\mathbf{0},\sigma_i]$. Finally, if $\rho(\mathbf{p},\tilde{\mathbf{y}}) > 0$ the *ith* consumer will be willing to devote *all* her resources to the most profitable activities, because this maximizes her wealth (let us recall here that consumers behave competitively, so that they make choices without taking into account any restriction other than wealth).

This allows us to express the *ith* consumer's wealth function as follows:

$$r_i(\mathbf{p},\tilde{\mathbf{y}}) \equiv \mathbf{p}\omega_i[1 + \max\{0, \rho(\mathbf{p},\tilde{\mathbf{y}})\}]$$

[which may not be defined for some pairs $(\mathbf{p},\tilde{\mathbf{y}})$].

Remark 10.1.- Note that this formulation implies, for $\rho(\mathbf{p},\tilde{\mathbf{y}}) > 0$, that consumers cannot trade with "future yields" before production takes place. For interpretative purposes we can think that consumers "invest" produced commodities at the beginning of the period, then production takes place, and finally consumers get paid and actually consume at the end of the period. We shall refer again to this question in the final section.

The *ith* consumer's demand is obtained as a solution to the following program:

$$Max. \; u_i(x_i)$$
$$\text{s.t.} \quad x_i \in X_i$$
$$\mathbf{p}x_i \leq r_i(\mathbf{p},\tilde{\mathbf{y}})$$

Then, the *ith* consumer's behaviour can be summarized by a demand correspondence $\xi_i : \mathbb{P} \times \mathbb{F} \to X_i$, such that $\xi_i(\mathbf{p},\tilde{\mathbf{y}})$ stands for a solution to the program above.

We have already described the technology and the consumption sector. Let us now refer to firms. A firm results from the application of resources to put into work some of the possibilities that the available technology offers. These resources have to be made available "before" production takes place [3]. Thus a firm can be described by the nature of its production activities and its feasible set (given by the amounts of factors available).

For every pair $(\mathbf{p}', \tilde{\mathbf{y}}') \in \mathbb{P} \times \mathbb{F}$, consumers will decide to set up firms by choosing the most profitable production activities and making available the inputs they own. In order to make things simpler, let us assume that there can be at most one firm per activity [4], and consider the following definition:

<u>Definition 10.1.-</u>

Given a point $(\mathbf{p}', \tilde{\mathbf{y}}') \in \mathbb{P} \times \mathbb{F}$, an **Input Allocation relative to** $(\mathbf{p}', \tilde{\mathbf{y}}')$ is a point $\tilde{\mathbf{a}} \equiv (\mathbf{a}_1, \mathbf{a}_2, \ldots, \mathbf{a}_n)$ in $\mathbb{R}_{-}^{kn}$, such that, for every $j = 1, 2, \ldots, n$, one has:

$$-\mathbf{a}_j = \sum_{i=1}^{m} \alpha_{ij}(\mathbf{p}, \tilde{\mathbf{y}})$$

An input allocation relative to $(\mathbf{p}', \tilde{\mathbf{y}}')$ is a way of allotting produced commodities to firms which is consistent with consumers' decisions. In particular, this implies that no firm will be created in those activities such that $\rho_j(\mathbf{p}', \mathbf{y}_j')$ is smaller than $\rho(\mathbf{p}', \tilde{\mathbf{y}}')$ (that is, $\rho_j(\mathbf{p}', \mathbf{y}_j') < \rho(\mathbf{p}', \tilde{\mathbf{y}}')$ implies $\mathbf{a}_j = \mathbf{0}$), and that $\sum_{j=1}^{n} -\mathbf{a}_j \in \sum_{i=1}^{m} I_i(\mathbf{p}, \tilde{\mathbf{y}})$. Needless to say that there are many input allocations relative to a given pair $(\mathbf{p}', \tilde{\mathbf{y}}')$, and that all of them are equally worthy from consumers' viewpoint.

Thus, given a price vector $\mathbf{p}' \in \mathbb{P}$, a vector of production plans $\tilde{\mathbf{y}}'$ in $\mathbb{F}$, and an input allocation $\tilde{\mathbf{a}}$ relative to $(\mathbf{p}', \tilde{\mathbf{y}}')$, the *jth* firm's feasible set is given by:

$$Y_j(\mathbf{p}', \tilde{\mathbf{y}}', \tilde{\mathbf{a}}) \equiv \{\mathbf{y}_j'' \in Y_j \ / \ \mathbf{a}_j'' \geq \mathbf{a}_j\}$$

The behaviour of firms can now be described as follows: Given a point $(\mathbf{p}', \tilde{\mathbf{y}}') \in \mathbb{P} \times \mathbb{F}$ and an input allocation $\tilde{\mathbf{a}}$ relative to $(\mathbf{p}', \tilde{\mathbf{y}}')$, the *jth* firm's supply is obtained by solving the program:

$$Max. \ \mathbf{p}' \mathbf{y}_j''$$
$$\text{s.t.}$$
$$\mathbf{y}_j'' \in Y_j \left(\mathbf{p}', \tilde{\mathbf{y}}', \tilde{\mathbf{a}} \right)$$

that is, the *jth* firm maximizes profits over its feasible set.

---

[3]This is an intuitive way of saying that Produced Commodities are essential inputs to production. The assumptions will make clear this point.

[4]It will be seen soon after that this implies no loss of generality, under the assumptions of our model.

Let $\lambda \in \mathbb{R}_+$ be a scalar, to be interpreted as a parametric rate of profits, and consider the following definitions which will enable to make precise (and non-vacuous) the equilibrium notion:

Definition 10.2.-
    The pair $(\mathbf{p}', \mathbf{y}_j') \in \mathbb{P} \times \mathbb{F}_j$, is an **equilibrium relative to** λ **for the** jth **activity**, if:
    (i) For $\mathbf{y}_j' \neq \mathbf{0}$,

$$\mathbf{p}'(-\mathbf{a}_j', \mathbf{0})\lambda = \mathbf{p}'\mathbf{y}_j' \geq \mathbf{p}'\mathbf{y}_j \;\; \forall \mathbf{y}_j \in Y_j \text{ such that } \mathbf{a}_j \geq \mathbf{a}_j'$$

    (ii) For $\mathbf{y}_j' = \mathbf{0}$, $\mathbf{p}'$ belongs to the closed convex hull of the following set:

$$\{\mathbf{q} \in \mathbb{P} \; / \; \exists \{\mathbf{q}^\nu, \mathbf{y}_j^\nu\} \subset \mathbb{P} \times [\mathbb{F}_j \backslash \{\mathbf{0}\}]$$

$$\text{with } \{\mathbf{q}^\nu, \mathbf{y}_j^\nu\} \to (\mathbf{q}, \mathbf{0}) \text{ and } \mathbf{q}^\nu \mathbf{y}_j^\nu = \mathbf{q}^\nu(-\mathbf{a}_j^\nu, \mathbf{0})\lambda\}$$

Definition 10.3.-
    A pair $(\mathbf{p}', \tilde{\mathbf{y}}') \in \mathbb{P} \times \mathbb{F}$ is a **Production Equilibrium relative to** λ if, for all $j = 1, 2, \ldots, n$, $(\mathbf{p}', \mathbf{y}_j')$ is an equilibrium relative to λ for the jth activity.

The jth activity is in equilibrium relative to λ when $\mathbf{y}_j' = (\mathbf{a}_j', \mathbf{b}_j')$ is a profit maximizing production plan at prices $\mathbf{p}'$, subject to the restriction of not using more produced commodities than those determined by $\mathbf{a}_j'$, and such that $\mathbf{p}'\mathbf{y}_j' = \mathbf{p}'(-\mathbf{a}_j', \mathbf{0})\lambda$. Since this places no restriction on prices when $\mathbf{y}_j' = \mathbf{0}$, we require in this case that $(\mathbf{p}', \mathbf{0})$ is a limit point of a sequence of pairs yielding a profitability equal to λ. A production equilibrium is a situation in which all activities are in equilibrium relative to λ, for the same price vector.

Consider now the following definitions:

Definition 10.4.-
    A **Classical Equilibrium relative to** λ is a price vector $\mathbf{p}^* \in \mathbb{P}$ and an allocation $[(\mathbf{x}_i^*), \tilde{\mathbf{y}}^*] \in \prod_{i=1}^{m} X_i \times \mathbb{F}$, such that:
    (α) $\mathbf{x}_i^* \in \xi_i(\mathbf{p}^*, \tilde{\mathbf{y}}^*), \forall i$
    (β) $\tilde{\mathbf{a}}^* \equiv (\mathbf{a}_1^*, \mathbf{a}_2^*, \ldots, \mathbf{a}_n^*)$ is an input allocation relative to $(\mathbf{p}^*, \tilde{\mathbf{y}}^*)$ [where these $\mathbf{a}_j^*$ are such that $\mathbf{y}_j^* = (\mathbf{a}_j^*, \mathbf{b}_j^*)$].
    (γ) $(\mathbf{p}^*, \tilde{\mathbf{y}}^*)$ is a Production Equilibrium relative to $\lambda = \rho(\mathbf{p}^*, \tilde{\mathbf{y}}^*)$.

(δ) $\sum\limits_{i=1}^{m} \mathbf{x}_i^* \leq \sum\limits_{i=1}^{m} \mathbf{y}_j^* + \omega$, with $p_h^* = 0$ for strict inequalities.

Definition 10.5.-

A **Canonical Classical Equilibrium** is a classical equilibrium relative to $\lambda = 0$.

That is, a Classical Equilibrium is a price vector and an allocation such that: (a) Consumers maximize preferences within their budget sets; (b) Consumers voluntarily provide all inputs which are needed for production purposes; (c,1) All firms maximize profits at given prices subject to their feasible sets; (c,2) All active firms are equally profitable; (c,3) The common rate of return is the maximum profitability attainable across sectors; and (d) All markets clear. In the case of a Canonical Classical Equilibrium, it is also true that the common rate of return is $\rho(\mathbf{p}^*, \tilde{\mathbf{y}}^*) = 0$. Observe that part ($\gamma$) of the definition implies that we are discarding those trivial equilibria obtained by setting $\mathbf{y}_j = \mathbf{0}$ for all j and finding a pure exchange equilibrium.

Let $A(\omega)$ stand for the set of attainable allocations, that is,

$$A(\omega) \equiv \{[(\mathbf{x}_i), \tilde{\mathbf{y}}] \in \prod_{i=1}^{m} X_i \times \mathbb{F} \ / \ \sum_{i=1}^{m} \mathbf{x}_i \leq \omega + \sum_{j=1}^{n} \mathbf{y}_j\}$$

The projection of $A(\omega)$ over the *jth* production set gives us the set of attainable production plans for the *jth* activity.

In order to get a suitable bound for the rate of profits, for each λ in $\mathbb{R}_+$, define a set $A(\omega, \lambda)$ as follows:

$$A(\omega, \lambda) \equiv \{[(\mathbf{x}_i), \tilde{\mathbf{y}}] \in \prod_{i=1}^{m} X_i \times \mathbb{F} \ / \ \sum_{i=1}^{m} \mathbf{x}_i - \omega - \sum_{j=1}^{n} [\mathbf{a}_j(1 + \lambda), \mathbf{b}_j] \leq \mathbf{0}\}$$

Define now $\Lambda \equiv \{\lambda \in \mathbb{R}_+ \ / \ A(\omega, \lambda) \neq \emptyset\}$, that is, the set of profit rates for which $A(\omega, \lambda)$ is nonempty. Note that this set is an interval which will be nonempty whenever the set of attainable allocations be nonempty.

We are already prepared to present the basic assumptions of our model:

A.10.1.- For each consumer $i = 1, 2, \ldots, m$,
   (i) $X_i = \mathbb{R}_+^\ell$.
   (ii) $u_i : X_i \to \mathbb{R}$ is a continuous and quasi-concave utility function, satisfying local non-satiation.
   (iii) $\sigma_i >> \mathbf{0}$.

<u>A.10.2.-</u> For each $j = 1, 2, \ldots, n$,
   (i) Y_j is a closed set such that $\mathbf{0} \in Y_j$, and $Y_j - \mathbb{R}_+^\ell \subset Y_j$.
   (ii) The jth firm's attainable production set is compact. In particular, $\mathbf{a}_j = \mathbf{0}$ implies $\mathbf{b}_j \leq \mathbf{0}$.
   (iii) Y_j is input-distributive.

<u>A.10.3.-</u> Let $(\mathbf{p}, \tilde{\mathbf{y}})$ be a production equilibrium relative to $\lambda \in \Lambda$. Then, for all $i = 1, 2, \ldots, m$, $r_i(\mathbf{p}, \tilde{\mathbf{y}}) > 0$.

Assumption (A.10.1) differs from (A.9.1) in two respects. First because now we take X_i as $\mathbb{R}_+^\ell$ (i.e., we consider leisure rather than labour). Second, because ω_i is not (it cannot be) in the interior of X_i. Assumption (A.10.2) corresponds to (A.9.2) and a special case of (A.9.3). Observe that production requires using up some produced commodities (this translates the idea that inputs have to be made available "before" production takes place), and that production sets are input-distributive. This property implies that all firms exhibit non-decreasing returns to scale (see section 9.3). Finally, assumption (A.10.3) introduces the cheaper point requirement over the set of production equilibria [this is necessary in view of (iii) of (A.10.1)].

Let us conclude this section by discussing the simplifying hypothesis of (at most) one active firm per activity. Suppose, for the sake of the argument, that any number of firms can be created in a given sector. Note that, under assumption (A.10.2), there can only be production activities with non-decreasing returns to scale. For those sectors exhibiting constant returns to scale, the number of firms is actually irrelevant (since production sets are convex cones, and thus satisfy additivity and divisibility). As for those sectors with increasing returns to scale, observe that, in equilibrium, there can only be one active firm in each activity. Otherwise $(\mathbf{p}^*, \tilde{\mathbf{y}}^*)$ would not be a Production Equilibrium relative to $\lambda = \rho(\mathbf{p}^*, \tilde{\mathbf{y}}^*)$. Therefore, modelling one firm per activity has only served the purpose of simplifying the writing of the model, without any loss of generality.

10.3 CANONICAL CLASSICAL EQUILIBRIUM

This section refers to canonical classical equilibria (i.e., the case in which $\rho(\mathbf{p}^*, \tilde{\mathbf{y}}^*) = 0$), whereas classical equilibrium with positive profits will be analyzed in the next one.

Let us start by presenting the main result of this section:

Proposition 10.1.-

Let E be an economy satisfying assumptions (A.10.1), (A.10.2) and (A.10.3). Then:

(i) A Canonical Classical Equilibrium $[\mathbf{p}^*, (\mathbf{x}_i^*), \tilde{\mathbf{y}}]$ exists.

(ii) There is no feasible allocation $[(\mathbf{x}_i'), \tilde{\mathbf{y}}]$, such that $u_i(\mathbf{x}_i') \geq u_i(\mathbf{x}_i^*), \forall i$, with at least a strict inequality, and $\mathbf{a}_j' \geq \mathbf{a}_j^*$ for all j.

Proof.-

(i) Let $\hat{E}$ be an economy whose data (consumers, technology and initial endowments) are identical to those in E, but in which consumers and firms behave according to the following pattern:

a) The ith consumer maximizes utility at given prices, within her budget set, which is defined by the following wealth function:

$$\hat{r}_i(\mathbf{p}, \tilde{\mathbf{y}}) = \mathbf{p}\omega_i$$

b) The jth firm's feasible set corresponds to Y_j and behaves according to a pricing rule ϕ_j, which is defined as the intersection of average cost and input-constrained profit maximization [that is, $\phi_j(\mathbf{y}_j) \equiv \phi_j^{AC}(\mathbf{y}_j) \cap \phi_j^{IC}(\mathbf{y}_j)$].

Observe that a canonical classical equilibrium for E corresponds precisely to a Scarf equilibrium for $\hat{E}$. To apply the existence result in corollary 9.2, we have to show that assumption (A.4.5) holds (see proposition 8.1). To do so suppose that $\hat{r}_i(\mathbf{p}, \tilde{\mathbf{y}}) \leq 0$ for some i. This is only possible if $p_t = 0$ for $t = 1, 2, \ldots, k$ (i.e., all produced commodities are free goods at $\mathbf{p}$). Then, $q_{jt} \geq p_t$ for all these t's, and (A.4.5) is trivially satisfied. This proves the existence of a canonical classical equilibrium.

(ii) The argument here is standard, and included for the sake of completeness:

Let $[\mathbf{p}^*, (\mathbf{x}_j^*), \tilde{\mathbf{y}}]$ be a canonical classical equilibrium, and suppose now that there is another feasible allocation $[(\mathbf{x}_j^*), \tilde{\mathbf{y}}]$ such that: (1) $u_i(\mathbf{x}_i') \geq u_i(\mathbf{x}_i^*)$ for every i, with a strict inequality for some consumer; and (2) $\mathbf{a}_j' \geq \mathbf{a}_j^*$ for every j. Since this allocation is feasible, it must be the case that

$$\sum_{i=1}^m \mathbf{x}_i' \leq \omega + \sum_{j=1}^n \mathbf{y}_j'$$

Now notice that non-satiation implies that

$$\mathbf{p}^* \sum_{i=1}^m \mathbf{x}_i' > \mathbf{p}^* \sum_{i=1}^m \mathbf{x}_i^* = \mathbf{p}^*\omega + \mathbf{p}^* \sum_{j=1}^n \mathbf{y}_j^*$$

Therefore substituting we get

$$\mathbf{p}^* \sum_{j=1}^n \mathbf{y}_j' > \mathbf{p}^* \sum_{j=1}^n \mathbf{y}_j' = 0$$

This implies that there is some j for which $\mathbf{p}^*\mathbf{y}'_j > 0$. This j cannot exist if we require that $\mathbf{a}'_j \geq \mathbf{a}^*_j$, according to the definition of canonical classical equilibrium. Therefore, such an allocation cannot exist.♠

Proposition 10.1 tells us that there exist canonical classical equilibria under fairly general assumptions. These equilibria may be regarded as describing a market situation where production is carried out, based on consumers' rational behaviour, in order to exploit the benefits derived from technical knowledge. Consumers maximize utility subject to their budget constraints. Firms are created only when they yield the highest profitability attainable at given prices, and maximize profits subject to their feasible sets. Proposition 10.1 ensures that all these actions are compatible for some pair $(\mathbf{p}^*, \tilde{\mathbf{y}}^*)$. It also establishes that there is no feasible way of making consumers better-off, preserving the distribution of produced commodities between firms. Even though this is a mild efficiency property, let us recall here that, in the presence of increasing returns, equilibrium allocations typically fail to satisfy Pareto optimality (see chapter 7).

Let $N = \{1, 2, \dots, n\}$ denote the set of indices identifying the firms of the economy. Assuming that (iii) of (A.10.2) holds, these firms can be divided into two categories: firms with constant returns to scale, and firms with increasing returns to scale. One can thus write $N = N_0 \bigcup N_1$, where N_0 is the set of indices corresponding to constant returns to scale firms, and N_1 its complement.

The following Corollary is an immediate consequence of proposition 10.1:

Corollary 10.1.-
Let $[\mathbf{p}^*, (\mathbf{x}^*_i), \tilde{\mathbf{y}}^*]$ be a canonical classical equilibrium. Then, those firms in N_0 behave as (unconstrained) profit maximizers at given prices.

Thus a canonical classical equilibrium gives us a picture of an economy where constant returns to scale firms behave as unconstrained profit maximizers, while natural monopolies maximize profits subject to their feasible sets, and all firms do break even. All these actions are compatible with consumption and "investment" decisions. If N_1 is empty, then all firms behave as (unconstrained) profit maximizers at given prices and the notion of canonical classical equilibrium coincides with that of a competitive economy.

Consider now the following assumption, which restricts the model to a case where produced commodities are not consumed:

<u>A.10.4.-</u> Produced commodities $h = 1, 2, \ldots, k$, are pure inputs, so that they do not enter the preferences of consumers.

The following result is an immediate application of theorem 9.1:

Proposition 10.2.-

Let E be an economy satisfying assumptions (A.10.1), (i) and (ii) of (A.10.2), (A.10.3) and (A.10.4). Suppose furthermore that $Y_0 = \sum_{j=1}^{n} Y_j$ is distributive. Then there exists a canonical classical equilibrium which is in the core.

This proposition provides us with sufficient conditions for the efficiency and social stability of some equilibrium allocations. Note that it says that there exists a canonical classical equilibrium which is in the core (not that every equilibrium allocation is a core allocation).

10.4   POSITIVE PROFITS

Let us address now the question of whether there exist classical equilibria with (strictly) positive profit rates, in this static framework. The answer depends very much on the specifics of the model under consideration. The existence of classical equilibria with positive profits cannot be ensured in general, although it might be so under certain circumstances. We shall briefly discuss here a particular case of the model in section 10.2, in which positive profits and classical equilibria turn out to be compatible.

Note first that in a classical equilibrium with positive profits, no consumption of produced commodities with positive prices can occur. This is so because in this case consumers devote *all* their initial endowments to production activities (in order to maximize wealth), and hence in equilibrium these commodities are actually *used up* by firms. Unless this condition holds, zero would be the only profit rate compatible with the existence of equilibrium. Hence it is natural to consider again the case in which initial endowments consist only of production factors which do not enter the preferences of consumers.

The following result is obtained:

Proposition 10.3.-

Under assumptions (A.10.1) to (A.10.4), for any given λ in Λ, there exists a Classical Equilibrium relative to λ.

Proof.-

(i) Consider an economy $E(\lambda)$, for $\lambda > 0$, which is identical to the original one except in the following:

a) The ith consumer's initial endowments are given by:

$$w_i(\lambda) \equiv w_i(1 + \lambda)$$

b) The jth production set, is now defined as:

$$Y_j(\lambda) \equiv \{\mathbf{s} \in \mathbb{R}^\ell / \mathbf{s} = [\mathbf{a}_j(1 + \lambda), \mathbf{b}_j], \text{ with } (\mathbf{a}_j, \mathbf{b}_j) \in Y_j\}$$

whose elements will be denoted by $\mathbf{y}_j(\lambda)$.

This economy satisfies assumptions (A.10.1) to (A.10.3), so that we can apply proposition 10.1 which ensures the existence of a canonical classical equilibrium for the $E(\lambda)$ economy, $[\mathbf{p}^*, (\mathbf{x}_i^*), \tilde{\mathbf{y}}^*(\lambda)]$.

(ii) Let us now show that $[\mathbf{p}^*, (\mathbf{x}_i^*), \tilde{\mathbf{y}}^*]$ is a classical equilibrium relative to λ for the original economy. First note that $[(\mathbf{x}_i^*), \tilde{\mathbf{y}}^*]$ is an attainable allocation. To see this observe that, by assumption,

$$\sum_{i=1}^m \mathbf{x}_i^* - w(\lambda) - \sum_{j=1}^n \mathbf{y}_j^*(\lambda) = \mathbf{0} \qquad [1]$$

The structure of the model and assumption (A.10.4) allow us to write

$$\sum_{i=1}^m \mathbf{x}_i^* = \begin{bmatrix} \mathbf{0} \\ \mathbf{c} \end{bmatrix}, \quad w(\lambda) = \begin{bmatrix} \sigma(1 + \lambda) \\ \mathbf{0} \end{bmatrix}, \quad \sum_{j=1}^n \mathbf{y}_j^*(\lambda) = \begin{bmatrix} \mathbf{a}(1 + \lambda) \\ \mathbf{b} \end{bmatrix}$$

Then equation [1] can be rewritten as follows:

$$\begin{bmatrix} \mathbf{0} \\ \mathbf{c} \end{bmatrix} - \begin{bmatrix} \sigma(1 + \lambda) \\ \mathbf{0} \end{bmatrix} - \begin{bmatrix} \mathbf{a}(1 + \lambda) \\ \mathbf{b} \end{bmatrix} = \begin{bmatrix} \mathbf{0} \\ \mathbf{0} \end{bmatrix}$$

which implies that $\mathbf{c} = \mathbf{b}$, $-\sigma(1 + \lambda) = \mathbf{a}(1 + \lambda)$, and, consequently, $-\sigma = \mathbf{a}$. Therefore it follows that

$$\sum_{i=1}^m \mathbf{x}_i^* - w - \sum_{j=1}^n \mathbf{y}_j^* = \mathbf{0}$$

It is easy to see that, for each j, $\mathbf{p}^* \mathbf{y}_j^* \geq \mathbf{p}^* \mathbf{y}_j$ for all $\mathbf{y}_j$ such that $\mathbf{a}_j \geq \mathbf{a}_j^*$. For suppose not, that is, suppose that there exists a firm j and a production plan $\mathbf{y}'_j$ such that $\mathbf{p}^*\mathbf{y}'_j > \mathbf{p}^*\mathbf{y}^*_j$, with $\mathbf{a}'_j \geq \mathbf{a}^*_j$. In that case we would also have that $\mathbf{p}^*\mathbf{y}'_j(\lambda) > \mathbf{p}^*\mathbf{y}^*_j(\lambda)$, against the hypothesis that $[\mathbf{p}^*, (\mathbf{x}^*_i), \tilde{\mathbf{y}}^*(\lambda)]$ is a classical equilibrium for the $E(\lambda)$ economy.

It remains to show that $\mathbf{x}^*_i$ is the *ith* consumer's demand in the original economy. But this follows immediately from the way in which the $E(\lambda)$ economy has been constructed.♠

Proposition 10.3 says that there exists an equilibrium with a rate of profits $\rho(\mathbf{p}^*, \tilde{\mathbf{y}}^*) = \lambda$, for any pre-established $\lambda \in \Lambda$. This points out a strong indeterminacy in the model: there may be many possible equilibria with different profit rates and, consequently, different income distributions, employment levels, etc. Profits are to be interpreted as the rents of those scarce factors which are required in order to carry out production activities. The profit rate may be seen as a parameter of the way in which the total surplus is distributed across agents. Yet the informative content of this parameter is rather ambiguous, except in very specific models [as in Sraffa (1960)].

The following Corollary is of interest:

Corollary 10.2.-
Let an economy satisfying assumptions (A.10.1), (i) and (ii) of (A.10.2), (A.10.3) and (A.10.4). Then,
(i) If N_1 is empty (i.e., all firms exhibit constant returns to scale), for every $\lambda \in \Lambda$, there is a Pareto Optimal Classical Equilibrium relative to λ.
(ii) If $\mathbf{Y}_0 = \sum_{j=1}^n \mathbf{Y}_j$ is distributive, then there exists a classical equilibrium relative to λ which is Pareto optimal, for every $\lambda \in \Lambda$.

Corollary 10.2 is simply a rephrasing of corollary 10.1 and proposition 10.2 within this new context (so the proof will be omitted). Nevertheless, it is worth noticing that it shows the existence of efficient equilibrium allocations in the presence of positive profits.

10.5   FINAL REMARKS

We have presented a model of a market economy with competitive features, in which there may be several industries with non-decreasing returns to scale. Rational consumers set up firms by applying their resources to the most profitable production activities, and maximize utility subject to their budget sets. Firms' behaviour consists of maximizing profits at given prices. A classical equilibrium is a situation in which all these actions are simultaneously feasible. Existence results have been provided, distinguishing between the cases of zero and positive equilibrium profits. Some efficiency properties have also been analyzed.

From a formal standpoint, the model is mostly an application of the results in sections 9.2 and 9.3. Yet, it provides us with an endogenous way of determining the input restrictions.

It is interesting to note the connection between this model and some other general equilibrium models. When production sets are convex cones (constant returns to scale), a canonical classical equilibrium corresponds to a standard Arrow-Debreu competitive equilibrium. When the economy consists of a single distributive firm, a canonical classical equilibrium is a social equilibrium à la Scarf. Many equilibrium models in the classical tradition (von Neumann, Leontief, Sraffa, and their variants) may be interpreted as particular cases of this one. It is also worth noticing the connection with the literature on *coalition production economies* [see for instance the model developed in Ichiishi (1993, ch.5)].

Let us conclude by commenting on the treatment given here to commodities, transactions and profits.

The rationale of the division between produced commodities and new goods is twofold. On the one hand it improves the descriptive power of the model, stressing the picture of a society which develops production activities in order to obtain commodities which are not available. On the other, it provides a natural basis for the analysis of classical equilibria with positive profits.

It was already pointed out (see Remark 10.1) that one may interpret the model as including a *sequence* of transactions within the period. Investment decisions are taken first, then firms are created and production occurs, and finally income is realized and consumption takes place. This sequential feature is relevant again for the analysis of equilibria with positive profits. For suppose that consumers can spend, before production takes place, the profits that will result from production activities. Then, whenever $\rho(\mathbf{p},\widetilde{\mathbf{y}}) > 0$, consumers will use their profits $\mathbf{p}[\sigma\rho(\mathbf{p},\widetilde{\mathbf{y}}), 0]$ to buy additional endowments, and spend the additional future yields to buy even more endowments, and will repeat this process again and again before deciding their consumption. But this income cannot be realized as an equilibrium, so that the only possible equilibria would be the canonical ones.

Needless to say that a sharper way of capturing this sequential character of transactions would be to set up a two-period model. Yet, this framework would necessarily involve some equilibrium "interest rate", which would obscure the nature of pure profits as rents of scarce factors, that we wanted to stress.

REFERENCES

Alós, C. & Villar, A. (1995), Clarke Cones and Marginal Pricing: An Exposition of the Key Results, **mimeo**, University of Alicante.

Arrow, K.J. & Enthoven, A.C. (1961), Quasi-Concave Programming, **Econometrica**, 29 : 779-800.

Arrow, K.J., Hurwicz, L. & Uzawa, H. (1961), Constraint Qualifications in Maximization Problems, **Naval Research Logistics Quarterly**, 8 : 175-186.

Arrow, K.J. & Hahn, F.H. (1971), **General Competitive Analysis**, Holden Day, San Francisco.

Aumann, R.J. & Shapley, L.S. (1974), **Values of Nonatomic Games**, Princeton University Press, Princeton, New Jersey.

Barten, A.P. & Böhm, V. (1982), Consumer Theory, Chapter 9 in K.J. Arrow & M.D. Intriligator (Eds.), **Handbook of Mathematical Economics**, vol. II, North-Holland, Amsterdam, 1982.

Bazaraa, M.S. & Shetty, C.M. (1979), **Nonlinear Programming**, John Wiley, New York.

Beato, P. (1982), The Existence of Marginal Cost Pricing Equilibria with Increasing Returns, **Quarterly Journal of Economics**, 389 : 669-688.

Beato, P. & Mas-Colell, A. (1983), Gestion au Côut Marginal et Efficacité de la Production Aggregé: un Example, **Annales de L'INSEE**, 51 : 39-46.

Beato, P. & Mas-Colell, A. (1985), On Marginal Cost Pricing with Given Tax-Subsidy Rules, **Journal of Economic Theory**, 37 : 356-365.

Benassy, J.P. (1991), Monopolistic Competition, in W. Hildenbrand and H. Sonnenschein (Eds.), **Handbook of Mathematical Economics (vol. IV)**, North-Holland, Amsterdam, 1991.

Billera, L.J. & Heath, D.C. (1982), Allocation of Shared Costs: A Set of Axioms Yielding a Unique Procedure, **Mathematics of Operations Research**, 30 : 32-39.

Billera, L.J., Heath, D.C. & Raanan, J. (1978), Internal Telephone Billing Rates -A Novel Application of Non-Atomic Game Theory, **Mathematics of Operations Research** 26 : 956-965.

Böhm, V.(1986), Existence of Equilibria with Price Regulation, in W. Hildenbrand & A. Mas-Colell (Eds.), **Contributions to Mathematical Economics. Essays in Honor of Grard Debreu**, North-Holland, Amsterdam, 1986.

Boiteaux, M. (1956), Sur la Gestion des Monopoles Publiques Astreints à l'Equilibre Budgétaire, **Econometrica**, 24 : 22-44.

Bonnisseau, J.M., (1988), On Two Existence Results of Equilibria in Economies with Increasing Returns, **Journal of Mathematical Economics**, 17 : 193-207.

Bonnisseau, J.M. (1991), Existence of Equilibria in Presence of Increasing Returns: A Synthesis, *Laboratoire d'Econométrie*, working paper n° 328.

Bonnisseau, J.M. & Cornet, B. (1988a), Existence of Equilibria when Firms follow Bounded Losses Pricing Rules, **Journal of Mathematical Economics**, 17 : 119-147.

Bonnisseau, J.M. & Cornet, B. (1988b), Valuation Equilibrium and Pareto Optimum in Non-Convex Economies, **Journal of Mathematical Economics**, 17 : 293-308.

Bonnisseau, J.M. & Cornet, B. (1990a), Existence of Marginal Cost Pricing Equilibria in Economies with Several Nonconvex Firms, **Econometrica**, 58 : 661-682.

Bonnisseau, J.M. & Cornet, B. (1990b), Existence of Marginal Cost Pricing Equilibria: The Nonsmooth Case, **International Economic Review**, 31 : 685-708.

Border, K.C. (1985), **Fixed Point Theorems with Applications to Economics and Game Theory**, Cambridge University Press, Cambridge.

Bös, D. (1987), Public Sector Pricing, Chapter 3 in A.J. Auerbach and M. Feldstein (Eds.), **Handbook of Public Economics**, North-Holland, Amsterdam, 1987.

Brown, D.J. (1991), Equilibrium Analysis with Nonconvex Technologies, Ch. 36 in W. Hildenbrand & H. Sonnenschein (Eds.), **Handbook of Mathematical Economics (vol. IV)**, North-Holland, Amsterdam, 1991.

Brown, D.J. & Heal, G.M. (1979), Equity, Efficiency and Increasing Returns, **Review of Economic Studies**, 46 : 571-585.

Brown, D.J. & Heal, G.M. (1982), Existence, Local Uniqueness and Optimality of a Marginal Pricing Equilibrium with Increasing Returns, Social Science Working Paper 415, California Institute of Technology.

Brown, D.J. & Heal, G.M. (1983), The Optimality of Regulated Pricing: A General Equilibrium Analysis, in C. Aliprantis and O. Burkinshaw (Eds.), **Advances in Equilibrium Theory**, Springer-Verlag, Berlin, 1983.

Brown, D.J., Heal, G., Khan, M.A. & Vohra, R. (1986), On a General Existence Theorem for Marginal Cost Pricing Equilibria, **Journal of Economic Theory**, 38 : 371-379.

Brown, D.J., Heller, W.J. & Starr, R.M. (1992), Two-Part Marginal Cost Pricing Equilibria: Existence and Efficiency, **Journal of Economic Theory**, 57 : 52-72.

Calsamiglia, X. (1977), Decentralised Resource Allocation and Increasing Returns, **Journal of Economic Theory**, 14 : 263-283.

Chipman, J.S. (1970), External Economies of Scale and Competitive Equilibrium, **Quarterly Journal of Economics**, 84 : 347-385.

Clarke, F. (1975), Generalized Gradients and Applications, **Transactions of the American Mathematical Society**, 205 : 247-262.

Clarke, F. (1983), **Optimization and Nonsmooth Analysis**, New York, Wiley.

Corchón, L. (1988), Cost-Prices with Variable Returns, **Metroeconomica**, 40 : 93-99.

Cornet, B. (1986), The Second Welfare Theorem in Nonconvex Economies, C.O.R.E. Discussion Paper 8630, Université Catolique de Louvain.

Cornet, B. (1988), General Equilibirum Theory and Increasing Returns, **Journal of Mathematical Economics**, 17 : 103-118.

Cornet, B. (1990), Existence of Equilibria in Economies with Increasing Returns, in B. Cornet & H. Tulkens (Eds.), **Contributions to Economics and Operations Research: The XXth Anniversary of the C.O.R.E.**, The MIT Press, Cambridge Ma., 1990.

Deaton, A. & Muellbauer, J. (1980), **Economics and Consumer Behavior**, Cambridge University Press, Cambridge.

Debreu, G. (1959), **Theory of Value**, Yale University Press, New Haven.

Dehez, P. (1988), Rendements d'Echelle Croissants et Equilibre General, **Revue d'Economie Politique**, 98 : 765-800.

Dehez, P. & Drèze, J. (1988a), Competitive Equilibria with Quantity-Taking Producers and Increasing Returns to Scale, **Journal of Mathematical Economics**, 17 : 209-230.

Dehez, P. &Drèze, J. (1988b), Distributive Production Sets and Equilibria with Increasing Returns, **Journal of Mathematical Economics**, 17 : 231-248.

Dierker, E. (1986), When does Marginal Cost Pricing Lead to Pareto Efficiency ?, **Zeitschrift fur Nationalokonomie**, Suppl. 5 : 41-66.

Dierker, E, Guesnerie, R. & Neufeind, W. (1985), General Equilibrium where some Firms Follow Special Pricing Rules, **Econometrica**, 53 : 1369-1393.

Dierker, H. & Neufeind, W. (1988), Quantity Guided Price Setting, **Journal of Mathematical Economics**, 17 : 249-259.

Dieudonné, J. (1969), **Foundations of Modern Analysis**, Academic Press Inc., New York.

Edlin, A.S. & Epelbaum, M. (1993), Two-Part Marginal Cost Sharing Equilibria with n Firms: Sufficient Conditions for Existence and Optimality, **International Economic Review**, 34 : 903-922.

Fitzroy, F.R. (1974), Monopolistic Equilibrium, Non-Convexity and Inverse Demand, **Journal of Economic Theory**, 7 : 1-16.

Florenzano, M. (1981), **L'Equilibre Economique General Transitif et Intransitif: Problèmes d'Existence**, Editions dy CNRS, Paris.

Gabsewicz, J.J. & Vial, J.P. (1972), Oligopoly " à la Cournot" in General Equilibrium Analysis, **Journal of Economic Theory**, 4 : 381-400.

Greenberg, J. & Shitovitz, B. (1984), Aumann-Shapley Prices and Scarf Social Equilibrium, **Journal of Economic Theory**, 34 : 380-382.

Guesnerie, R. (1975), Pareto Optimality in Nonconvex Economies, **Econometrica**, 43 : 1-29.

Guesnerie, R. (1990), First-Best Allocation of Resources with Nonconvexities in Production, in B. Cornet & H. Tulkens (Eds.), **Contributions to Economics and Operations Research: The XXth Anniversary of the C.O.R.E.**, The MIT Press, Cambridge Ma., 1990.

Hart S. & Mas-Colell, A. (1989), Potential Value and Consistency, **Econometrica**, 57 : 589-614.

Herrero, C., (1982), Sobre la Compacidad de los Conjuntos Alcanzables de Producción y Consumo, **Estadística Española**, n° 96 : 63-68.

Herrero, C. & Villar, A. (1988), General Equilibrium in a Nonlinear Leontief Framework, **The Manchester School**, 56 : 159-166.

Ichiishi, T. (1993), **The Cooperative Nature of the Firm**, Cambridge University Press, Cambridge.

Ichiishi, T. & Quinzii, M. (1983), Decentralization for the Core of a Production Economy wwith Increasing Returns, **International Economic Review**, 24 : 397-412.

Jouini, E. (1988), A Remark on Clarke's Normal Cone and the Marginal Cost Pricing Rule, **Journal of Mathematical Economics**, 17 : 309-315.

Kamiya, K. (1988), Existence and Uniqueness of Equilibria with Increasing Returns, **Journal of Mathematical Economics**, 17 : 149-178.

Khan, M. A. & Vohra, R. (1987), An Extension of the Second Welfare Theorem to Economies with Nonconvexities, **Quarterly Journal of Economics**, 102 : 223-241.

Koopmans, T.C. (1957), **Three Essays on the State of Economic Science**, McGraw-Hill, New York.

Kuhn, H.W. & Tucker, A.W. (1951), Nonlinear Programming, in J. Neyman (Ed.), **Proceedings of the Second Berkeley Symosium on Mathematical Statistics and Probability**, University of California Press, Berkeley, 1951.

Llinares, J.V. (1995), Existence of Maximal Elements in a Binary Relation Relaxing the Convexity Condition, **A Discusión**, w.p. 9510.

MacKinnon, J.G. (1979), Computing Equilibria with Increasing Returns, **European Economic Review**, 12 : 1-16.

Malinvaud, E. (1972), **Lectures on Microeoconomic Theory**, North-Holland, Amsterdam.

Mantel, R. (1979), Equilibrio con Rendimientos Crecientes a Escala, **Anales de la Asociación Argentina de Economía Política**, 1 : 271-283.

Marshall, A. (1890), **Principles of Economics**, Macmillan, London.

Mas-Colell, A. (1974), An Equilibrium Existence Theorem without Complete or Transitive Preferences, **Journal of Mathematical Economics**, 1 : 237-246.

156

Mas-Colell, A. (1987), **Lecciones sobre la Teoría del Equilibrio con Rendimientos Crecientes**, Segundas Lecciones Germn Berncer, Valencia, Generalitat Valenciana.

Mas-Colell, A. & Silvestre, J. (1989), Cost-Share Equilibria: A Lindahlian Approach, **Journal of Economic Theory**, 47 : 239-256.

Mirman, L.J., Samet, D. & Tauman, Y. (1983), An Axiomatic Approach to the Allocation of a Fixed Cost Through Prices, **Bell Journal of Economics**, 14 : 139-151.

Mirman L.J. & Tauman, Y. (1982), Demand Compatible Equitable Cost Sharing Prices, **Mathematics of Operations Research**, 7 : 40-56.

Mirman, L.J., Tauman, Y. & Zang, I. (1985), Supportability, Sustainability, and Subsidy-Free Prices, **Rand Journal of Economics**, 16 : 114-126.

Mirman, L.J., Tauman, Y. & Zang, I. (1986), Ramsey Prices, Average Cost Prices and Price Sustainability, **International Journal of Industrial Organization**, 4 : 1-18.

Moulin, H. (1988), **Axioms of Cooperative Decision Making**, Cambridge University Press, Cambridge.

Nadiri, M.I. (1982), Producers Theory, Chapter 10 in K.J. Arrow & M.D. Intriligator (Eds.), **Handbook of Mathematical Economics**, vol. II, North-Holland, Amsterdam, 1982.

Negishi, T. (1961), Monopolistic Competition and General Equilibrium, **Review of Economic Studies**, 28 : 196-201.

Quinzii, M. (1982), An Existence Theorem for the Core of a Production Economy with Increasing Returns, **Journal of Economic Theory**, 28 : 32-50.

Quinzii, M. (1991), Efficiency of Marginal Pricing Equilibria, in W. Brock and M. Majumdar (Eds.), **Equilibrium and Dynamics: Essays in Honor of David Gale**, MacMillan, New York, 1991.

Quinzii, M. (1992), **Increasing Returns and Efficiency**, Oxford University Press, New York

Ramsey, F. (1927), A Contribution of the Theory of Taxation, **The Economic Journal**, 37 : 47-61.

Reichert, J. (1986), **Strategic Market Behavior**, Ph.D. Dissertation, Yale University.

Roberts, J. & Sonnenschein, H. (1977), On the Foundations of the Theory of Monopolistic Competition, **Econometrica**, 45 : 101-113.

Ruggles, N. (1949), The Welfare Basis of the Marginal Cost Pricing Principle, **Review of Economic Studies**, 17 : 29-46.

Ruggles, N. (1950), Recent Developments in the Theory of Marginal Cost Pricing, **Review of Economic Studies**, 17 : 107-126.

Samet, D. & Tauman, Y. (1982), The Determination of Marginal Cost Prices under a Set of Axioms, **Econometrica**, 50 : 895-910.

Scarf, H.E. (1986), Notes on the Core of a Productive Economy, in W. Hildenbrand & A. Mas-Colell (Eds.), **Contributions to Mathematical Economics. Essays in Honor of Gerard Debreu**, North-Holland, Amsterdam, 1986.

Schmeidler, D. (1971), A Condition for the Completeness of Partial Preference Relations, **Econometrica**, 39 : 403-404.

Sen, A.K. (1970), **Collective Choice and Social Welfare**, Holden Day, San Francisco.

Shafer, W.J. (1974), The Nontransitive Consumer, **Econometrica**, 42 : 913-919.

Shafer, W.J. & Sonnenschein, H. (1975), Equilibrium in Abstract Economies without Ordered Preferences, **Journal of Mathematical Economics**, 2 : 345-348.

Sharkey, W.W. (1979), Existence of a Core whre there are Increasing Returns, **Econometrica**, 47 : 869-876.

Sharkey, W.W. (1980), **The Theory of Natural Monopoly**, Cambridge University Press, Cambridge.

Sharkey, W.W. (1989), Game Theoretic Modelling of Increasing Returns to Scale, **Games and Economic Behavior**, 1 : 370-431.

Silvestre, J. (1977), General Monopolistic Equilibrium under Non-Convexity, **International Economic Review**, 18 : 425-434.

Silvestre, J. (1978), Increasing Returns in General Non-Competitive Analysis, **Econometrica**, 46 : 397-402.

Sraffa, P. (1920), The Laws of Returns under Competitive Conditions, **The Economic Journal**, 26 : 535-550.

Sraffa, P. (1960), **Production of Commodities by Means of Commodities**, Cambridge University Press, Cambridge.

Suzumura, K. (1983), **Rational Choice, Collective Decisions and Social Welfare**, Cambridge University Press, Cambridge.

158

Takayama, A. (1985), **Mathematical Economics**, 2nd.Ed., Cambridge University Press, Cambridge.

Ten Raa, T. (1983), Supportability and Anonymous Equity, **Journal of Economic Theory**, 31:176-181.

Villar, A. (1991), A General Equilibrium Model with Increasing Returns, **Revista Española de Economía**, 8 : 1-15.

Villar, A. (1992), **Operator Theorems with Applications to Distributive Problems and Equilibrium Models**, Springer-Verlag, Berlin.

Villar, A. (1994a), Existence and Efficiency of Equilibrium in Economies with Increasing Returns: An Exposition, **Investigaciones Económicas**, 18 : 205-243.

Villar, A. (1994b), Equilibrium with Nonconvex Technologies, **Economic Theory**, 4 : 629-638.

Vohra, R. (1988a), On the Existence of Equilibria in a Model with Increasing Returns, **Journal of Mathematical Economics**, 17 : 179-192.

Vohra, R. (1988b), Opimal Regulation under Fixed Rules for Income Distribution, **Journal of Economic Theory**, 45 : 65-84.

Vohra, R. (1990), On the Inefficiency of Two-Part Tariffs, **Review of Economic Studies**, 57 : 415-438.

Vohra, R. (1991), Efficient Resource Allocation under Increasing Returns, Stanford Institute for Theoretical Economics, Tech. Rep. no.18.

Vohra, R. (1992), Marginal Cost Pricing under Bounded Increasing Returns, **Econometrica**, 60 : 859-876.

Walker, (1977), On the Existence of Maximal Elements, **Journal of Economic Theory**, 16 : 470-474.

NOTATION

(Listed in approximately the order it appears in the text)

The **convention for vector comparisons** is the following: let $\mathbf{x}, \mathbf{y} \in \mathbb{R}^n$; then, $\mathbf{x} >> \mathbf{y}$ means that $x_h > y_h$ for all h; $\mathbf{x} > \mathbf{y}$ means that $x_h \geq y_h$ for all h, with $\mathbf{x} \neq \mathbf{y}$; and $\mathbf{x} \geq \mathbf{y}$ means that $x_h \geq y_h$ for all h.

$\mathbf{x}_i$ consumption plan for the *ith* consumer

$X_i \subset \mathbb{R}^\ell$ consumption set for the *ith* consumer

$(\mathbf{x}_i) \in \prod\limits_{i=1}^{m} X_i$ consumption allocation

$u_i : X_i \to \mathbb{R}$ *ith* consumer's utility function

r_i wealth (function) for the *ith* consumer

$\gamma_i(\mathbf{p}, r_i)$ *ith* consumer's budget set

$\xi_i(\mathbf{p}, r_i)$ *ith* consumer's demand

$b_i(\mathbf{p}) = \text{Min } \mathbf{px}_i$ on X_i

ω_i *ith* consumer's initial endowments

$\omega \in \mathbb{R}^\ell$ (aggregate) initial endowments

$\mathbf{y}_j$ production plan for the *jth* firm

$Y_j \subset \mathbb{R}^\ell$ production set for the *jth* firm

$\mathbb{F}_j$ *jth* firm's set of (weakly) efficient production plans

$\prod\limits_{j=1}^{n} \mathbb{F}_j \equiv \mathbb{F} \subset \mathbb{R}^{\ell n}$

$\widetilde{\mathbf{y}} = (\mathbf{y}_1, \ldots, \mathbf{y}_n)$ a point in $\mathbb{F}$

$\mathbb{P} \equiv \{\mathbf{p} \in \mathbb{R}_+^\ell / \sum_{h=1}^{\ell} p_h = 1\}$ the price simplex

$\phi_j : \mathbb{P} \to \mathbb{P}$ *jth* firm's pricing rule

$[(\mathbf{x}_i), \widetilde{\mathbf{y}}] \in \prod\limits_{i=1} X_i \times \mathbb{F}$ an allocation

$A(\omega) \equiv \{[(\mathbf{x}_i), \widetilde{\mathbf{y}}] \in \prod\limits_{i=1} X_i \times \mathbb{F} \ / \ \sum_{i=1}^{m} \mathbf{x}_i - \omega - \sum_{j=1}^{n} \mathbf{y}_j \leq \mathbf{0}\}$ the set of attainable allocations

160

$\mathbb{F}'_j$ the *jth* firm's set of efficient and attainable production plans.

$K = \{ \mathbf{z} \in \mathbb{R}^\ell \ / \ | \, z_h \, | \le k, , \ for \ all \ h = 1, \dots, \ell \}$ cube with edge $2k$.

$K_+ = K + \mathbb{R}^\ell_+$ (big enough to contain in its interior any attainable production or consumption set)

$\mathbb{F}^*_j = K_+ \cap \mathbb{F}_j$ (it contains in its relative interior the set $\mathbb{F}'_j$).

K^n_+ n-fold replica of K_+

$\mathbb{F}^* = \mathbb{F} \cap K^n_+$

$\mathbf{e} = (1, 1, \dots, 1)$ unit vector in $\mathbb{R}^\ell$

$\perp_Y(\mathbf{y})$ cone of perpendicular vectors to Y at $\mathbf{y}$

$\mathbb{N}_Y(\mathbf{y})$ Clarke normal cone to Y at $\mathbf{y}$

$\phi^{MP}_j : \mathbb{F}_j \to \mathbb{P}$ marginal pricing rule for the *jth* firm.

(q_{ij}) hook-up system $(j = 1, \dots, n, i = 1, \dots, m)$.

θ_{ij} *ith* consumer's participation in the *jth* firm's profits

$\phi^{PM}_j : \mathbb{F}_j \to \mathbb{P}$ profit maximization pricing rule for the *jth* firm

$\phi^{AC}_j : \mathbb{F}_j \to \mathbb{P}$ average cost pricing rule for the *jth* firm

$\phi^{IC}_j : \mathbb{F}_j \to \mathbb{P}$ input-constrained profit maximization pricing rule

$\phi^{OC}_j : \mathbb{F}_j \to \mathbb{P}$ output-constrained profit maximization pricing rule

$\rho(\mathbf{p}, \tilde{\mathbf{y}})$ maximum profitability attainable at prices $\mathbf{p}$ when production is $\tilde{\mathbf{y}}$.

$$A(\omega, \lambda) \equiv \{ [(\mathbf{x}_i), \tilde{\mathbf{y}}] \in \prod_{i=1}^m X_i \times \mathbb{F} \ / \ \textstyle\sum_{i=1}^m \mathbf{x}_i - \omega - \sum_{j=1}^n [\mathbf{a}_j(1+\lambda), \mathbf{b}_j] \le \mathbf{0} \}$$

DEFINITIONS

(By alfabetical order)

Attainable Allocations (Def. 3.4, p. 44)

Average Cost Pricing (Def. 8.4, p. 118)

Canonical Classical Equilibrium (Def. 10.5, p. 142)

Clarke Normal Cone (Def. 5.3, p. 73)

Classical Equilibrium relative to λ (Def. 10.4, p. 141)

Competitive Equilibrium (Def. 8.3, p. 115)

Complete preferences (p. 15)

Continuous preferences (Def. 2.1, p. 17)

Convex preferences (p. 20)

Core (Def. 7.2, p. 103)

Efficient Production Plan (Def. 3.1, p. 41)

Equilibrium (Def. 4.1, p. 53)

Equilibrium Relative to λ for the *jth* Activity (Def. 10.2, p. 141)

Hook-up System (Def. 6.1, p. 85)

Input Allocation (Def. 10.1, p. 140)

Input-Constrained Profit Maximization (Def. 9.1, p. 122)

Input-Distributive Sets (Def. 9.2, p. 126)

Limsup of a Correspondence (Def. 5.1, p. 68)

Loss-Free Pricing Rule (Def. 8.1, p. 112)

Marginal Pricing (Def. 5.4, p. 76)

Monotone preferences (p. 22)
Non-satiation (p. 22)
Output-Constrained Profit Maximization (Def. 9.3, p. 131)

Output-Distributive Production Sets (Def. 9.4, p. 132)

Pareto Optimality (Def. 7.1, p. 93)

Perpendicular Vectors (Def. 5.2, p. 71)

Pricing Rule (Def. 3.5, p. 46)

Pricing Rule with Bounded Losses (Def. 3.8, 47)

Production Equilibrium (Def. 3.6, p. 46)

ASSUMPTIONS

RESULTS

164

Vol. 393: B. Lucke, Price Stabilization on World Agricultural Markets. XI, 274 pages. 1992.

Vol. 394: Y.-J. Lai, C.-L. Hwang, Fuzzy Mathematical Programming. XIII, 301 pages. 1992.

Vol. 395: G. Haag, U. Mueller, K. G. Troitzsch (Eds.), Economic Evolution and Demographic Change. XVI, 409 pages. 1992.

Vol. 396: R. V. V. Vidal (Ed.), Applied Simulated Annealing. VIII, 358 pages. 1992.

Vol. 397: J. Wessels, A. P. Wierzbicki (Eds.), User-Oriented Methodology and Techniques of Decision Analysis and Support. Proceedings, 1991. XII, 295 pages. 1993.

Vol. 398: J.-P. Urbain, Exogeneity in Error Correction Models. XI, 189 pages. 1993.

Vol. 399: F. Gori, L. Geronazzo, M. Galeotti (Eds.), Nonlinear Dynamics in Economics and Social Sciences. Proceedings, 1991. VIII, 367 pages. 1993.

Vol. 400: H. Tanizaki, Nonlinear Filters. XII, 203 pages. 1993.

Vol. 401: K. Mosler, M. Scarsini, Stochastic Orders and Applications. V, 379 pages. 1993.

Vol. 402: A. van den Elzen, Adjustment Processes for Exchange Economies and Noncooperative Games. VII, 146 pages. 1993.

Vol. 403: G. Brennscheidt, Predictive Behavior. VI, 227 pages. 1993.

Vol. 404: Y.-J. Lai, Ch.-L. Hwang, Fuzzy Multiple Objective Decision Making. XIV, 475 pages. 1994.

Vol. 405: S. Komlósi, T. Rapcsák, S. Schaible (Eds.), Generalized Convexity. Proceedings, 1992. VIII, 404 pages. 1994.

Vol. 406: N. M. Hung, N. V. Quyen, Dynamic Timing Decisions Under Uncertainty. X, 194 pages. 1994.

Vol. 407: M. Ooms, Empirical Vector Autoregressive Modeling. XIII, 380 pages. 1994.

Vol. 408: K. Haase, Lotsizing and Scheduling for Production Planning. VIII, 118 pages. 1994.

Vol. 409: A. Sprecher, Resource-Constrained Project Scheduling. XII, 142 pages. 1994.

Vol. 410: R. Winkelmann, Count Data Models. XI, 213 pages. 1994.

Vol. 411: S. Dauzère-Péres, J.-B. Lasserre, An Integrated Approach in Production Planning and Scheduling. XVI, 137 pages. 1994.

Vol. 412: B. Kuon, Two-Person Bargaining Experiments with Incomplete Information. IX, 293 pages. 1994.

Vol. 413: R. Fiorito (Ed.), Inventory, Business Cycles and Monetary Transmission. VI, 287 pages. 1994.

Vol. 414: Y. Crama, A. Oerlemans, F. Spieksma, Production Planning in Automated Manufacturing. X, 210 pages. 1994.

Vol. 415: P. C. Nicola, Imperfect General Equilibrium. XI, 167 pages. 1994.

Vol. 416: H. S. J. Cesar, Control and Game Models of the Greenhouse Effect. XI, 225 pages. 1994.

Vol. 417: B. Ran, D. E. Boyce, Dynamic Urban Transportation Network Models. XV, 391 pages. 1994.

Vol. 418: P. Bogetoft, Non-Cooperative Planning Theory XI, 309 pages. 1994.

Vol. 419: T. Maruyama, W. Takahashi (Eds.), Nonlinea and Convex Analysis in Economic Theory. VIII, 306 pages 1995.

Vol. 420: M. Peeters, Time-To-Build. Interrelated Investment and Labour Demand Modelling. With Applications to Six OECD Countries. IX, 204 pages. 1995

Vol. 421: C. Dang, Triangulations and Simplicial Methods IX, 196 pages. 1995.

Vol. 422: D. S. Bridges, G. B. Mehta, Representations o Preference Orderings. X, 165 pages. 1995.

Vol. 423: K. Marti, P. Kall (Eds.), Stochastic Programming Numerical Techniques and Engineering Applications. VIII 351 pages. 1995.

Vol. 424: G. A. Heuer, U. Leopold-Wildburger, Silverman' Game. X, 283 pages. 1995.

Vol. 425: J. Kohlas, P.-A. Monney, A Mathematical Theory of Hints. XIII, 419 pages, 1995.

Vol. 426: B. Finkenstädt, Nonlinear Dynamics in Eco nomics. IX, 156 pages. 1995.

Vol. 427: F. W. van Tongeren, Microsimulation Modellin of the Corporate Firm. XVII, 275 pages. 1995.

Vol. 428: A. A. Powell, Ch. W. Murphy, Inside a Modern Macroeconometric Model. XVIII, 424 pages. 1995.

Vol. 429: R. Durier, C. Michelot, Recent Developments in Optimization. VIII, 356 pages. 1995.

Vol. 430: J. R. Daduna, I. Branco, J. M. Pinto Paixão (Eds.) Computer-Aided Transit Scheduling. XIV, 374 pages. 1995

Vol. 431: A. Aulin, Causal and Stochastic Elements i Business Cycles. XI, 116 pages. 1996.

Vol. 432: M. Tamiz (Ed.), Multi-Objective Programmin and Goal Programming. VI, 359 pages. 1996.

Vol. 433: J. Menon, Exchange Rates and Prices. XIV, 31 pages. 1996.

Vol. 434: M. W. J. Blok, Dynamic Models of the Firm VII, 193 pages. 1996.

Vol. 435: L. Chen, Interest Rate Dynamics, Derivative Pricing, and Risk Management. XII, 149 pages. 1996.

Vol. 436: M. Klemisch-Ahlert, Bargaining in Economi and Ethical Environments. IX, 155 pages. 1996.

Vol. 437: C. Jordan, Batching and Scheduling. IX, 17 pages. 1996.

Vol. 438: A. Villar, General Equilibrium with Increasin Returns. XIII, 164 pages. 1996.